Y0-CLA-999

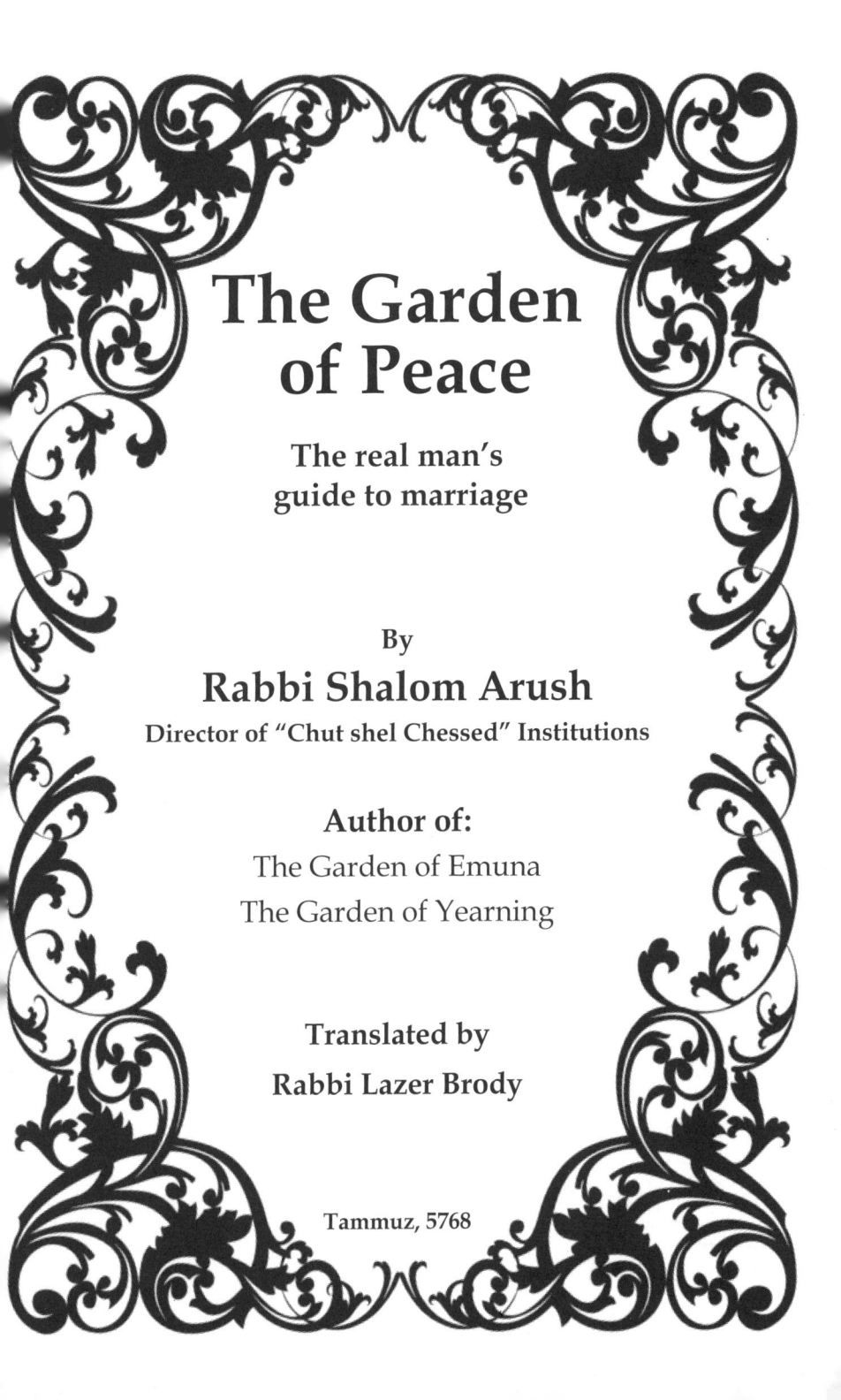

The Garden of Peace

The real man's guide to marriage

By
Rabbi Shalom Arush
Director of "Chut shel Chessed" Institutions

Author of:
The Garden of Emuna
The Garden of Yearning

Translated by
Rabbi Lazer Brody

Tammuz, 5768

COPYRIGHT © 2008

by Chut Shel Chessed Institutions

All rights reserved. No part of this book may be reproduced in any form without written permission of the author.

No part of this publication may be translated, reproduced, stored in any retrieval system or transmitted in any form or by any means without prior permission of the author, except by a reviewer who wishes to quote brief passages in connection with a review written for inclusion in magazines or newspapers.

In all matters relating to this book, please contact:

Chut Shel Chessed Institutions

POB 50226, Jerusalem, Israel

Telephone

972-52-2240696

or

972-2-5812210

Design and Layout:
Eye See Productions
972-2-5821453

Distribution:
Tel: 972-52-2240696
www.myemuna.com

Printed in Israel

The Garden of Peace

The real man's guide to marriage

Approbations

Rabbi Eliezer Berland Shlit'a

Rosh Yeshiva, Shuvu Banim Institutions, Jerusalem

15 Av, 5767

I am awed to the depth of my soul with this most important and rare book, "The Garden of Peace," that deals with peace in the home and the wife's honor, with the holiness of the covenant and with hastening the full redemption of our people by invoking the Divine Presence into every household, by way of true marital peace and mutual respect, so neither spouse will seek to rule over the other, Heaven forbid.

It's an absolute obligation on every person to purchase this book and to encourage others to do so as well. One should distribute this book among relatives, friends, and acquaintances until there is no home without this rare gem of a book.

Anyone who purchases this book will be blessed with blessings from Above and will merit in seeing our rebuilt Holy Temple speedily, amen.

With the blessings of our pure and holy Torah,

Your servant,
Eliezer Berland

Grand Rabbi Naftali A. Y. Moscowitz Shlit'a

Melitzer Rebbe, Ashdod, Israel

20 Teveth, 5768

I hereby strengthen the hands of he who performs a great mitzvah, my esteemed friend who is well-known for his enormous dissemination of Torah and Outreach, the brilliant Rabbi Shalom Arush shlit'a, Director of the "Chut Shel Chessed" Institutions of Jerusalem. Rabbi Arush's magnificent books and recorded lessons have already been widely accepted around the globe, and now he has written "The Garden of Peace," a manual that deals with marital peace and family solidarity. This is a book that is sorely needed in our generation, for we see with our own eyes how many households are destroyed by quarrel and dissension. Children from such homes suffer both materially and spiritually, for it is impossible to educate children without tranquility in the home.

Therefore one benefits society by helping to distribute this book, teaching it to himself and to others. Happy is he who builds his home according to the foundations of Torah and tradition. I convey my blessing to the noble author, may Hashem grant him long and good days, and may Hashem be with him to see the fruits of his labors. May his words be heeded to bring hearts closer to our Father in Heaven, and may he succeed in all his endeavors.

Signed with admiration and esteem,

Naftali Moscowitz

Table of Contents

An Important Message from the Author	16
Translator's Foreword	17
The Road to Paradise	20

Chapter One: The Most Important Mitzva — 24

- Remaining single 24
- The Exalted Sage and Pillar of Compassion Shlit'a 29
- The true purpose 33
- Practice makes perfect 34

Chapter Two: No Comments, Please — 36

- This is her honor 37
- The first foundation 38
- Emphasis 38
- The wife is a mirror 39
- Observe and understand 42
- Your personal mirror 43
- Magnifying glass 44
- Mirror or suffer 45
- Mirroring the inner self 46
- A mirror for the worthy 47
- Why did Sarah laugh? 48
- The Sun and the Moon 48
- The Speaker System 49
- The Tape Deck 50
- 1. Comments are debilitating 52
- 2. Remarks don't help 53
- 3. Remarks are degrading 54
- 4. One who criticizes is arrogant 54

6. The pedant can't teach 55
7. Remarks are dangerous 55
8. The remarks are a boomerang 55
Clarification 56
How will she change? 56
The right way 58
The middle road 60

Chapter Three: First Place   62

The central axis 62
The needless list 62
A woman's oxygen 64
Devoting the time 65
Don't be caught off guard 67
Guarding your investment 67
Big profit 69
The root 69
Communication breakdown 70
Foresight 71
"You shall desire your man" 73
Like an ape 74
Education 75
The compassionate father 77
A big savings 78
Stepchildren 78
Livelihood 79
Career 79
No comparisons! 80
Guarding one's eyes 80
Walking in the door 82
Honor, to what extent? 83
This is the Torah 84
Calm down 85
A Wife is a hidden Tzaddik 87

"Mine and yours is hers" 88
An urgent meeting 90
Listen to the Rabbi 91

Chapter Four: Be a Man   95

A lost cause? 95
Start being a man 99
A reminder 106

Chapter Five: Honor your Wife   109

Her beauty 110
Why complain? 112
You have clothing, be our ruler (Isaiah 3) 114
Honor 117
Who's the man in the house? 118
Fulfilling obligations 121
To illuminate, and not to make comments 123
Honor and be honored 125

Chapter Six: Facing each other   127

A good 'way' (Derech) 128
This problematic body 128
Attention or lust 130
Love or hatred 131
The Mitzvah of 'Her Time' 133
Vicious cycle 135
Get out of Purgatory 136
Holiness 138
Peace to the distanced 139
The greatest punishment 140
Don't destroy 142
Let's get to work 143
There is hope 143
Important warning! 144

Chapter Seven: The House of Prayer — 149

This is your correction 150
Moving up a level 151
Our efforts are all for the best 152
A good ending 153
Peace in the home through prayer 156
The power of an hour 158
An amazing change 160
Repentance – Teshuva 161
Sweetening of judgments 161
"I will make him a helper – against him" 164
Every man has his hour 165

Chapter Eight: The way to a happy home — 167

Heaven in this world 169
The importance of guidance 170
The Torah Scholars 172
The perfection of creation 173
"It is not good for man to be alone" (Genesis 2:18) ... 175
Loving-kindness 176
A red carpet 177
The poor of your household come first 178
Gratitude 179
Homework 181
Learning to smile 182
Yuck! Ingrate! 183
Ultimately, he will deny Hashem's loving-kindness ... 183
Gratitude to Hashem 185

Chapter Nine: How great is peace! — 187

Homework 188
The source of all good 190
Above everything else 190

No loss, all gain 191
Who is the King of Glory? 192
Peace is priceless 194
Mercy or cruelty? 194
Dear parents: Peace! 197
Stand by her 198
All its ways are peace 198
Wanting the best 199
The obstacle 200
The truth comes to light 203
A great gulf 205
There are no mistakes 206
Holy Constriction 207
The light in the Torah 208
No short cuts 209
This against that 209
The Wise man's eyes are in his head (Ecclesiastes 2:14) 213
Approaching married life 214

Chapter Ten: The true test   215

Peace commensurate with emuna 216
Happy with their lot in life 217
Get out the house 217
Everything's fine with me 220
Take the hints 220
The only problem is lack of emuna 221
Irresponsible advice 221
A new start 222
An amazing gift 222
At the right time 223
"I'm guilty." 223
A recovery plan 225
Divorce 228
The eyes of emuna 230

Proper guidance..230
Wounds of the heart..231
Remove anger from your heart..232
The end of the arguments, or just the beginning? 233
The true solution...234
Lack of knowledge 235
Lust...236
Who's the trouble-maker? 237
Spiritual crisis...237
It's not too late..238
Look forward..238
Forgiveness...239
Learning from the past 240
The children's future 241
Life goes on..242

Chapter Eleven: A man of valor — 245

Assuming responsibility..246
It's your problem 246
The light of a wife's soul..247
A bride's jewels 248
Don't be petty...249
Forget about money..249
Go to work..250
Proper management..250
Don't be stingy 253
That's mine!..253
A good husband..255

Chapter Twelve: A Garden of Eden — 257

Difficult times...257
The first year of marriage...259
Know the difference 261
The essence of woman 262

The husband cheers the wife 264
The heart 266
A listening ear 267
A wife's honor 270
Love 272
Shining faces 274
A helping hand 276
The scale of merit 278
Emuna 280
Two Women in the Home 282
Laziness 284
Wronging one's wife 286
Entrenched in arguments 288
A Tyrant in the House 291
Quelling arguments 294
No Pressure 297
Lies 300
Self Correction 303

Chapter Thirteen: Finding a Mate   307

Good advice 307
Success 308
Preparation with prayer 308
Hashem sees the heart 308
Paving the way 309
Good character traits 310
The task begins 311
The arrogant lose 312
The choice is up to you 313
The current circumstance is what counts 314

Chapter Fourteen: Premarital instruction   315

The most beautiful life 315
Prepare yourself for life 315

The wedding day 317
Stage One – The Ketuba 317
Text of the Ketuba 319
The power of giving 320
She looks to you 321
Get a job! 322
Cherish 323
Faithfully 323
Conjugal rights 325
Kosher witnesses 325
Kosher ketuba 326
Married already? 326
Stage Two – Veiling the bride 326
Stage Three – Under the Chuppa 328
Blessing of the wine 329
Betrothal 329
Consecration and ring 330
The Shehechiyanu Blessing 331
Reading of the Ketuba 331
Acquisition, oath, and signature 331
The Seven Marriage Blessings 332
Remembrance of the destruction 336
Summary 336
Enjoy the sweetness 337
The main preparation 339
Prayers on the wedding day 341

Glossary   343

An Important Message from the Author

Every married individual should feel that he or she alone bears the responsibility for peace in the home. Both partners in the marital union must learn their respective responsibilities and obligations and do their utmost to fulfill them. Neither should police the other; a person that's occupied with finding fault in someone else fails to see his or her own faults.

The Garden of Peace is a marriage manual for men. As such, it places the burden of marital peace on men. I therefore strongly discourage women from reading this book. Women who read this book will likely misuse the lofty standards that it sets for husbands as a weapon against their husbands. In that respect, this book will undermine their marital bliss instead of enhancing it. I hope that the women will be prudent enough to listen to me.

Since the husband and the wife fulfill different functions, each needs individual guidance. At the time of this writing, I've already embarked on the project of preparing a marriage manual for women. Please be patient for a little longer; with Hashem's loving help, I hope to complete it in coming months.

I bless every woman who resists the temptation to read this book with all the very best of material and spiritual abundance, marital bliss, and gratification from their children, who with Hashem's help will grow up in the path of the righteous in strength of body, mind, and soul.

Shalom Arush, Jerusalem

Sivan, 5768

Translator's Foreword

Rabbi Shalom Arush's first English-translated book, **The Garden of Emuna**, made its debut less than two years ago. His golden message has opened up new gateways of hope and happiness to hundreds of thousands of people around the globe. As one reader wrote me, "My life is divided into two parts – before I read **The Garden of Emuna** and after I read **The Garden of Emuna**." Anything more is superfluous.

Rabbi Shalom's words are a cool drink for a parched soul. He – like our teacher and master Rebbe Nachman of Breslev of blessed and saintly memory - is a master physician of the soul who adeptly cures all people's ills with one secret spiritual remedy – *emuna*, the pure and complete faith in The Almighty.

Hashem has granted me the rare privilege of basking in the light of Rabbi Shalom Arush for over a dozen years already, both as the dean of the Ashdod branch of his renowned rabbinical seminary, "Chut Shel Chessed" and as his English translator and understudy. More than anyone I've ever seen, Rabbi Shalom meticulously practices what he preaches. He is the undisputed pillar of emuna and marital peace in this generation.

Thousands of people in Israel alone flock to Rabbi Shalom Arush's door, many of whom suffer from apparently irreconcilable marital difficulties. My own eyes have witnessed the enormous number of marriages that he has saved. Virtually unable to continue private counseling, Rabbi Arush wrote a rare gem of a marriage manual for men in Hebrew, **B'Gan HaShalom**. Like Rabbi Arush's **B'Gan Ha'emuna**, this book became an overnight best-seller in Israel within weeks.

The Garden of Peace – the English-language version of **B'Gan HaShalom** - is a book for men that want to be winning husbands. An old adage says that winners don't need to make excuses why they won the game, yet losers are full of excuses why they lost the game. In that vein, Rabbi Shalom's track record is no less than phenomenal – he's a winning marital coach with a better track record than any marital counselor alive. His advice, girded firmly in the foundations of Talmudic and Jewish esoteric thought, is crystal clear and reader friendly. I have never seen a person that implemented Rabbi Shalom's advice who did not see a major subsequent improvement in his marriage.

This book will undoubtedly improve your marriage too. Whether you've already celebrated your Golden Anniversary or whether you've just began to contemplate marriage, **The Garden of Peace** will quickly become your trusty companion and guide.

With Hashem's loving guidance, I have tried my utmost to preserve the flavor, intent, and beautiful simplicity of Rabbi Shalom's original style. Even so, any deficiency in this book is surely that of the translator and not of the author. My sincere thanks and blessings go to (alphabetically) Sam Green, R. Levy, Shelly Perluss, R.T. Salkover, Avi Weiss, and Aaron Yosef for their dedicated assistance in making **The Garden of Peace** a reality.

I wish to express my deepest gratitude to Rabbi Shalom Arush himself, who so selflessly has illuminated my mind and soul with his noble teachings. May Hashem bless him, his family, and his pupils with the very best of spiritual and material abundance always.

My cherished wife Yehudit deserves the credit for this book and for everything else I do. May Hashem bless her with long and happy days, success, and joy from all her offspring. May they walk courageously in the path of Torah and emuna until the end of time, amen.

With a song of thanks to the Almighty and a prayer for the full and speedy redemption of our people Israel,

Rabbi Lazer Brody

Ashdod, Tammuz 5768

The Road to Paradise

About thirty years ago, before I was married, I asked my teacher and spiritual guide, Rabbi Eliezer Berland, to coach and prepare me for marriage. Rabbi Berland gave me two short but cogent pieces of advice, that in essence are advice for life itself. This book is the product of these two bits of advice, which I've tried my best over the years to learn, internalize, and implement to the fullest extent. From these two priceless gems of advice, I have derived a set of foolproof guidelines for *shalom bayit*, or peace in the home, that have since saved tens of thousands of people around the world from the bleak and bitter fate of a turbulent and broken home, constant strife, and divorce. A marriage *can* be happy.

A peaceful home surpasses any imaginable paradise. Those who live in a peaceful home have the feeling that they're walking around in an exotic garden of peace. Unfortunately, the opposite holds true as well. Purgatory is a kindergarten compared to a home with marital strife. Living in a home environment that's devoid of peace is most likely life's worst form of tribulation.

The entire *Geula*, or full redemption of our people, depends on peace in the home. A peaceful home is a worthy sanctuary for the *Shechina*, or Divine Presence. The more the Divine Presence fills this world, the closer we get to the *Geula*. Therefore, every family that builds a peaceful home hastens the *Geula*. Our sages say that peace is the best vessel there is for all kinds of blessings. By enhancing the peace in one's home, one merits every imaginable blessing. For that reason, it's worth making every effort to make our homes more peaceful.

We've entitled this book, "The Garden of Peace." As the newest addition to our series of "gardens" – "The Garden of Emuna" and

"The Garden of Yearning" - "The Garden of Peace" is intended to help you live a happier life.

During the year that I gathered the material for this book, I found myself again and again printing single pages from finished chapters, to answer the many questions I'm confronted with on the subject of *shalom bayit*. I'd send one page to a man that was on the verge of divorce as a solution to his problem; another page to a young groom the day before his wedding; and yet a different page to a troubled wife that was searching for someone to instruct her husband as to the true meaning of a relationship. People responded that the answers I sent to them were like a cool drink for a parched soul that saved them from imminent marital tragedies and illuminated their homes with peace and emuna.

The positive feedback served as an incentive to publish this book as fast as possible. Instead of a few random pages, what could be better than a whole book? That way, each person would be able to read about the entire subject of peace in the home and build for himself a truly wonderful household.

It's of utmost importance to read this book from beginning until end without skipping around. Even if a certain chapter seems unimportant or irrelevant to your specific needs, don't skip it. A pensioner married for fifty years still needs to know what a young bridegroom needs to know. Certain principles that we teach a bridegroom could save the marriage of a person who's already a grandfather. Even if you're not married, you'll need to learn every single chapter in this book in preparation for marriage.

I don't know how to thank Hashem, or how to adequately sing praise to His glorious Name for the infinite favors of loving-kindness, wondrous deeds, and outright miracles that He has performed in my life. Hashem has enabled me to pass the wonderfully sweet illumination of simple emuna to people from all backgrounds, all over the world, thus enabling them to break down borders and barriers and to get closer to Hashem - as is befitting for a beloved son or daughter. Especially, the illumination of peace in the home enhances the illumination of the Divine Presence in the world, for every peaceful household becomes an additional suitable dwelling place for Divine light.

My sincere blessings go to my esteemed teacher and spiritual guide, Rabbi Eliezer Burland, may Hashem grant him long and happy days. The wisdom in this book can be traced directly to Rabbi Burland's phenomenal teachings. May Hashem enable him to continue in his wonderful way of building pupils and pupil's pupils while enjoying good health and illumination from Above until the coming of Moshiach, amen.

Having the support of our spiritual leaders is a tremendous source of encouragement and strength. I therefore especially want to thank one of this generation's esteemed tzaddikim, Grand Rabbi Naftali Moscowitz of Ashdod, better known as the Melitzer Rebbe, for all his moral support, guidance, and suggestions that contributed so much to the preparation of this book. May Hashem bless him with good health, length of days, and gratification from all his offspring and pupils, amen.

My heartfelt thanks go to my beloved mother and teacher, Yamna bat Esther, may Hashem grant her life and length of days. May she enjoy gratification from all her children and offspring, and merit to see the light of Moshiach's countenance, speedily and in our days.

A special note of gratitude goes to my dedicated wife, an outstanding woman of valor - Miriam Varda, may Hashem bless her with a long, happy and healthy life – my partner in life and my very best friend. Her power and her merit are the source of all of my success, for she deserves all the credit for my accomplishments. Mine and yours is hers. May it be Hashem's will that we merit – together – to see the success of all of our offspring and pupils and the full redemption of our people Israel in the nearest future, amen.

My faithful friend and pupil, Rabbi Eliezer Raphael (Lazer) Brody, may Hashem guard over him, well-known author, translator of this book, and editor of our Breslev Israel English-language website, has tirelessly dedicated himself to spreading my teachings around the globe. His translation and adaptation of **The Garden of Emuna, The Garden of Yearning,** and of my CD lessons have already spread in the hundreds of thousands to every continent on earth. May Hashem grant him strength, success, and joy from his offspring, and may we continue together to spread emuna in the world until the age of 120.

Last but not least are my dear pupils Rabbi Yaakov Hertzberg and his wife Esther, may Hashem bless them, who have merited from above in assisting me with the composition of my books. May Hashem bless them with long and happy days, and may they see success from their children, and may the light of emuna – which they help spread – illuminate the world and their path in life.

May it be Your will, Father in Heaven, that we – together with all of Israel - walk in the path of truth and love, and may Your glorious kingdom be revealed on earth speedily, amen.

Chapter One

The Most Important Mitzva

Know full well – the most important thing in the service of Hashem is *shalom bayit* – peace in the home. Here a husband must invest all his efforts, for this is a mitzvah that obligates him the entire days of his life. As long as a person lacks a peaceful marriage, then he must devote as much as he can to learning about, praying for, and achieving *shalom bayit*.

A common misconception is that attending to a wife's needs is a waste of time, especially Torah-learning time. The opposite is true. *Shalom bayit* is a person's most important mitzvah, a barometer of his service to Hashem, his lifelong project, and his real test in life.

Remaining single

One's objective in life is to cling to Hashem, His Torah, and His commandments. Apparently, it's easier to do so as a bachelor, without the yoke of a wife, children, and livelihood. If so, one could surmise that Hashem would want us to remain single, so we could serve Him with no outside interference. Even the Gemara says that a married man has a millstone around his neck, in other words, a formidable burden. Yet, the reality is that Hashem doesn't want us to remain single.

Hashem punished Aaron's sons Nadav and Avihu because they didn't take wives and marry, even though they were – according to the Zohar – righteous men on the level of Moses. King Hezekiah, a pious and upright sage with the soul of Moshiach, in whose merit all of Israel learned Torah, received a Heavenly death sentence because he hadn't yet taken a wife. The sentence was only rescinded when he quickly married Isaiah's daughter.

This leads us to ask, why is it so important to get married? Why were those that didn't marry punished so severely? Nadav, Avihu, and Hezekiah simply wanted to fulfill the mitzvoth and learn Torah without any disturbances, to cling to Hashem, and to enjoy the sublime spiritual delights of the next world in this world. So why does Hashem require a person to marry? Doesn't the mitzvah of taking a wife and providing for all of her needs tie a person down to this lowly, material world?

Here's the answer: the purpose of creation – one's observance of Torah and attaining a *tikkun*, or correction of the soul – can only be achieved within the context of a marital relationship and a peaceful home. Therefore, marriage is senseless without *shalom bayit*, peace in the home. Without marital peace, why marry? Why commit transgressions and make your wife miserable? Since one can observe the Torah fully and attain a *tikkun* only as a married man, if he doesn't get married, he renders himself superfluous in the world. Even worse, the world can't be fully corrected if the individual doesn't fulfill his purpose...

Let's elaborate on the above concept with the help of the two following parables, which describe situations that each one of us can relate to: The Holy Celibate *Shlit'a*.[1]

In his earliest days, the Holy Celibate Shlit'a decided that his soul yearns for Torah. He concluded that his very best move would be

---

1. Shlit'a is the Hebrew abbreviation for, "May he merit long and good days," and is used as a titular suffix to the names of leading scholars and rabbis. Here, Rav Arush's intention is tongue-in-cheek.

to remain single and to find a secluded house of study where he could devote the days of his life to Torah and to Divine service. Soon, the Holy Celibate Shlit'a discovered a tiny clapboard synagogue in a rural village far off the beaten track. He asked permission from the local beadle to eat, sleep, and drink within the confines of the synagogue, which also served as the village house of study. He solemnly promised not to disturb a soul. The beadle agreed.

The Holy Celibate Shlit'a would quietly sit in the corner, learning day and night with no disturbance or interruption. He barely left the house of study. He limited his food intake to a few dry crusts of bread. Denying himself any semblance of bodily pleasure, he drank water from the tap, and slept on a hard wooden bench. Days, months, and years transpired in this manner, until the fateful day when the beadle found the elderly Holy Celibate Shlit'a lying lifelessly on the floor of the synagogue.

The entire village escorted the Holy Celibate Shlit'a on the way to his final resting place. They couldn't find adequate words to express his holiness and asceticism. All the villagers were certain that such an individual, totally withdrawn and aloof from anything mundane, was surely a great tzaddik.

In fact, the Holy Celibate Shlit'a agreed with the villagers; he was sure that he was a tzaddik of lofty merits. As his soul ascended to the Heavenly Court, he was certain that he'd be greeted by an honor guard of history's greatest tzaddikim playing lyres and cymbals, accompanied by a choir of archangels singing in six-part harmony. He was positive that they'd be escorting him to his rightful station beneath the Heavenly Throne to bask in the sublime light of The Divine Presence.

The Holy Celibate Shlit'a suffered a horrifying shock of disappointment. No souls of the great tzaddikim arrived to greet him. He didn't hear any angels playing music in his honor. All he saw were the images of his parents and ancestors standing in front of him with dejected countenances. Without any further delay, he was ushered into the Heavenly courtroom, where he stood before a tribunal of very stern-looking tzaddikim.

The Chief Justice opened a large volume, the life story of the Holy Celibate Shlit'a. He reviewed all of the Holy Celibate Shlita's mitzvot, and then addressed him by his first name, ignoring the dignified title of 'Holy Celibate Shlit'a.' The Chief Justice said: "Yosske, you learned quite a bit of Torah, you prayed, you made the necessary blessings, you put on tefillin daily, and you wore tzitzit. You observed the Sabbath and the holidays, and you fasted even more than required. In fact, you've done a good job of observing the mitzvot. There's a problem though with all your good deeds – you didn't complete the mission that you were *supposed* to complete in the physical world. You learned Torah, but you failed to implement what you learned. Had you married, you would have seen how far away you are from true Torah observance, for then, you would have had to invest much more effort to fulfill each mitzvah."

Casting a chastising glance at the shocked soul of the Holy Celibate Shlit'a, the Chief Justice added: "Didn't you know that the entire purpose of learning Torah was to acquire emuna? The level of emuna that you attained is extremely inadequate. Had you married, you'd have been required to face a long list of trials and tribulations with your wife. When she would have hindered your Torah learning with her various demands, you would have failed the tests. Whenever she would have belittled or scolded you, you'd have tarnished your soul with anger and complaining; only then, would you have seen how weak your emuna really is. You thought you trusted in Hashem, but if you'd been faced with the challenge of providing for a wife and children, you'd have seen just how frail your trust in Hashem really is. Every time you'd have been faced with a financial problem, you would have sunk into a state of depression and despair."

The charges were getting more serious by the minute. But the Chief Justice hadn't yet finished his admonishment of the Holy Celibate Shlit'a: "The minute you'd have earned some money, you'd have developed a lust for money; then, you would have forsaken the Torah while trying to make more money. Trust in Hashem? You were far away from trust. Patience? You never received a test of patience. Indeed, you are intrinsically full of anger and impatience. Good character? Had you married, you'd have seen just how much you really needed to improve, for you never had to compromise with, or to give in to, another person. Happiness? Maybe you see yourself as a happy person, but had you married, you would have seen how far you actually were from happiness, and even more, how difficult it would have been to make your wife happy, while listening to all of her daily demands, complaints, and problems. And furthermore…"

"…if Hashem would have desired that you only fulfill the mitzvoth between God and man, then He wouldn't have sent your soul on a tour of duty to the lowly material world. Your mission down there was to arrive at the awareness of Hashem and to get to know Him; that can only be accomplished in the material world as a married man with all the relevant trials and tribulations…"

"…the Tribunal therefore concludes – in light of all the hard facts of your life – that you have failed to fulfill the vast majority of the mitzvoth between man and fellow man. You never gave of yourself to another person; you never sacrificed a thing for another person; nor have you ever surrendered your desires to the desires of another person. You have no idea about the meaning of compromise. You've done nothing to uproot or even mitigate your innate egotism."

The Chief Justice and the Tribunal showed Yosske just how miserably he had failed. Yosske stood in front of the court, while the fires of humiliation scorched his soul. He had utterly failed to perform his tikkun. He was forced to realize just how badly he had failed to understand his task in the world by failing to take a wife. If only he'd have married and raised a family, while striving to build a peaceful home…

The Exalted Sage and Pillar of Compassion Shlit'a

Now, we shall tell the story of the Exalted Sage and Pillar of Compassion Shlit'a:

The Exalted Sage and Pillar of Compassion Shlit'a began his life as a child of remarkable talent, wonderful personality and razor-sharp mind. As he grew, he became known in his hometown as a genius, and he was fortunate to marry the daughter of one of the area's leading families. The Exalted Sage and Pillar of Compassion Shlit'a developed his aptitudes to the hilt. He learned Torah with exceptional perseverance. Despite his lofty level, he never failed set aside time for outreach and for teaching Torah to the town's simple laborers.

As for charity projects, the Exalted Sage and Pillar of Compassion Shlit'a had no equal. He freely loaned money to the poor or helped them attain loans from other sources. He arranged food for orphans and widows. He speedily became a leading public figure whom everyone loved and admired. Even the generation's great spiritual leaders became fast friends with the Exalted Sage and Pillar of Compassion Shlit'a.

The Exalted Sage and Pillar of Compassion Shlit'a had one "small" flaw in his impressive personal dossier – his wife! She neither respected him nor admired him. On the contrary, she constantly complained about him and spoke to him with utter disdain. More often than not, the Exalted Sage and Pillar of Compassion Shlit'a would arrive home in the wee hours, only to find his wife bitter, angry, and about to explode. He would try to ignore this unpleasant side of his life, and therefore spent little time at home.

The Exalted Sage and Pillar of Compassion Shlit'a regarded his wife's complaints as the product of her faulty character and her weak observance of the Torah. She obviously failed to recognize the merits of a true Torah sage, and to respect him accordingly. All she did was to constantly hinder him with petty demands and baseless accusations. He always made an effort to give her the money she needed, but in a begrudging way. His entire marriage was no more than a never-ending hassle. Rather than contend with his wife, he preferred to stay away. Even on Shabbat and on holidays, he always had a prearranged obligation, such as a Torah lecture to deliver. Rather than "rotting" at home, he preferred to devote his time to Torah and to charitable deeds in the outside world.

As is the way of the world, the final day of the Exalted Sage and Pillar of Compassion Shlit'a also arrived. The same car with the loudspeaker that drives through the neighborhoods declaring an emergency or the death of a tzaddik, announced in a mournful tone all over town: "…the Holy Ark has fallen captive! Darkness has prevailed over the angels of holiness! The funeral of the Minister of Torah and loving-kindness, the holy Exalted Sage and Pillar of Compassion Shlit'a, will begin at two o'clock this afternoon and proceed toward the Grand Rabbinical Section of Mount Tranquil Cemetery. All of Israel shall mourn the loss this righteous soul…"

Thousands escorted the Exalted Sage and Pillar of Compassion Shlit'a along the way to his place of eternal rest. Two dozen police directed the traffic. The city's spiritual luminaries eulogized the Exalted Sage and Pillar of Compassion Shlit'a, sparing no platitudes. Thousands of Yeshiva boys in black hats wailed. The sidewalks were lined with hundreds of sobbing women. Lying in the middle, aware of everything around him, the Exalted Sage and Pillar of Compassion Shlit'a was ever so smugly gratified – such a funeral takes place once in a decade.

When the Exalted Sage and Pillar of Compassion Shlit'a left the threshold of the physical world, a platoon of formidable accusing angels with metal-spiked clubs of fire and black strike-force uniforms grabbed him and yanked him not-so-gently into the Heavenly Court. The Exalted Sage and Pillar of Compassion Shlit'a protested the harsh treatment, screaming that there must be some mistake. He was certain the he'd receive the same honor and prestige upstairs that he did downstairs. He was in for a rude awakening.

The trial of the Exalted Sage and Pillar of Compassion Shlit'a began. The members of the Heavenly Tribunal perfunctorily reviewed his mitzvoth, obviously unimpressed. When they looked down the list and arrived at the underlined and highlighted subject listed as **Marriage**, their countenances changed in a fear-invoking manner. The Chief Justice's wrath grew as he counted the number of times that the Exalted Sage and Pillar of Compassion Shlita's wife had cried. The other judges gasped as they measured the volume of her tears. The prosecuting attorneys approached the bench with sonogram-photographic evidence of her blood-stained and broken heart, showing thousands of scars of loneliness, humiliation and insult. They asked the Sergeant of Arms to dim the lights in the Heavenly Courtroom, and then projected a vivid wide-screen video documentary showing the wife sitting alone at the Shabbat table, while no one acknowledged the fresh challas that she had baked and the delicacies that she had spent so much time preparing for the ungrateful individual that just waited for the moment that he could escape from the table. The film showed her starving soul – never a thank-you, never a gift, never a nice word. It was a blatant example of the Exalted Sage and Pillar of Compassion Shlita's mistaken and misplaced priorities.

The Chief Justice ignored the fictitious titles of honor of the deceptive material world, and addressed the accused by his real name. Summarizing, he declared: "Bentzy, even though you learned a lot of Torah and performed many charitable deeds, you neither completed your assignment nor attained your tikkun, your soul correction. You have been an arch-egotist, concerned only about yourself, your own prestige, and your success. All of your learning has gone to the Dark Side, giving power to the forces of evil in the world. Your acts of charity can't possibly atone for your sins, for charity begins at home. If there's no charity at home, then all the charity done on the outside is lacking.

"You should have directed your compassion first of all to your wife, for she was literally your own flesh. You gave to strangers while ignoring her; this proves that you were not at all charitable, just a seeker of prestige. You had patience to listen to strangers' problems for hours, yet you never had two minutes a day to listen to your wife. You looked at her like a waste of time. You delivered ridiculous sermons about your warped notion of marriage, and you gave your students the worst marital advice that can be. Because of your negative influence, they too have become as terrible a husband as you were…"

"…with all your book learning, you failed to understand that life's principal test is to live in peace and harmony with your wife. You regarded the wonderful mitzvoth that a husband should do for a wife as a nagging hindrance. You disdained true loving-kindness."

With an accusing finger, the Chief Justice bellowed: "Had you invested in your *shalom bayit*, you'd have discovered how far you really are from the Torah and its values. The Torah is geared to bring a person to emuna. Your lack of emuna shows that you never really learned Torah. Hashem gave you so much natural intelligence, yet you failed to understand that when your wife was trying to talk to you, Hashem was trying to talk to you. When your wife was begging you to spend some time at home, Hashem was begging you to spend some time at home. Hashem was speaking by way of her vocal chords. By ignoring your wife, you, in your blind arrogance, were repeatedly ignoring Hashem. Torah should have brought you to humility. Was disdaining your wife the act of a humble man? True compassion is in the heart; so why was your heart so cold and uncompassionate toward your wife? You see, you lacked genuine compassion! Why did you give everything to strangers, leaving nothing – not even a minute – for your own wife? Did you ever change a diaper? Did you ever offer to sit up late at night and comfort one of your sick children? She did all of that. You never lifted a finger to help." Bentzy's embarrassment knew no bounds in realizing how he had utterly wasted an entire lifetime in ignorance of man's prime mitzvah – *shalom bayit*, peace in the home.

* * *

The above two parables mock the prototypes that the unsuspecting public holds in high regard. Despite their other apparent achievements, these two individuals failed to complete their principal task, that of living in peace with their wives. Without the latter achievement, the former accomplishments lose their value. Such seemingly-righteous people aren't regarded in the Heavenly Court with anywhere near as much esteem as a simple, unassuming person who has succeeded to build a home of marital peace and harmony.

The true purpose

Rebbe Nachman of Breslev teaches (Likutei Moharan II: 37) that a man's true purpose is to serve Hashem and to walk in His ways. This enables us to recognize Hashem and to get to know Him. One should have no other intent in the service of Hashem than faithfully fulfilling His will.

Since our purpose on this earth is to get to know Hashem, each of us should know that there's no chance of getting to know Hashem without successfully withstanding the test known as "*shalom bayit*," or peace in the home. Therefore, *shalom bayit* is the main way that we fulfill our true purpose.

In order to attain true peace in the home, we must strive to attain emuna and humility – the two most important assets in serving Hashem. By attaining emuna and humility, we also achieve our soul correction, our particular mission on earth. As such, striving to build a successful marriage with *shalom bayit* is the key to fulfilling our true purpose in life and perfecting ourselves.

Practice makes perfect

Dear reader, please don't think that one reading of this book will revolutionize your marriage. Each chapter and each principle should be learned and reviewed over and over until it becomes second nature.

Some of the leading tzaddikim of this generation have mentioned that stern judgments and their manifestations – sickness, strife, financial difficulties, and the like – are frequently the outcome of a woman's distress in the face of her husband's disregard or disrespect for her. Therefore, one will find an enormous added dividend that the more he invests in *shalom bayit*, the more he invokes Divine blessings in his life.

Let this book be your companion. By implementing and striving to implement each point, you are doing yourself the greatest favor in the world.

Chapter Two
No Comments, Please

This chapter teaches one of the most important foundations of *shalom bayit,* or peace in the home. First, I'd like to share a true story with you:

A husband came to me with a long list of things that he does for his wife. He devotes time to her every day. He's attentive to her needs and buys her everything, even spoils her. Apparently, she should be the happiest of women. But no – she's miserable, and they don't have peace in their home. Even worse, she frequently lashes out at him in anger. What's going on here?

To my dismay, this phenomenon is quite familiar; it was clear why the husband had a turbulent home. I told him that his frequent comments about everything she does were destroying her happiness. By the look in his eyes, I knew that I was right on target. All the gifts and niceties in the world aren't worth a constant stream of comments and criticism. The wife of a critical husband is broken, depressed, pained, and has no vitality.

One of the most important foundations of *shalom bayit* is that a husband should never criticize, or comment about his wife under any circumstance.

Before we clarify and elaborate on this principle, we should understand that marital peace is impossible as long as a husband continues to criticize his wife and to comment about everything she does. Every tiny comment is a crack in the wall of marital bliss. With more and more cracks, the home eventually crumbles to the ground, Heaven forbid.

Hashem created the marital relationship in such a way that a husband's criticism can do terrible damage to it; a person has to be insane to try and change a law of creation. Therefore, don't expect your wife to get used to comments and criticism. Don't demand "maturity" or "rational behavior" from her. The comments and criticism literally destroy her, for that's the way Hashem created her.

This is her honor

First of all, we should know that the spiritual source of a woman's soul is honor. Her entire vitality and happiness is dependent on the way her husband honors her. Therefore, any affront to her honor damages her soul, weakens her vitality, and virtually kills her, both spiritually and materially.

The worst breach of a woman's self-respect comes from her husband's comments. Even if his criticism is gentle and delicate, she suffers; even more so when the comments and criticism are cutting and brutal. A woman wants to be perfect in her husband's eyes – this is her honor, her happiness, and her security. Her husband's snide remarks destroy her self-image and her security. Each morsel of criticism is his statement that she's not perfect – to her that means she's nothing! A wife that's subjected to comments and criticism finds life unbearable.

The principle that comments are the opposite of honor is seeded within religious law. One is not allowed to make remarks to one's parent or rabbi, for this is a breach of honor. Even if a son sees a father committing an outright transgression, he's not allowed to comment or criticize, only hint in a round-about manner.

Whether or not the father understands the hint is not the son's responsibility.

Later, we'll learn alternate ways to influence a wife. Comments and criticism are certainly not the way. A wife's honor is even more sensitive that a father's honor. We're allowed to hint to a father, but we're not even allowed to hint criticism at a wife.

The first foundation

Many husbands come to me with their marital issues, with a long list of complaints about their wives. I listen to them, but then tell them that they don't have marital peace because they criticize their wives.

I have never had a case of a husband that admitted to the mistake of comments and criticism – and then made a firm resolution to change – that didn't see a dramatic improvement in his marriage.

Frequently, women complain about their husbands with a long list of grievances. Most of the time, the wife doesn't know how to put her finger on the real source of her anguish – her husband's comments and criticism.

Husbands complain that their wives make mountains out of molehills. They tell me that their wives are always complaining about apparently miniscule problems. The truth is that when she's broken and sad from her husband's constant comments and criticism, every tiny thing upsets her. When he criticizes her, she can't understand him or be considerate of him in any way. She becomes argumentative, hostile, and displeased with everything he does.

Emphasis

I can't sufficiently emphasize the importance of this foundation principle in building a marriage: never comment or criticize. Criticism is so devastating to a wife that it can actually lead to physical ills and health complications.

As long as a husband continues to criticize his wife, it's pointless to deal with other factors that affect marital peace. This first foundation must be corrected before we deal with any other issues in the marriage. A husband should therefore appeal to Hashem for help in refraining from commenting or criticizing his wife in any way.

Husbands are amazed to see the striking difference in their relationship with their wives as soon as they begin working on this point. Now, we'll explain on a deeper level why refraining from comments and criticism in the home is so very important.

The wife is a mirror

Let's stop and contemplate Hashem's exact, tailor-made Divine Providence for a moment: Since everything is under Hashem's control and designed to facilitate a person's individual soul correction and the correction of the world in general, then there must be a rationale behind why Hashem has instilled zero tolerance of her husband's comments and criticism in a wife. Why is this so? What's the lesson we need to learn from this? Why can't her soul tolerate criticism?

My esteemed teacher, Rabbi Eliezer Berland shlit'a provides the answer. As a young man, I asked him to teach me the foundations of marital peace. He taught me the following two principles:

First, the wife is a mirror of the husband (this principle comes from the holy Ariza'l). Any deficiency he sees in her is actually his own deficiency.

Second, never make any remarks, comments, or criticism about anything she does, even if she's done a gross misdeed.

Rabbi Berland told me that everything I see in my wife is a message for me. Frequently, a wife's unpleasant behavior is an indication of something askew in the husband's service of Hashem, or of something else that needs correcting. On a more basic level, a wife's disrespect of her husband merely mirrors the husband's disrespect for his wife. If he places her on a pedestal, then she'll do likewise.

The above two principles are interdependent. Since any deficiency that a husband sees in his wife is really his own shortcoming, then he certainly shouldn't try to correct her, especially by reprimanding or criticizing. Instead, he should evaluate himself and correct what needs correcting. When he does so, she'll automatically change for the better.

Rav Berland emphasized that these two principles – knowing that a wife is the husband's mirror and refraining from comments and criticism no matter what – saved his own marriage. With ignorance of these two principles, a husband can't possibly avoid criticizing his wife, particularly when he feels like he's doing her a service by correcting her actions. Since the wife can't stand criticism, they lose their marital peace.

One who is equipped with the knowledge of these two principles will never comment on or criticize his wife's actions, even the biggest mistake she might make. Knowing that she is his mirror, he searches to correct within himself the flaws he sees within her.

This is the rule: Hashem shows a husband what he needs to correct by way of the wife. Any negative characteristic he sees in her, every flaw, and every mistake she makes, shows him what he needs to rectify. His looking at her is exactly like his looking in a mirror. The shortcomings he sees in her are actually his own.

The reason a wife is so sensitive to comments and criticism is because Hashem doesn't want him to criticize her in the least, but rather, only to correct himself instead.

If Hashem would have desired that a husband correct his wife, then He would have implanted within her a soul that tolerates criticism. But, as the husband corrects himself, the wife is corrected too, since she mirrors his behavior.

So, one can effect a change within one's wife by correcting oneself, without saying a single word to her!

The entire mitzva of marriage is designed as a soul correction for the husband, for according to the dry law, a woman isn't obligated to get married. She can live a life on her own, while he is commanded to get married and to have children.

From an esoteric standpoint, the Ariza'l teaches that a woman has been corrected already; she comes to this earth to facilitate her husband's soul correction.

A wife is "programmed" to facilitate her husband's teshuva. Any flaw, mistake, or shortcoming on his behalf triggers a reaction from the wife. This works in the opposite manner as well: any improvement or spiritual reinforcement in the husband elevates the wife. We'll soon learn how to interpret her reactions.

With eyes of emuna, we see that a wife's characteristics are designed to help her husband become a righteous person.

Observe and understand

Since the wife is the husband's mirror, he should know how to interpret what he sees in that mirror in order to reach the proper conclusions. We'll illustrate a few examples of how a wife serves as a mirror for her husband. Each husband should pray to Hashem for the wisdom to understand what he observes within his "mirror."

A. Hashem governs the world according to the "ATFAT" principle (A Turn For A Turn). For example, if a wife fails to respect her husband, then the husband is not properly respecting Hashem. If the wife doesn't obey the husband, then the husband is most certainly disobeying Hashem, and so forth.

B. Hashem shows the husband what he must correct by displaying that particular flaw within the wife. A woman's anger is indicative of a husband's tendency to lose his temper. A woman's disdain of a certain mitzvah – modesty, for example – indicates her husband's failure to observe that very same mitzvah. If he looks at other women, she'll most certainly try to attract the attention of other men.

C. Hashem uses a breach in marital peace to stimulate a correction within the husband. For example, as soon as a husband acts arrogantly in the slightest, his wife opposes him. If a husband has lewd desires, his wife won't stand him. If he desires other women, pornography, and debauchery, then she'll be disgusted with him. It turns out that the status of their marital peace is an indication of what he needs to correct.

D. King Solomon said (Proverbs, chapter 27): "As water reflects one's countenance, thus one heart reflects another's heart." Her behavior toward him is a mere reflection of his behavior toward her. If he treats her like a queen, he'll be a king. But, if he treats her like a floor mop, he'll be a wet rag.

E. Our sages said that a person with a nasty wife is spared from purgatory. The Gemara teaches that we must therefore accept the tribulation of a difficult wife with love, for a husband's suffering atones for his sins.

My esteemed teacher Rabbi Levi Yitzchak Binder, of blessed and saintly memory, told me that not only a wife that curses and hits is called a "nasty wife," but any woman that causes sorrow and anguish to her husband is regarded likewise. If she's unkempt and disheveled, she also falls into this category. The Gemara says (tractate Yevamot, 63) that even if she prepares him a wonderful meal, but she does something to upset him such as ignoring him or turning her back on him, then she's also regarded as a "nasty wife."

A woman who is overly meticulous about cleanliness and order is also a "nasty wife," for it's difficult to live within the confines of a museum.

Let's clarify: a wife doesn't become a "nasty wife" on her own accord. If she torments her husband, then he deserves to be tormented, for there are no tribulations without prior transgression. Whatever Hashem gives a man – a woman that's clean, messy, angry, or patient is exactly what he deserves. So, if she's what he deserves, why complain about her? Is it her fault that the Heavenly Court has sentenced him to suffer? The wife is only a stick in Hashem's hands. Instead of reprimanding her, let him open his heart and ears to Hashem's reprimand, take positive action, and do teshuva.

Your personal mirror

The principal that a wife mirrors her husband enables a person to refrain from criticizing his wife. The flaws she exhibits are the flaws he needs to rectify. She is his exact reflection.

If you see in the mirror that your hat's on crooked, don't try to straighten the mirror – it won't do any good. Likewise, comments and criticism do nothing to correct a wife; they only destroy her joy in life.

One with no spiritual awareness is upset by the flaws he sees in his wife. He becomes embittered and regrets his misfortune in marrying such a woman. He also thinks that his solemn obligation is to criticize everything she does, to lecture, reprimand, and sermonize. He can't love her either, because he only sees her faults. Such an attitude is the root cause of strife in a marriage.

As long as a husband thinks that his wife must correct herself, especially when he eggs her on with comments and criticism, there can never be peace in the home. Their lives become a purgatory on earth.

You didn't get married to correct your wife. You got married to correct yourself, by using your wife as a mirror of you.

Magnifying glass

A wife isn't just a mirror that reflects life-size images. She's much more than that; she's a high-powered electron microscope that reveals all of her husband's flaws. For example, if he has the slightest streak of anger, Hashem will show him his flaw within his wife. She is liable to exhibit disproportionate levels of anger, just so that her husband will get the message.

One might ask, is this fair? Why does Hashem make the wife overreact? The answer is simple: no man is capable of objectively seeing his own faults. If Hashem would send subtle suggestions for character improvement, the husband would probably brush them aside. His wife's extreme magnifications of his behavior are designed to elicit a responsive effort to improve. Our sages said that a hint is enough for a wise man, but a fool needs to be hit over the head.

Mirror or suffer

Understandably, a wife is a mirror only for a husband that respects her and does his best to refrain from comments and criticism. But, if he's forever tearing her down with his remarks and criticism, then her anger is a result of her own frustration and unhappiness. In such a case, the husband must make immediate teshuva for upsetting his wife.

In the face of their wife's expressions of rage, some husbands – rather than understanding where she's coming from – react smugly and say: "Why can't you control your temper like I do? Why can't you work on yourself and learn a little patience?" Such a husband is light years away from teshuva. His only hope is to learn this book and pray to implement it.

In most cases, a husband's calm in the face of his wife's anger is not an expression of commendable character, for at other times – when he should be calm and collected – he flies into a fury. When his wife is angry, he enjoys showing himself off as 'Mister Chill', the epitome of serenity, in an attempt to make her look like the wicked witch. This is nothing more than sinister and spiteful behavior on his part.

Her sorrow should have touched his heart, and aroused him from his smug apathy. He should understand that her angry reactions are a sign of distress. The husband, by correcting his own faults, rescues his wife from distress.

If a person is a model husband that never criticizes his wife, and yet she still exhibits outbursts of anger, then he should know that he still has inclinations of anger that he needs to uproot.

Mirroring the inner self

A wife mirrors a husband's inner dimension more than she does his outer dimension. With serious soul-searching, a person could evaluate himself if he truly wanted to, but human nature tends to whitewash one's flaws and character blemishes. People like the comfort of feeling that everything is fine. But, if a person believes that his wife is the mirror of his inner self, then he earns a rare opportunity to discover the truth, to see his own innermost flaws as reflected in his wife, and to work to correct them.

Many husbands come to me with complaints about their wives. When I tell them that she is a mirror of the husband's shortcomings, they refuse to accept what I'm saying. This shows a denial of their faults and an unwillingness to correct them.

When a husband has a genuine desire to improve, and he does an hour of daily self-assessment and hitbodedut, trying his best to improve what he can, then Hashem shows him what he needs to correct via his hitbodedut. Such a husband doesn't need the wake-up calls of an irate wife, and therefore enjoys a good measure of tranquility. Even if he doesn't succeed in discerning all of Hashem's hints during hitbodedut, then Hashem will augment the Divine messages with gentle messages from the wife.

A husband that prefers burying his head in the sand like an ostrich and ignoring his faults requires a shock treatment, which he receives from his wife. If this doesn't arouse him to work on himself, then it's a sign that he's far away from teshuva and self-correction.

A mirror for the worthy

The holy 16th Century CE Kabbalist, Rabbi Avraham Azulai of blessed and saintly memory, author of the classic "Chessed L'Avraham" and great grandfather of the renowned Rabbi Chaim Yosef David Azulai (the "Chida"), writes about the principle of the wife as a mirror of her husband. He explains that Hashem runs the world by implementing a turn for a turn. **The way a person acts with Hashem is exactly the way his wife will act with him.** For example, if a person revolts against Hashem, then his wife will revolt against him.

It's common for a man to consider himself a good husband; he therefore fails to understand why his wife doesn't listen to him. This is a result of the ATFAT principle (a turn for a turn). She revolts against him in the same manner that he has revolted against Hashem. This is not a punishment, but on the contrary; it's Divine compassion designed to encourage him to mend his ways and come closer to Hashem.

"Therefore," writes Rabbi Avraham Azulai, "every upright young man whose wife revolts against him shall know that he himself is the cause."

What does Rabbi Azulai mean? If a person is not an upright young man, then his wife won't act like a mirror. The answer is that he who fails to behave in the way of the Torah would obviously react brutally and violently if his wife would make a remark about him, much less if she'd dare yell at him or disparage him. A wife is deathly afraid of such a husband. She is subservient because she's emotionally vanquished and terrified of how he might react.

She can't possibly be a mirror, because he has shattered her long ago.

Only a person with the will to improve himself and with a delicate and forgiving manner is worthy of a wife that mirrors him. The kind, loving, and respectful husband can attribute his wife's irrational behavior to his own shortcomings. Rather than being upset with her, he makes a greater effort to improve himself.

Why did Sarah laugh?

The Torah in Parshat Vayera relates how the angels promised Abraham a son within the coming year. From inside her tent, Sarah heard them and laughed. Hashem reprimanded Abraham and asked: "Why did Sarah laugh? Doesn't she believe in my ability to give her a child, despite her old age?"

The question is, why did Hashem reprimand Abraham? Our sages tell us that Sarah was a prophet too, on an even loftier spiritual level than he was. Why didn't Hashem reveal Himself directly to her and ask her why she laughed?

From here, we learn that everything a wife does is rooted in her husband. Although we have no concept of Abraham and Sarah's legendary spiritual plateau, at their level, her laugh was a reflection of a slight blemish in emuna on his part. This explains why Hashem reprimanded Abraham for something that Sarah did. Her manifest flaw is actually his.

The Sun and the Moon

According to Kabbalah, an important principle of creation is that the male is the giver and the female is the receiver. The husband resembles the sun and the wife resembles the moon. She has no light of her own, only the light that he shines on her. Therefore, her darkness is a sign of his insufficient illumination. A husband who fails to work on himself and improve his character can't possibly shine the light on his wife that she needs.

Since the husband is the giver, he must honor his wife, grant her warmth, love, joy, and security. He must be a living example of emuna for her. But, when a husband comes home looking for a handout – demanding respect, understanding, attention and the like – then he assumes the spiritual characteristic of a female. Even though a woman often gives, this is the outcome of Hashem's desire to give him a pat on the back and encourage him further.

A person will definitely get what he deserves – whether encouragement and respect, or a slap in the face and verbal abuse.

The Speaker System

Hashem completely programs the woman. Not only is she her husband's mirror, she is also Hashem's speaker system. Hashem speaks to the husband through the wife. Imagine that you're listening to your FM stereo. You've invested in an expensive speaker system with tweeters, bass and woofers, housed in an expensive mahogany casing. You're listening to a radio broadcast, and the speakers start hurling all kinds of insults and epithets at you. Would you be angry at your speaker system, grab your speakers one by one and smash them on the floor? Of course not! The guilty party could be broadcasting from a studio that's hundreds or even thousands of miles from your whereabouts. Your speaker system certainly isn't responsible, despite the fact that it emitted the sounds.

The same goes for your wife's anger, yelling, disrespect, and verbal abuse. She's not the one who's talking – Hashem is! For that reason, the husband should listen to what she has to say, even when it stings. He should no sooner be upset with her than he would be at his stereo speaker system.

The Tape Deck

A wife also resembles Hashem's tape deck. He inserts the disc that her husband needs to hear. When Hashem wants to encourage the husband, the wife speaks words of kindness and reinforcement. When Hashem wants to arouse a husband to teshuva, the wife speaks words of insult and anger. Does it now make sense to blame a distasteful CD recording on the tape deck? In essence, that's what the wife is – Hashem's tape deck. Arguing with her or retaliating is like arguing and retaliating against a tape deck, a totally absurd notion. Rather than fighting against Hashem's tape deck, the husband should open his ears and listen to Hashem's message, no matter how unpleasant it may be.

We often see that apparently 'model' husbands still suffer insults from their wives. Despite the husband's outer conduct, Hashem knows his innermost dimensions. Hashem therefore does what's needed to stimulate self-assessment and teshuva.

Sometimes, a wife reacts in a way that certainly doesn't seem to reflect the husband's behavior. This is a clear sign that Hashem is relaying a message for him by way of her.

Let's assume that Marty is a model husband. He always comes straight home from work. He helps around the house as much as he can. One day, he came home after doing all the food shopping for Shabbat. He spared no expense in buying his wife's favorite meats and sweets. He walks in the door, and boom! She's like a Howitzer that fires a 105mm bombshell right between his eyes. He can't understand what's happening to him. Marty did everything to please her, and now she's pouring hot coals of anger and insult all over him. Why is she so angry? Why did Hashem insert a CD of wrath into her throat?

While shopping, Marty was staring at a strange woman, contaminating his eyes and blemishing his soul. His wife has no idea what he did, but Hashem knows exactly where, when, and what Marty did. Hashem made her react the way she did. He injected her with a dose of anger and frayed nerves so that she'd trigger her husband's urgent soul-searching. That way, Marty would realize that he did something wrong that required immediate teshuva.

When a person walks in the street and looks at women, even if he comes home with baskets full of gifts, wine, and sweet song, his wife will still shoot him down. This is a message from Hashem: "You looked at what you weren't supposed to? You were bombarded!"

The principle that a wife is her husband's mirror, tape deck, and speaker system is the main reason why he should never criticize her. Let's examine a few more reasons why one should never make comments to, or criticize his wife:

1. Comments are debilitating

Rebbe Nachman of Breslev explains that a person that isn't worthy of reprimanding others shouldn't make comments and remarks to people, especially to his wife. Rebbe Nachman says:

"Even though chastisement is a lofty thing, and each Jew has a duty to chastise his neighbor when the latter acts awry, for it is written: "You shall chastise your neighbor," even so, not everyone is worthy of reprimanding others. Rabbi Akiva said: "I'm surprised if there's anyone in this generation that's worthy of reprimanding others." If Rabbi Akiva said that about his generation [a generation of spiritual giants and holy men – LB], then we certainly can't reprove others in this generation…"

Rebbe Nachman continues to explain that chastisement from an unworthy person is not only ineffective, but damaging as well. It's remindful of an object with a foul odor; as long as you don't push and prod the object, it doesn't exude a bad smell. But, as soon as you move or prod the object, it exudes its foul odor. The same goes for a soul. If the soul has transgressed, then chastisement is like prodding the soul and arousing the soul's blemishes and uncorrected traits which give off a spiritually foul odor that cuts these souls off from their source of Divine abundance.

"A soul thrives from aroma. So, when the person who chastises arouses the foul odor of the soul, that soul is debilitated and consequently cut off from Divine abundance. But, when the person that chastises is a worthy of reprimanding others, then his chastisement arouses the good aroma of that soul, for one's chastisement must be on the level of Moses' chastisement (Likutei Moharan II:8)".

In order to reprimand other people, a person must be on the spiritual level of Moses. And if Rabbi Akiva said that there was no one in his lofty generation of the *Tannaim* (the Mishnaic sages) that was qualified to reprove others, and Rebbe Nachman of Breslev said the same about his generation (also a generation of giants such as the Chozeh from Lublin, the Koznitzer Maggid, and Rebbe Mendele of Rimnov), then we certainly can't make even the slightest remark to another person, especially our wives. Those who continue to remark and comment about others and to criticize them are making a grave mistake.

The Torah requires a person to reprimand his fellow man, only if he doesn't do harm to that person. True chastisement is designed to release the burden of sin from a person's shoulders. The reprimands that come from the mouth of an unworthy person simply call attention to the burden of sin and make it an even more unbearable burden.

Most reprimands weaken people and break their hearts. They say to themselves: "If I'm such a loser and everything I do is wrong, how can there ever be hope for me?" Many fall into despair and give up their struggle to improve. Some may even fall by the wayside and throw off the yoke of Torah and mitzvoth altogether. So, rather than helping others, the person that criticizes and chastises does grave damage.

The Chazon Ish of blessed and saintly memory, gave a ruling that there is no one that properly knows how to reprimand in this generation and therefore we must show love toward our neighbor.

Up until now, we've been speaking about man and his fellow man. A wife is all the more in need of her husband's sensitivity, respect, and constant encouragement. Comments and criticism are devastating to her. A wife's entire vitality depends on her husband's kind words to her.

2. Remarks don't help

By nature, a woman can't acknowledge a fault or a mistake, even when someone gently reproves her. Even more so, when strongly reprimanded, no wife will accept her husband's words. Therefore, a husband's remarks are useless. Our sages say that just as it is a mitzvah to chastise one that heeds, it's a mitzvah to refrain from chastising a person that doesn't heed. Since the wife can't listen to her husband's criticism, then his remarks will only increase tension and animosity; they might even turn her accidental misdeed into a willful transgression.

3. Remarks are degrading

In a wife's eyes, not only criticism, but the slightest delicate uncomplimentary remarks – even said with the purest of motives - are premeditated affronts to her dignity. She is insulted, angered, and unforgiving, certain that her husband doesn't love her. If he truly loved her, why would he be trying to find fault in her all the time? The famed Kabbalist Rabbi Avraham Azulai paraphrased the Mishna in tractate Avot and said: "Don't look at a person during his hour of failure or weakness, for then, that person hides so no one will see him, and when you discover his failure, he'll think that you take joy in his misery."

If a husband was sensitive, he'd feel just how insulting and degrading remarks and criticism are to a wife, even when said with utmost kindness and with positive intent. If he knew how sharply his remarks pierce her heart, he wouldn't say them.

4. One who criticizes is arrogant

The truth is that husbands who criticize aren't gentle and well-meaning in so doing. Many have a drive to constantly remark, comment, criticize, complain, and find fault in those close to them. This drive stems from arrogance, cruelty, and an utter lack of self-control.

A husband must therefore ask himself where his comments and criticism are coming from. If he's honest with himself, he'll discover that his compulsive drive to make comments and criticize all the time is a sign of his own arrogance, character flaws, and cruelty that he needs to work on.

5. Remarks are damaging

Many people have a tendency to tear themselves down; women especially. Woman often feel that they're not doing enough, that they're not good enough, or that they're not satisfying their husbands. A criticizing husband adds fuel to the fire of self-persecution and a low self-image. Such a husband justifies and reinforces a wife's negative feelings about herself. In extreme cases, his remarks and criticism put her right on the psychiatrist's sofa, Heaven forbid.

6. The pedant can't teach

A pedantic husband can't have marital peace. Our sages teach (Mishna, tractate Avot, ch. 2) that a pedant can't teach. Therefore, a husband won't be able to effect a change in his wife by way of comments and criticism.

7. Remarks are dangerous

A person that reprimands his wife will almost surely fall into the traps of several outright Torah transgressions such as anger, humiliating one's fellow man, and causing anguish to one's fellow man. Ironically, a husband that chastises his wife for doing a minor misdeed ends up committing major transgressions, upsetting the peace at home, and chasing away the Divine Presence from his midst. What's worse, her minor misdeed or his major transgressions? The remarks are dangerous.

8. The remarks are a boomerang

The old adage says that people who live in glass houses shouldn't throw stones. A husband should know that the minute he criticizes his wife, he's exposing himself to criticism.

Clarification

Everything we said until now applies to a situation when a husband comments or criticizes **after the fact**. But, if he sees that his wife might make a mistake or commit a misdeed, he can guide her gently **before** she does something wrong. There's a world of difference between guidance and criticism.

How will she change?

One of the arguments that the Yetzer Hara (Evil Inclination) uses to incite a husband to comment and criticize is that the criticism is for her ultimate spiritual and material benefit.

The Yetzer Hara hides in his thoughts and says: "Nobody's perfect! People want to improve. They want to make progress in life. How's my wife going to get ahead if I don't help her? She should be grateful for my comments and criticism! If I really love her, how can I ignore the damages she does to herself with her mistakes? How will she ever change if I don't help her?"

Before we dismantle the Yetzer's mental landmines, let's see what happens inside a woman's heart when her husband criticizes her:

The moment a husband makes a remark about something his wife does – no matter how gentle or justified, even more so if the remark is unfair or brutal – her heart withers and her soul darkens. She sees herself as a nothing, worthless and unsuccessful. She loses all will to improve. All she has left is her need to survive. Therefore, like a threatened and wounded she-wolf, she tries to salvage what's left of her dignity by holding her ground and justifying herself, even if it goes against all logic. At such times, she exposes her fangs.

For a woman to admit to a mistake or shortcoming is worse than death. She'll therefore do anything to protect her dignity, which like oxygen, is the source of her vitality. Taking away her dignity is consequently tantamount to threatening her life.

The husband thinks that *his* wife is the only woman in the world that's so sensitive to criticism. He says to himself: "What kind of woman is this that denies the truth? She never in her life apologized for her mistakes!" The husband becomes heartbroken; he doesn't realize that every woman is just like his wife and can't admit to a fault even if she wanted to. When he sees that she can't admit to the truth or accept constructive criticism, he is simultaneously saddened and angered. He disdains her lack of integrity and accuses her of arrogance.

A husband especially disdains his wife's visible mistakes, which the Yetzer Hara is all too ready to amplify. He can't understand why she can't admit that the food is burnt - the whole kitchen smells like charcoal! The more he tries to explain to her that the casserole should have been baked for 45 minutes and not for two hours, the more she fights to the death to defend herself.

Now, the husband has more complaints against his wife and the vicious downward spiral continues: the more he complains and disdains, the more he destroys her and invokes her anger and irrational reactions. The more he humiliates and tramples her, the more she chokes. Her heart fills with hatred and despair, and she despises her husband like she despises a person that attempts to stab her in the heart.

A husband that doesn't understand a woman's sensitivity to remarks and criticism considers her reactions an expression of insanity. "What did I say? I didn't even intend to criticize? Why is she reacting so violently? Has she lost control?" He doesn't realize that one doesn't need to curse or hit to be called an abusive husband. As long as he continues to comment and criticize, her life isn't worth living.

Experience shows that women who are subjected to comments and criticism suffer extreme emotional anguish, to the point of shattered nerves and total breakdown. The hate their husbands and whatever he stands for. If a husband criticizes in the name of the Torah, the wife will hate the husband, his Torah, and even Hashem, G-d forbid. She's liable to take off her hair covering and to throw away religion altogether, even to search for forbidden consolation, Heaven forbid.

Now that we know what happens to a wife when her husband makes a remark or criticizes her, let's ask the husband: Do you still think you can change your wife with your comments and criticism? Do you still ask yourself: "How will she change?" Are you still prepared to risk destroying your life, her life, and your children's lives with your criticism?

The right way

Everything we said until now boils down to one solid conclusion: **A husband must avoid criticizing his wife at all costs.**

Maybe you'd like to ask, OK, everything's fine and dandy in theory, but how is it possible to ignore a wife's shortcoming in practice? We're not angels, and there are things that she does that upset us. If we keep quiet, we're liable to explode one day! So how do we get her to mend her erroneous ways, both in the material and the spiritual areas of her life? Isn't there any way to get her to improve or to do teshuva? Isn't this our duty as husbands? Didn't the Gemara say that if a husband doesn't guide his family then he gets caught for their sins? Is it truthful to stand by and let a wife transgress or make mistakes without doing anything? What's the right way?

Here's the answer: In addition to the eight additional reasons why we shouldn't comment or criticize, let's remember our main reason – a wife is her husband's mirror. If we see an unsightly image, do we break the mirror? No! We correct the image. In truth, a husband must know that he need not correct his wife. Instead, he should roll up his sleeves and begin working on himself. Once he's corrected, she'll be corrected automatically.

The salient point here is that all of a wife's shortcomings, failures, and mistakes are all reflections of what the husband needs to correct. Even if he suffers, then he can rest assured that he deserves whatever tribulations he suffers from her. His only resort is teshuva.

Refraining from commenting and criticizing is not enough. A husband must strive to see only the good in her. He should know that in her own right, she's a fabulous person. But unfortunately, she's now reflecting his negative attributes so that he can understand how to make teshuva.

This brings us to Rebbe Nachman's classic teaching about finding the good points, as brought down in Likutei Moharan I: 282:

"Know that one must always judge every person fairly, even a totally wicked person, one should look to discover the morsel of good within him, for by judging him fairly, one uplifts him to a level of good, and in this way initiates his full repentance…"

The principle of invoking a favorable reaction by judging a person fairly is seemingly illogical. One would think that improvement stems from showing a person his mistakes and encouraging him to rectify them. In extreme cases, severe reprimanding and punishment further this goal, according to conventional thought.

In Chassidic thought, the opposite is true: the way to help a person improve is by showing him his good points. By judging a person fairly, we give a person the joy and vitality of knowing that others think favorably of him. This gives him the willpower and the incentive to improve his ways.

This ploy of judging others favorably is so strong that it works even when we only *think* favorably about another person, without even saying a word to him. Kind words accelerate the other person's efforts to improve so much more.

Especially in a marriage, when a husband only looks for the good in his wife and compliments her incessantly, he gives her the desire and incentive to truly please him. No woman is an ingrate – she'll look for all kinds of ways to repay her husband's kindness.

When a wife is happy, she has the inner strength to work on herself. When she's the brunt of painful remarks and criticism, she won't have the strength to boil a pot of water.

A husband must remember that the same holy Rebbe that warned against chastising and criticizing is the Rebbe that teaches us to look for a person's good points and to judge others favorably. A husband that internalizes both pieces of advice is a winner in two ways. First, he sees no faults in his wife, and therefore is never dissatisfied with her. Second, he sees the good in her and therefore loves her, which gives her the power and incentive to gratify him all the more.

The middle road

If, after everything we've learned, the husband still desires to speak with his wife and try to correct something she's doing wrong, he should remember that as soon as he sees something askew, he must not comment! The Vilna Ga'on says that we must learn from Hashem, who turned away His eyes while Adam and Eve were sinning by eating the forbidden fruit. Hashem spoke to them only after they covered themselves with fig leaves. A husband must do the same. If he sees his wife doing something wrong, he should wait 2 or 3 days before mentioning anything about it.

Before he speaks to his wife, he should pray to Hashem that his wife won't be slighted or saddened and will accept what he has to say lovingly.

The husband should express himself in a positive manner, for example: "What a pleasure it is not to slander a single human being" or, "How wonderful it is to be a positive role model for our children."

He should speak to her during a time of loving intimacy, like when they're taking a walk together or dining alone. He should clothe his message with words of love, understanding, and concern for her welfare. Instead of chastising her for staying up too late, he should say: "Sweetheart, I'm really concerned about your health. You need a minimum amount of rest to function and for your beauty to shine. You work so hard during the day – you deserve proper rest…"

The key words are love, consideration, understanding, and concern.

Once again, this mode of gentle remarks is not the best road to take. It's a middle road for those that haven't yet accustomed themselves to refraining from all comments and criticism. But, a man with a strong heart and a will to serve Hashem in truth knows that *shalom bayit* is dependent on him alone, and the environment he creates in the home. Nothing creates such a wonderful home atmosphere as a husband that refrains from comments and criticism.

Chapter Three
First Place

The central axis

Marital bliss and success rotates around one central axis – a wife's knowledge that she holds the first place in her husband's list of priorities. She wants to be the most important part of his life. He should strive to make her feel that way.

A husband should seize every opportunity to show her that she's first place. He should constantly remind her that he loves her more than anyone else and that she's top priority and his actions should bear witness to his words all the time. When she needs something, he should jump to do it. When she opens her mouth, he should lend an ear as if she's about to say the most important thing in the world.

When a wife sees that a husband does everything in his power to please her, then she'll really feel like she's in first place in his life. This feeling gives her indescribable joy, strength, and vitality. He is ultimately the one that benefits from all his sacrifices for her. Her payback is tenfold from whatever he invests in making her feel like she's number one.

The needless list

The principle of "First Place" encompasses one's entire life with a wife, as the following example shows:

A quarreling young couple came to me to bridge their disagreements. The wife read a long list of complaints that she had about her husband, written on a piece of folio paper.

Her first complaint was that whenever she needs her husband to come home at a certain hour – to enable her to attend a lecture, an exercise class, or whatever – he's always late. Despite his promises to come home on time, he never does.

I asked the husband why he fails to come home on time. He answered: "Rabbi, believe me that I don't waste time. My overtime is for the benefit of my wife and kids. Would I come home late without a good reason? What can I do? Urgent situations arise that need my attention…"

"You're dead wrong," I answered. "Your wife should be your first priority. Even if your business is for her benefit, you can't be successful in the long run unless she is happy. Her needs come before anyone else's. Therefore, you have to put a limit on your overtime. And if you're working extra hours because of your debts, you have to limit this too. The way to invoke Divine assistance in escaping debt and financial difficulties is to make your wife happy."

"All your problems," I continued, "are because your wife isn't your highest priority. Up until now, you've let everything else come before her. She must now assume first place in your life."

I explained to the husband that his chronic lateness is because everything is more important to him than his wife is. If he really cared about her needs, he'd come home on time, especially when it means so much to her. And, coming home on time so that she can attend her favorite evening Torah lecture is not enough; he must do it willingly and with a smile.

With the wife's list of complaints in hand, I told the husband that all of his wife's grievances rotate around the central issue that she's less than highest priority in his life. Here he speaks to her, but his eyes are glued to the newspaper. There he comes home late, and his wife misses an important wedding. She asked him to pick up her meat order from the local butcher on the way home from work, and it slipped his mind. Her needs always seem to be ignored or forgotten. These things recur because she's not first place in his life.

The wife listened to my dialog with her husband, and her eyes opened wide in amazement. "Rabbi, what a bulls-eye! I myself didn't know how to put a finger on what was really bothering me most. You just did it! You described my feelings to the tee. I can't stand being second or third class in my husband's eyes!"

I asked the wife if anything else was bothering her. She answered, "Nothing! If my husband is capable of understanding what you summed up in one sentence, Rabbi, then my whole list of complaints is needless."

A woman's oxygen

To understand the underlying rationale behind the principle of making your wife first place, we must realize that Hashem created women in such a way that a woman's vitality comes from her sense of dignity. King David alluded to this in Psalm 45 when he said: "The entire dignity of a princess is internal." In other words, a woman's soul thrives on dignity. A slight to her honor and prestige, or failing to respect her, is like robbing her lungs of oxygen.

Don't think that living with a woman is like living with a friend or a business partner. Between men, the tacit agreement of: "If I'm OK with you, then you must be OK with me," works fine.

The rules of living with a woman are different. One must know what makes her tick, how she thinks, what she likes, and what she despises. More than anything, one must understand that honor and respect are basic needs to her soul – without them, she withers. She derives her honor first and foremost from the feeling that she's the most important thing in her husband's life and loved more than anyone else. As long as a husband fails to give his wife that feeling, they'll never be happy together.

In this chapter, we'll illustrate what it means to make your wife happy. Even if the husband puts on a good act and fulfills our recommendations, as long as he doesn't internalize the feeling that his wife is first place in his life – and radiate that message to her - she won't be truly happy.

The Yetzer Hara, or evil inclination, is constantly trying to destroy a person's marital bliss. Even if a man learns how to be a good husband, the Yetzer will try to trip him up all the time. One would therefore be well-advised to pray to Hashem for help in implementing each of the teachings in this book.

Devoting the time

A couple came to me with marital problems. The wife complained that the husband has no time for her or for the children. The husband countered that his schedule was simply jammed from morning till night, and that it's not his fault...

A husband has no time when his family scores low on his scale of priorities. Those who place career and corporate success before true success – *shalom bayit* – rationalize that if they're left with some time at the end of the day, then they'll throw a few crumbs to the wife and children. But since the husband is a go-getter with aspirations, then his entire waking day is centered on chasing what he wants. Everything – tennis with the boss, dinner with a prospective client, a late meeting downtown - takes preference to his withering wife at home.

The above husband shrugged his shoulders and asked me what he's supposed to do if he's occupied with making a living all day long. I answered that his question shows that he has no idea of what I'm talking about.

"If you'd realize that truly the biggest success in your life is marital bliss, and if you'd understand how important putting your wife in first place is, then you'd find a way to move other commitments aside and to devote the time to her that she needs. But," I continued, letting my words sink in, "if you come home with an impatient and begrudging attitude, then she'll be just as upset as if you didn't come home at all. You should give her the feeling that coming home to her is the biggest treat there is. Give her a warm greeting and a big smile when you walk in the door. Break up the long day with a phone call or two telling her how much you look forward to seeing her."

Many husbands go through the motions and do what their wives want them to do, but they lack sincerity. Sure, they don't want wars and arguments. But, their wives are still far from being first place in their lives. In such a circumstance, a wife remains dissatisfied with her husband. Some husbands justify themselves: "I do everything for her, and she still complains all the time. She's never satisfied!"

True. Even diamonds and ocean cruises won't satisfy her, as long as she's anything but first place in his life.

Don't be caught off guard

Suppose you've been trying to do everything right. You want to show your wife that she's your top priority in life. Yet at a certain the moment, you're deeply involved in something and she needs you. Caught off guard, you answer her with impatience and give her the feeling that she's a nuisance. From that moment on, consider all your efforts down the drain. Now you'll have to work triple hard to repair the damage and to give her back the feeling that she's in first place.

Damage control requires much more time and effort than simply giving her the proper attention when she needs it, even if you are busy with something else, no matter how vital. As long as one hasn't deeply internalized the necessity of making his wife first place in his life, he'll continually be caught off guard in those situations that reveal his true priorities. One can't put on an act in the long run. To make a wife feel like she's top priority, a husband must internalize the absolute necessity of making her top priority.

When a husband looks at his watch and begrudges the time he has to devote to his wife, then he'll end up devoting triple the time to putting out the fires of arguments and marital crises. When a husband fulfills a wife's requests lovingly and devotes to her the time that she needs, he'll end up with marital peace that costs a minimal investment of time. The opposite also holds true: When a husband fails to fulfill a wife's requests lovingly and begrudges her the time that she needs, he'll end up with marital hurricanes whose damage will require a major investment of time *and* money to repair.

Guarding your investment

No woman can stand the feeling of being second fiddle, even when her husband is devoting his attention to something that's important to her, such as making a living. As soon as she feels that something is more important to her husband than she is, peace in the home disintegrates.

Suppose that a husband is a good guy, meets his wife's needs and tries to do everything she wants, but she's still not happy. He doesn't understand what in the world she wants. In such a case, he has likely flunked her test at a critical time. Maybe she asked him for a favor while he was watching the Super Bowl and he inadvertently ignored her. That's all it takes to give her the feeling that she's second place to the Dallas Cowboys. She can't stand that. She wants to be first place *all the time*.

Let's view a different scenario: Suppose the wife knows just how passionate her husband is about football. She's cooking and he's watching his favorite team play an important semifinals game. She cuts her finger while chopping vegetables, and she calls him to the kitchen for consolation and to help her bandage the wound, despite the fact that it's only a slight sliver…

Beware! This is a test! Guard your investment; don't lose everything you've worked hard for in a split second. Get up, express your concern, and put the bandaid on her finger. Let her feel that for you, her tiniest scratch is a cause for concern.

If the husband passes the test, and lovingly jumps to his wife's call no matter what it is, then she'll be truly pleased with him.

Don't forget that meeting her needs is not enough. A husband must be loving, willing, and quick on his feet to help her. If he does so out of fear, or to get rid of her so that he can go back to his game, then she'll sense that she's not highest priority and the husband goes back to square one. The more he disappoints her, the harder he'll have to work to convince her that she's first place in his life.

Big profit

Once a wife feels like she's first place in her husband's life, she has everything! She's happy and fulfilled, and she doesn't need him to hold her hand all day long. She'll respect him and will give him the freedom to develop his career, build his business, concentrate on his learning, or excel in whatever his field of endeavor is. Once he invests the time to give her the secure feeling that she comes first in his life, he's virtually free to do as he pleases. When a wife lacks that security, the husband will find himself investing hour upon hour in trying to placate her.

A smart husband realizes that any investment in a marriage yields big profits. When he invests the time and effort in giving his wife the feeling and security that she's first place, he hits the jackpot.

The root

The principle of making your wife top priority in your life is rooted in wisdom. When you find that your presents, the time you invest, and all your efforts in trying to satisfy your wife never seem to succeed, it's because she doesn't yet feel like she's first place in your life. As long as you haven't internalized the feeling that she must be the most important thing in your life, no matter what you do for her or what you spend on her, she won't be satisfied. A wife wants to be first place in her husband's life, and therefore won't accept any substitutes.

The petty complaints that wives have against their husbands are frequently expressions of a frustration that they themselves don't know how to express – they want to be top priority and they're not! In such a situation, the wife will have grievances about her husband all the time. She complains about his tardiness or that he doesn't help her with the dishes. Lo and behold, he comes home on time and even does the dinner dishes, and she's still complaining! She complains that she doesn't have enough money for household expenditures, and he gives her more money. Yet, she still complains! Why? As long as he continues to treat her any less than the most important thing in his life, she'll continue to complain no matter what he does or what he gives her.

The gains that a husband will attain both on a spiritual and a material level defy description, once a husband gets to the root of his marital problems and makes his wife first place. The nagging and the complaints will disappear, as well as the petty requests and the demands on his time. The husband will feel the benefit of enhanced *siyata dishmaya*, or Divine assistance, and will succeed in whatever he does. In such a situation, when he realizes that his success and happiness depend on her feeling of marital security, he'll be happy to drop anything in order to fulfill her needs.

Communication breakdown

What so many husbands fail to understand is that a wife doesn't need to tie her husband to her apron strings. On the contrary, she functions a lot better when she has her space and he's not breathing down her neck. A wife doesn't like to be under constant scrutiny – it makes her nervous. But, when she feels that she's less than first priority in her husband's life, she'll demand that he spend more time at home. Also, she'll come up with a long list of complaints about her husband. The fact is that she's grabbing at straws because she doesn't know how to express what's really bothering her. Even when he does what she says, she's still not happy.

Naturally, the husband has no idea about what his wife wants. He feels frustrated, and says to himself: "Hey, I've done everything she asked; what more does she want? Nothing I do satisfies her!" Oftentimes, he tells her so to her face. Then an argument erupts.

To justify herself, the wife looks for another reason to complain, because once again, she doesn't know how to vocalize what's really upsetting her. She's unhappy, but can't put her finger on what she's so unhappy about.

We now have a classic communication breakdown. The wife has grievances. The husband can't understand what she's complaining about. Both are miserable. This is the type of volatile situation that leads to marital crises, G-d forbid.

Even if the couple goes to a counselor or mediator, they'll merely succeed in attaining a ceasefire until the next skirmish. The only way to solve the problem and break the spiral of complaint, communication breakdown, and marital strife is for the husband to give his wife the security that she's the most important thing in his life.

Foresight

A successful husband needs a good measure of foresight. Without it, he's a loser. For example, suppose the wife asks for an hour of his time to go food shopping together. He grumbles and refuses, failing to understand why she can't go to the supermarket by herself. She feels slighted, for other things are more important to him than she is. With all the tension, arguments, and damage control that follow, he loses ten hours. With a little foresight, he'd have gladly granted her the hour of his time, and that way, he'd have been a winner on all counts.

A husband should definitely not insist on being right. This leads to arguments. Arguments show that he doesn't value her opinion – that means that she's not first place in his life. Therefore, he should let her be the one that's right. He should let her have her say and give her the feeling that she's the one who decides, and that he backs her decisions.

Recurrent arguments are like acid that corrodes a woman's heart. Therefore, the husband must pray extensively for humility, empathy, and understanding – the tools that are needed to avoid arguments and to give her the feeling that she's the most cherished part of his life.

It's better to be wise than to be right.

Despite the fact that a husband realizes the need of making her first place, the Evil Inclination is constantly looking for opportunities to destroy the peace in the home. The Yetzer will tell the husband: "This time, you must put her in her place," or "don't let this go by without saying anything," or "look how she's committing an outright sin! You must call her down on this issue!" The Yetzer's seemingly justified complaints are simply tests of the husband's emuna. In such a sensitive situation, he must stop and think: "Hashem wants me to cherish my wife and make her feel like she's first place. If I criticize her or argue with her, then she won't feel like that. So, how can I call her down for doing something wrong? That's not what Hashem wants!"

Here's an example of how to pray for Divine assistance in this issue:

Master of the Universe, have mercy on my wife, on my children, on me, and on all those who are dependent on me. Let me understand that my happiness and success depends on my wife's happiness, namely, that she feels that she's the most important part of my life. Master of the Universe, have mercy on me and instill in my heart an abundance of love for my wife, a love that is greater than anything in the world. Have mercy on me so that my heart won't tempt me in any way whatsoever. Help me to successfully withstand all the trials and tests that come my way in this area, and that I will always place my wife and her needs, aspirations, and desires above everything else. Let me internalize the knowledge that this is Your desire in Your Divine wisdom. Let my wife feel that's she's truly the most important part of my life...

At this point, you can add your own personal prayers according to your own needs and circumstances.

"You shall desire your man"

Nothing must detract from or compete with a wife's rightful status as number one in her husband's life, not even children, Torah learning, career, work, hobbies, or the husband's rabbi and / or spiritual guide. A man must pray not only for success in every endeavor, but also that whatever he's doing doesn't slight the wife's feeling of being in first place in any way.

Hashem instilled in the woman the burning desire to be on the highest rung of her husband's priorities. The Torah says (Breishit, ch. 3): "You shall desire your man and he shall govern you," meaning that a husband governs his wife's moods. She can attain genuine happiness only through him, through his attention, love, and respect for her. She is therefore totally dependent on him.

Why did Hashem instill in a woman the dependence on her husband?

First, since Eve tempted Adam and as such caused the advent of death in the world, for before she sinned there was no death, therefore all women are compelled to receive their vitality from their husbands, for without the husband's attention, the wife's life tastes like death.

Time and again, we see that a woman may have almost everything – diamonds, gold, career success, fame, status, recognition, and more – yet, if she doesn't have her husband's total love and respect, her life taste like ashes to her. She has no joy. Nothing can substitute for the ultra VIP treatment she needs from her husband.

Second, Adam was created with immortal powers. His sin reduced him to the level of a mere mortal. Therefore, all men are compelled to reduce their own self-importance by caring for their wives before they care for themselves. This includes giving her empathy, sympathy, understanding, and a listening ear. It also means sacrificing his own desires for her desires, as well as respecting her, protecting her, and always siding with her against everyone else. The need for a husband to give so much to his wife provides the husband with a necessary soul correction, namely, uprooting arrogance and his inherent tendency to care for himself first. On an esoteric level, this is also a correction of Adam's sin.

By subjugating his will to her will, the husband eradicates the blemish of the heretical attitude of "the might of my hand" from his soul. This opens the path to emuna, which is the loftiest acquisition he can dream of in this world. A husband that willingly subjugates his will to his wife's will avoids marital strife, arguments, headaches, and bad feelings. With marital bliss, he's free to devote his time and energy to whatever vital task he needs to be doing. Prayer, teshuva, and humility help him to reach this goal.

Third, since Adam willingly heeded Eve in sinning, a husband must now heed his wife even if it goes against his will.

Like an ape

Love, respect, devotion, dedication, empathy, sympathy, understanding, and a listening ear aren't enough to make a wife feel like she's first place. A husband must add kind words and frequent compliments, giving her the feeling that she's the best, the most beautiful, the smartest, and so forth.

The Zohar says that Adam praised Eve, saying that she was the most beautiful of women, and that all others looked like apes compared to her. That's the way a husband should talk about his wife's cooking, her interior decorating, and everything else she does. He has to show her that no one can ever replace her in his life, so her status as his highest priority won't be threatened in any way, ever. And – if she does feel threatened in any way – he should reassure her. This requires sensitivity and alertness on the part of the husband. If he senses that she considers herself inferior to anyone else in his life, he should immediately show her and convince her otherwise.

Education

Maintaining the wife's security that she's first place is a basic requirement for peace in the home. If a husband remembers this, he'll spare himself indescribable headaches and anguish.

This principle is especially true in child education. Sometimes a mother loses patience with her children. As a result, she might react with anger, a raised voice, or even a slap to one of the children. This is a critical test of the husband: If he defends the children against the mother, her wrath will double. She will construe that he places the children above her. Now that she feels that she's not first place in his life, he can forget about peace in the home.

The husband's compassion for his "persecuted" children is one of the Yetzer's traps. In this case, compassion for the children is cruelty against the mother. Why was he compassionate on them and cruel with her? The answer is simple – they are more important to him than she is.

Stop and think: Is your wife yelling because she's happy and content? Of course not; a happy wife is a patient and content mother. Her short temper shows that she's not happy, for her husband fails to give her what she needs – the feeling that she comes first, even before her children.

Instead of justifying her and building her confidence and feeling of security, the unwitting husband does the opposite by scolding her and defending the children. He is proving to her that her feelings of frustration and discontent are justified, for she certainly is not number one in his life. Understandably, she's now angrier and more frustrated than she was before.

If the husband would have placed his compassion in the right place – with her and not with the children – he would have been a big winner, as follows:

First, the wife would have felt that he's on her side; her anger would have subsided immediately; and in that respect, he would have rescued the children from her fury.

Second, situations like this are golden opportunities to show her that she's the most important person in his life. Preferring her to his own children is the ultimate proof of his loyalty to her. She knows full well how much he loves his children, so when he places her above them, she's *really* happy. This is one of the biggest compliments he can give her, for his actions speak so much louder than his words.

Third, once things calm down, the husband can educate his children in the proper manner. He can reassure them how much he loves them and explain them the importance of listening to their mother rather than upsetting her. He can itemize all the wonderful things that their mother does for them, many of which they take for granted. He should show them just how wonderful she is and how fortunate they are, and perhaps conclude the discussion with a story from our sages about honoring parents.

The scenario of a confrontation between wife and children is a true test of the husband's priorities. If the feeling that his wife is first place is not deeply embedded in his heart, then it's doubtful that the husband will pass this test under fire.

If the husband is fortunate enough to internalize the necessity of doing everything to elevate his wife's status above everything and everyone else in his life, then such potentially volatile situations as a flare-up between her and the children won't be a test for him at all. It's clear to him that first and foremost, he stands by her side. This is true compassion for his children, for when she's happy she won't have to dump a payload of anger and frustration on their heads.

The compassionate father

A father is the role-model for his children. His greatest influence on them is by his personal example. When the father demonstrates outstanding character traits – compassion, patience, forgiveness, humility, and the love of peace, then the children will follow suit.

In those unfortunate homes where a father yells, threatens, and hits, the children's souls suffer inestimable damages. On the other hand, when the mother is the one with the short fuse, the damage to the children is much less. The children know that behind the shrill voice is a mother's heart.

The husband that elevates his wife to first place in his life is also a compassionate father. A wife who feels that she's first place in her husband's eyes, and whose life is free of criticism and comments, becomes a calm, contented mother that will rarely raise her voice against her children.

A big savings

Once again, we see that the husband's small investment of giving in to his wife is a big savings in terms of the time and effort that restoring her trust and self composure would require, if he would have done otherwise.

Life's tests in general and marital challenges in particular behoove a husband to avoid instinctive reactions, which often are impulsive and erroneous. When a husband considers his wife before he considers himself, he becomes a winner on two counts: First, he neutralizes the Yetzer Hara, who tries everything to upset the peace in the home. Second, he gives his wife the feeling that she's first place. That alone will save him untold tribulations and difficulties.

Each point of implementation requires much prayer. Therefore, a husband would be best advised to devote a few minutes of his daily personal prayers to asking Hashem to help his wife truly feel like she's first place in his life.

Stepchildren

There are situations where a husband's children from a former marriage come to live with him. The husband often perceives that every remark, criticism, and complaint that his wife makes about his children are unfounded since they're not her children, she resents them, dislikes them, and the like.

This is a mistake! Her grievance is not against them, but against the fact that they're more important to him than she is. His actions show that he loves them more than he loves her. She therefore feels threatened, insecure, and on edge, especially in the company of his children with whom she has to compete for his love. By making her first place, he once again saves himself tons of headache, heartache, and constant strife in the home.

Livelihood

Another example of a test of whether a man's wife is really first place in his life is in the area of livelihood.

Our sages said that a man must spend more on his wife than he can afford. If a husband has arguments with his wife about money and spending, he should ask himself if she's really number one in his life, more than his money or anything else.

Therefore, anytime she asks for money, he should give it to her willingly, for it's his responsibility according to Torah not only to provide for her, but to make her happy. She'll be happy as soon as she feels "first place" in his life.

Career

A well-known performer who was working on an exciting new project encountered a major domestic crisis at home with his wife. She had the impression that the project was more important to him than she was. She became his fiercest opponent, yelling at him and hindering all his efforts. The entire household turned into a battleground.

The performer came to me and spilled his heart out. I taught him the principle of "first place", and advised him to convince his wife that the entire project isn't worth one minute of her happiness.

The performer did a wonderful job of implementing my advice. Before long, his wife was urging him to complete the project. She became his biggest fan.

No comparisons!

A woman's biggest rival is *any* other woman. A husband must therefore be careful to avoid mentioning the names of other women to her. By praising another woman – even his mother or his sister - he's destroying his relationship with his wife with his own two hands.

Comparing your wife with any other woman is disastrous. Even if a husband does so innocently, he's still pushing his wife out of the number-one slot in his life. A wife can't stand when a husband praises his mother's cooking, his sister's orderliness, or the neighbor's patience with her children.

The worst thing a husband can do is to give a wife the feeling that she's competing for her husband's love and/or admiration, no matter what the competition is. Her soul thrives when she's first place in his eyes; second place and bottom rung of the ladder are the same misery to her. He shouldn't even compare her to her own mother, whom she loves with all her heart. It goes without saying that he shouldn't compare her to his mother, Heaven forbid. As soon as he compares her to any other woman, she'll hate that woman. So, if a husband wants his wife to get along with his mother, he should show her that he loves her more than he does his own mother.

Guarding one's eyes

Guarding one's eyes means that a husband should refrain from looking at other women. This is essential if a husband truly desires to make his wife first place in his life, for if he looks at other women, he arouses his natural male drives. The moment he covets another woman, his wife is no longer first place in his life and trouble starts.

If a husband's looking at other woman is bad, then looking at other women when he's with his wife is catastrophic. Few things are more insulting to a wife than when her husband sets his eyes on other women. One woman told me that as soon as she caught her husband looking at other women, a demon-like feeling of competition penetrated her heart. Instead of devoting her spare time to spiritual development, personal prayer, and Torah learning, she began spending hours in front of a mirror. Her life became bitter, and she wanted a divorce.

The husband who lets his eyes wander destroys his marriage with his own two hands. Instead of being a haven of peace and blessings, his home becomes a warehouse of materialism. His wife demands outrageous sums for cosmetics, beauty creams, clothes, shoes and spas – the list goes on and on. Oftentimes, she contaminates herself with trashy books and magazines. She acts compulsively and irrationally in her "struggle" to look more beautiful. Inside though, she feels dejected and ugly.

Husbands who complain to me that they don't love their wives are surely looking at other women; that's why their hearts stray from their wives. Keeping in mind the importance of making one's wife first place, woman-gazing becomes a criminal act, for the wife of a woman-gazer can never be first place in her husband's wandering eyes. The only way a husband can preserve his love for his wife is by guarding his eyes from looking at any other woman.

A husband that guards his eyes and preserves his gazes for only his wife can reach a spiritual level where his wife actually appears to be stunningly beautiful, even though on a physical level she might even be homely. Such a husband can tell his wife that she's gorgeous, and truthfully so. By looking at her only – his true soul mate – the husband sees the exquisite radiance of her soul that was meant for his eyes only. With prayer and effort, a husband can reach such a spiritual level where his wife is both first place and beautiful in his carefully-guarded eyes.

Walking in the door

A rule of thumb in spirituality says that everything goes according to the beginning. That's why a husband's first step inside the door after a long and difficult day's work plays a key role in marital bliss. This is an ideal time to show a wife that she's first place in her husband's eyes. Even if the children greet him at the door, his first question should be: "Where's mommy?"

A husband's greeting to his wife should be loving, animated, and flavored with sweet words to show her how happy he is to come home to her. He should first inquire how she's feeling and how her day went. This must show his genuine concern for her welfare. Putting his own selfish needs aside and devoting his attention to her when he first walks in the door scores major points in *shalom bayit*.

A woman thrives on sharing her life with her husband. She loves to tell him everything that happened to her during the time they were apart. The husband should listen with intent to what she has to say, even if it seems trivial and unimportant to him. That gives her the wonderful feeling that she can tell her husband anything. Therefore, if a husband criticizes her in any way, it's as if he's breached her trust. She doesn't open her heart for the purpose of her husband to stick a knife in it. By letting her pour her heart out, the wise husband saves her from telling gossip and slander to her girlfriends. And, even if she's speaking gossip and slander about other people to her husband, he should filter them in his heart and refrain from reprimanding her.

Honor, to what extent?

One of my students was preparing to say *Mincha*, the afternoon prayer service. His wife phoned him and asked him to come home immediately. He told her that in two minutes he was about to pray Mincha with the other students at our yeshiva, and asked if she agreed that he'd come home in another half an hour. She said no and asked him to come home immediately – that's just what he did, and rightfully so, even if it meant praying alone at home.

Let me qualify – the above example is talking about an upright young man who's not looking for excuses to shirk his responsibilities, such as prayer in a *minyan* with ten other men. Our sages said that sometimes we fulfill Torah by putting our Torah books back on the shelf. Once a wife has the security that she's first place and that her husband will be there whenever she needs him, then she'll allow her husband to do virtually whatever he wants.

My esteemed and beloved teacher Rabbi Eliezer Berland would always tell those of his pupils that had marital problems: "Listen to whatever your wife says. If she tells you to come home, go home right away, stay with her at home, and afterwards she'll give you a month's vacation."

If Jewish Law can be stretched for the purpose of peace at home - in other words, if the Torah is willing to allow a person to miss a Torah lesson or a prayer in a minyan - then a husband should certainly be willing to put aside his own plans, work, or hobbies to fulfill his wife's requests.

When a husband complains that his wife locks him in jail, then that husband hasn't given her the feeling that she's first place. When she perceives that other things are more important to him than she is, she fights against them. Not only that, but her anguish is indescribable when he prefers other interests rather than being with her. So, as soon as he gives her the feeling that she's highest priority in her life, his "jail cell door" becomes unlocked.

This is the Torah

Don't misunderstand what we've said until now: No one should receive the false impression that he's allowed to violate the Torah in order to make his wife feel like she's first place. Heaven forbid! The commandments of the Torah must be observed to the letter. A husband must therefore be wise enough to give his wife the feeling that she's first place without compromising on *halacha,* Jewish law.

A husband should give his wife the feeling that he's there whenever his wife needs him. This is done by the attention he gives her, by the way he listens to what she has to say, and by the brisk manner that he runs to fulfill her wishes. This feeling can be reinforced by loving responses to her requests, such as: "Right away, sweetheart!" or, "my greatest pleasure, honey." She needs to feel that he cares.

Usually, kind words and a swift response will make her happy. Maybe the husband paid the price of missing a prayer in public or a Torah lesson, but with a secure wife, he'll then be able to enjoy hundreds of prayers in public and Torah lessons with no interruptions.

A wife's occasional urgent need for her husband's help and attention is a golden opportunity for him to show her that she's number one in his life. When he answers her call quickly and willingly, she'll get the feeling that she doesn't have to compete for his love and attention. This gives her deep gratification and joy. She'll then happily allow him to pursue his own interests, especially when they are Torah learning and prayer.

Any normal wife understands that if she calls her husband to come home from work, she's damaging her own income. But, a husband should never tell her so. Even though she knows that he has required work, prayer, and study hours, she still wants to hear and feel like she's first place. So, when she needs him, he should respond immediately.

Sometimes a wife's call is only a test – conscious or unconscious – of her husband. She wants to see and hear if she's really number one. His granting her that very feeling is the greatest gift he can give to her.

Calm down

Enthusiastic Torah students, especially *baalei teshuva* (newcomers to Orthodox Judaism) who have made great strides in their Torah observance, with hearts burning and yearning for Hashem, ask themselves: "How can I possibly place my wife ahead of Hashem?"

It's clear to everyone – especially to a wife – that Hashem and His commandments come first. Even concerning such an important commandment as honoring one's parents, if a parent tells a child to ignore one tiny law of Torah, then the child should not obey the parent.

The answer is that a husband should give his wife the feeling that she doesn't have to compete with anything or anyone for her husband's attention, not even with Hashem. Hashem wants a husband to honor his wife in such a manner.

Suppose that the husband wants to attend an important Torah lecture, but his wife wants him to stay at home. If he reacts sanctimoniously like some husbands do, and says: "What are you talking about? Stay at home? Hashem commands me to learn

Torah, day and night! I have to do Hashem's will before I do yours…", then not only will he upset her, but he'll be creating a fierce opponent to everything he wants to do. This is not the way to talk to a wife. Instead, he should say: "Sweetheart, you and your needs are the most important thing in my life. If you need me at home, then I'm right here for whatever you need." With soft words like these, a difficult or tense marital situation turns itself completely around.

Once a husband gives his wife the warmth of love and the security that he's there for her whenever she needs him, he'll discover that she no longer hounds him or tries to lock him in jail. All she cares about is that she doesn't have to compete with anyone for her status as number one in his life.

Let's emphasize again that the wife doesn't expect to be more important than Hashem and His Torah. But, if he's constantly using the Torah and mitzvoth as an excuse for neglecting her, then she'll hate religion and everything associated with it. Even worse, she's likely to throw off the yoke of Torah and its commandments, Heaven forbid. Therefore, a husband must do virtually anything and everything to give his wife the feeling that she's highest priority in his life. When a religious man treats his wife like a queen, then she'll do everything to strengthen her faith and her observance.

Bridging the gap between a wife's needs and a husband's other obligations is seldom easy. That's why a husband must pray constantly to Hashem for guidance and Divine assistance, so that he can make his wife feel like she's highest priority without compromising his own observance of every single commandment. Here are some key guidelines:

1. There are many areas where one can be flexible. A husband's "zealous nerves" (the result of the *Yetzer Hara* prodding him

to be more stringent) cause him to fantasize that his wife is resisting him against the will of Torah.

2. Hashem doesn't give a person a trial or tribulation that the person is incapable of coping with. If a man stops and thinks, he can find a way to do his wife's wishes without compromising on religious law.

3. If the husband gives his wife the feeling that she's first priority in all the halachically permissible areas, then she won't demand things that are outside the context of what Judaism allows. A wife opposes the Torah only when a husband makes her sick of the Torah and makes her feel like she's competing against the Torah for his love and attention.

4. If a husband gives in to his wife's wishes, she'll give him back double in return. This is what our sages meant when they said that sometimes putting the Torah aside is the very observance of Torah. When a husband closes his Gemara to do a favor for his wife or to help her, he is observing the very teachings of the Gemara itself.

5. When in doubt as to how you can placate your wife and observe the Torah's commandments at the same time, consult a qualified rabbi.

A Wife is a hidden Tzaddik

A wife that feels like she's first priority in her husband's life has the inner peace, joy, and strength that enable her to weather any difficulty. She is the perfect partner. She'll say "yes" to her husband instead of "no", and will back him up and help him in everything he does.

In addition to her conscious assistance, her happiness will invoke an abundance of Divine blessings both material and spiritual. That's why our sages warned us to be extremely careful about honoring our wives, for the blessing in a man's home is by virtue of his wife.

A woman's merits, deeds, and influence are not always visible. She acts behind the scenes. A husband is visible to the public and is praised for his good deeds. People don't notice the actions of a wife, the daughter of The King whose honor is veiled from the public eye (see Psalm 45).

On the outside, it appears that success and income are dependent on the husband. In actuality, abundance secretly descends from Above by virtue of the wife. The more a husband honors her, the more he'll benefit from enhanced material and spiritual wealth.

"Mine and yours is hers"

The old adage says that behind every successful man is a great woman. When Rebbe Akiva returned to his hometown with tens of thousands of pupils accompanying him, he said: "Mine and yours are hers!" He attributed all of his lofty achievements to his wife.

Let's take a deeper look at what Rebbe Akiva said. Are his success in Torah and his tens of thousands of understudies really his wife's doing? She's the one who agreed that he spend years away from home learning Torah, but he's the one that devoted himself to his studies day and night. Is everything really hers?

Rebbe Akiva was no fibber, Heaven forbid. He knew that his success was thanks to the illumination of his wife's soul. As a great sage, he knew better than to take credit for all his achievements.

The Baal Shem Tov said that if his first wife would have remained alive, he could have risen to such a spiritual level that he could have ascended to the Heavens in a firestorm, from the middle of the vendors' market in Medziboz. He was alluding that his level would have been even higher than that of Elijah the Prophet, who ascended to the Heavens in a firestorm from the middle of the desert, far from the public eye. Had his first wife lived, the Baal Shem Tov could have ascended in front of everyone…

This sounds strange; what was the Baal Shem Tov lacking? Why did his first wife's death hamper his spiritual ascent?

We learn that when a man lives in peace with his wife, her soul truly merges with his. He therefore gains all the benefits of her wonderful spiritual attributes. She is like a spiritual afterburner that gives thrust to a rocket. She makes him whole. But without marital bliss, he is like dual-engine aircraft with a faulty engine – such a plane can't possibly fly at optimum speed and range. Even worse, it's in danger of cracking up.

Just because a husband's powers are visible and the wife's are not, doesn't mean that her influence is any less than his. With this in mind, we can understand just how deeply the Baal Shem Tov lamented over his first wife.

In conclusion, if while striving for spirituality, a husband neglects his wife or fails to fulfill her needs, particularly her need to be his first priority, then ultimately he'll forfeit his spirituality altogether. If he doesn't invest whatever is required in terms of time, attention, and resources, to instill in her the feeling that she's first priority, not only will he gain nothing, he could also lose everything.

An urgent meeting

Try this scenario: the husband has an urgent meeting somewhere and the wife doesn't want him to go. What should he do?

The answer is that Hashem decides whether or not he'll go, and he should subjugate his will to Hashem's will. So, the husband should therefore tell the wife that he's happy to abide by her decision, and to stay home if she wants him to. He should really mean what he says, take off his hat and coat and sit down beside her, or whatever the situation calls for. In his heart, he should pray: "Hashem, if You don't desire that I go to where I planned to, then help me accept this obstacle happily and with faith. Help me believe that this is Your will, so that I can accept Your decisions with full emuna and with joy."

A husband that sincerely tells his wife that he'll do anything to keep her happy, giving her the feeling that she's highest priority, will profit in two ways:

First, if she prevented him from going because she felt neglected, now that he has given her sincere and befitting respect and attention, giving her the feeling that she really is first place in his life, she'll let him go.

Second, by giving in to her, he's giving in to Hashem. That's exactly what Hashem wants. Once a husband nullifies his ego to Hashem, then Hashem doesn't need to send him obstacles in life that make him nullify his ego.

If at any rate she doesn't want him to go, that means there's an additional reason. Maybe the wife feels threatened or in competition with whatever her husband is going to do or whoever he's going to see. But once he shows her that she's first place in his life, she won't feel like she has to compete with anyone or anything. If she still resists him, then it's time for him to evaluate himself, do teshuva, and pray to Hashem. No matter what happens, the husband must accept his circumstance happily, with no frowns, complaints, or pouting.

Listen to the Rabbi

The Rostover Rebbe of blessed memory once gave a soul correction to his students, requiring them to spend the entire Succoth holiday every year in an isolated village in eastern Poland, no matter what hardships this might cause.

One of the Rebbe's younger students that lived far away from the said village informed his wife – without asking for her opinion – that he'd be leaving her for the duration of Succoth. It was a foregone conclusion in his mind that whatever the Rebbe says, he does! But the wife bitterly objected. Not only that, she was slighted that her husband would even think of leaving her alone on Succoth.

The young student didn't flinch. He had no doubt that the Rebbe's far-reaching holy spirit took precedence over his wife's mundane focus on day-to-day needs. Whose opinion is more important? So he made the journey without his wife's consent.

When he returned home, he discovered that someone had instilled in her a fierce opposition to him and to his Rebbe. She wasn't the same sweet girl that he married, but vicious and vindictive. She even refused to let him touch her.

Despite all this, the young man still intended to go away for the next Succoth holiday. He had no idea how things would develop. But with Hashem's lovingkindness, he met Rebbe Shlomo Hirsch, his first teacher in *cheder,* who had taught him the *aleph-bet.* Rebbe Shlomo was a man of pure and simple emuna, who had experience with the type of ambitious young men that seek lofty spiritual levels, while neglecting their marriages.

Rebbe Shlomo said, "This isn't the way, my son. When the Rebbe told you to make the journey, he didn't intend that you wreck your household. Your challenge was to be able to do the Rebbe's bidding while keeping your wife happy as well."

The young man asked: "How in the world do I do that? Last year, everything was fine between us, and she didn't want me to go. This year, I'll just have to persevere in dedication and go, no matter what…"

Rebbe Shlomo said: "That's neither perseverance nor dedication, but outright foolishness! Listen to me – go tell her that this year you don't intend to go away against her will. Give her your passport and apologize for your mistake, telling her that you received bad advice from your friends, who coerced you into going. Now tell her that after lengthy deliberation and soul-searching, you've decided that she's more important than this trip. Improve your behavior too, and give her the feeling that she comes first in your life. The only effort you need to make in your desire to make the journey again this year is to devote as much time as possible to teshuva and to personal prayer, begging Hashem to enable you to make the journey."

Rebbe Shlomo continued: "Once you've humbled yourself in complete teshuva and you've become a model husband, then you can gently approach your wife and ask for her consent to make the trip. If she shows the slightest reservation, then back off and accept that Hashem wants you to devote more time and effort to prayer and teshuva. Know full well, as King Solomon said, once Hashem is pleased with a person's ways, even his enemies reconcile with him."

The young man understood that his childhood Rebbe wanted only the best for him. Rebbe Shlomo's wisdom and common sense were apparent, as well as the pure truth of his advice. He implemented Rebbe Shlomo's advice to the letter. Later that year, he made the journey on Succoth with his wife's full support and blessings.

If your wife opposes what you want to do, tell her that she comes first. Give her the feeling that she doesn't have to compete with anyone or anything for your love and attention. Once a person accepts Hashem's will and reacts to obstacles with teshuva and prayer (and not with a sledgehammer), then the obstacles disappear. When a person is in need of salvation, a six-hour straight personal prayer session can move mountains.

Once a person prays enough and reaches the level where Hashem is pleased with his actions, then his "enemy" – his wife, as our sages tell us – will become his beloved ally.

Let's summarize:

1. In regard to his wife – she comes before anything else.

2. In regard to Hashem – he must be attentive to Hashem's messages, for Hashem often uses the person's wife as a mouthpiece. Teshuva and prayer mitigate the hard judgments that manifest themselves in a harsh wife.

By doing Hashem's will, harsh judgments become merciful grace.

Chapter Four

Be a Man

After learning the previous chapters of "No comments" and "First Place," hopefully the reader has understood them and accepted them; will continue to follow the advice in this book; and will enjoy all the blessings that come from having peace in his home. But if for some reason, one felt that the concepts in those chapters were strange, unclear, unrealistic, or impossible to apply - and he wasn't able to accept them - then he needs to read this chapter very carefully.

A lost cause?

I have counseled couples for many years now, and in the course of this time Hashem has blessed me, in His great mercy, to find in our holy Torah a wealth of instruction for peace in the home. On the whole, these instructions have worked wonders, and have been effective even for couples who were on the brink of divorce with no hope of saving their marriage.

On the other hand, there were other cases where whatever I said just didn't help.

I also noticed a pattern while writing 'The Garden of Peace.' After I completed each chapter, I would give out a few copies to married men for their feedback. The vast majority of them were deeply influenced by what they read. They told me that what they learned had changed their lives dramatically. Others, though, weren't touched at all by my words, and continued as if they hadn't read the sample chapters at all. They even complained to me: "But what about the women? How about some instruction for them? How will they ever change? What about their contribution to the marriage? When will you teach the women how to act?" Somehow, they'd missed the point.

Here's an example: A man came to me for advice because he was having problems at home with his wife. He told me what a good husband he was, how helpful and good he is to her, and so on. He claimed that she didn't do enough. In his opinion, all their problems were all her fault.

While I was listening to him, I thought to myself that I'd advise him to read some of the sample chapters from the 'Garden of Peace' that I had already completed. I was sure that once he read them, he would see the error of his ways. While I was waiting for him to finish his story, he suddenly pointed to those very chapters on my desk and said: "I have a friend that you gave these chapters to, and I also read them. Believe me, I do everything that it says in them, but it doesn't help, because she's the way she is."

That stumped me. If he'd read the chapters and yet still believed that the responsibility for peace in the home lay with his wife, and was waiting for her to make changes, then I had nothing more to tell him. I blessed him and sent him on his way, with a prayer in my heart that Hashem should grant him some understanding.

Divine Providence then arranged for this same husband to go home and tell his wife, in my name, that "she'd better change her ways, or else." Enraged, she called up and spoke to one of my secretaries and told him what her husband had said, how I was angry with her and had threatened her. The secretary told her that he didn't know what I'd said, but that he was willing to swear on a Torah scroll that I hadn't said such things. He told her that anybody who knew me knows that I never speak negatively to or about women. If she wanted, he would put her through to me, so I got to speak to her directly. I said to her: "You know your husband. How could you have believed him?"

In the ensuing conversation she told me all about how he constantly makes negative comments to her and torments her, in exact contradiction to all the rules of peace in the home that I had written in those chapters, which he claimed to have fulfilled to the letter.

This made me realize that there was a significant minority of men who somehow weren't getting the message of this book. I sat down and taxed my mind in an attempt to understand why this was. What was missing? After reading the previous chapters, how could a husband could still blame his *shalom bayit* problems on his wife?

Hashem then helped me to understand. Those husbands lacked an understanding of what a man's role is, namely, to give.

The principle of man's role as a giver is the backbone of this entire book. All the lessons and instructions stem from this one unifying root concept. This is why the book is only directed towards men, and will only help a husband who has desires to fulfill a man's role.

He created male and female. Men and women are complete opposites. Men are obligated to observe many commandments that women aren't. The role of men and women in the home is very different. The many differences between men and women teach us that Hashem created men as givers and women as receivers.

The lessons and instructions for achieving peace in the home are contingent on a husband's understanding and internalizing this difference, namely, that his task as a man is to give and his wife's task is to receive from him. As such, he now knows what to strive for. Peace in the home depends on both husband and wife fulfilling their true roles.

Another difference between men and women is that women don't need to be taught how to be women. Men, on the other hand, need extensive guidance as how to behave like a man, since in this generation many men have lost their male characteristics. This is a prime cause of problems in domestic peace. When men don't behave like men, it's impossible for there to be peace in their homes.

The Zohar compares the husband-wife relationship to that of the sun and the moon. The moon merely reflects the light that it receives from the sun, for it has no light of its own. So too, a wife's vitality depends upon the "spiritual light" that her husband shines on her. When he's kind and considerate, she radiates. When he's critical and stingy, she suffers in a dark cloud of sadness. Her state of mind and behavior depends on him.

This book was written for men only since it would be impossible to address both genders at once. For example, one can't write a book about children's education addressed to both teachers and children. A teacher's role is different from a child's.

By learning the "Garden of Peace" a husband can learn where he is deficient, where he is not fulfilling his role as a man, and then correct it. A serious husband who is willing to implement each detail in this book will find it to be a comprehensive guide to peace in the home. He will learn to shoulder responsibility and won't have complaints against his wife. Once the husband takes the initiative and begins to give without expecting to receive, he soon achieves marital peace and harmony.

Start being a man

For those husbands who somehow didn't grasp the message of this book's initial manuscript, I came up with a new idea. I told them to forget about all the concepts and they had heard from me or read in the book until now and focus all their efforts and prayers on one thing: becoming a man. I then explained to them what I meant by 'being a man.' This idea helped, and even worked wonders.

Allow me to define here what it means to be a man: A man gives. He pampers others; listens to others; pays attention to others; concedes his wants for the sake of others; is forgiving; doesn't seek honor; doesn't want to benefit from others; supports others; helps others and empathizes with others. A man can accept humiliation with love, and can also accept complaints and accusations without being offended or defensive.

To internalize all these traits, one must pray.

As long as a man lacks the desire to give to others and make them happy, then the instructions in this book will be difficult for him, because they will be going against his nature.

Telling the 'female' husbands to focus on becoming men certainly helped. They started to change. Their wives, who were generally already beyond despair and sure that divorce was the only answer, testified that amazing transitions had occurred in their husbands.

Once again: a man gives, a woman receives. This is a rule of creation and of procreation. The husband should give his wife honor and attention. He should be compassionate, forgiving and able to cope with life's difficulties. He should always be "illuminating" - happy and smiling. He should certainly never say: "She offended me" - because a man shouldn't get offended. When a man feels offended, it means that he wants honor, and this is a female trait. A true man can accept humiliation and continue giving to the one who humiliated him.

A true man expects nothing from his wife. He doesn't need her honor or attention. When a husband asks: "Why doesn't she honor me/understand me/compliment me/encourage me/support me?" he is hoping for everything that his wife hopes for. A husband who wants to receive behaves like a woman. In this vein, Our Sages said: "Her eyes are lifted to you, and your eyes are lifted to Hashem." The wife receives from her husband, and her husband should receive from Hashem.

Some husbands say: "I don't ask for much, just for a smile or a nice word. I don't want loads of compliments or lavish expressions of love. All I need is for her to express some care. That would give me the motivation to give to her. When she's so caustic and apathetic, not smiling or giving me any positive attention, it takes away my desire to do things for her." No matter how little he wants her to give him, the desire to receive is a female one, and there is no hope of peace in such a home.

Women can't stand a man who gets offended and insulted. Such men should pray: "Master of the world. Have mercy on me and help me to be a man, that I shouldn't want honor. I get offended because I want honor. Help me rid myself of this female trait."

As long as a man seeks to be a recipient rather than a giver, he can't have a successful relationship with his wife. The instructions for peace in the home are all methods of giving. The concepts of "First Place", "No Comments" and "The Wife is a Mirror" all revolve around giving.

The lesson of "First Place" is clearly all about giving. When a husband puts his wife's wishes before his and gives her priority over everyone and everything else, he is giving to her in a very cogent way. He concedes his desires, time, money and honor, just to make her happy. By doing this, he lets her know that she's the most important thing in his life.

The lesson of "No comments" is also giving. Comments detract from a wife's honor, make her feel inadequate and rob her of her self-confidence. Compliments, love and praise, on the other hand, increase her self-confidence, her happiness and her vitality. A husband who wants to make his wife happy showers her with the "light" of sincere compliments and praise, while shielding her from the "darkness" of derogatory remarks and criticism.

A true man gives because it's his nature to do so. He doesn't give with ulterior motives. He doesn't hope to get honor or concessions from his wife just because he gives to her. He wants to give. A man who feels that it's unfair that he should give to his wife without receiving anything in return is still plagued by female characteristics.

The lessons of the "Mirror" chapter explain giving in a different sense. Once a man knows that his wife is his mirror, he understands that whatever faults he sees in her are rooted in him. If he wants her to change, he works on himself. He knows that it makes no sense to comment and try to change her with his words. Comments exhibit a husband's lack of sensitivity, damage a wife's self-confidence, and show a lack of emuna. Every comment is an attempt to change things in a way not directed by Hashem, and at a time not directed by Hashem. A man with emuna knows that if he wants something to change he needs to pray for it, work on himself, and then wait. The change will happen when Hashem decides that the time is right.

The following story illustrates how a husband's behavior towards his wife determines her behavior towards him: A rich miser once came to his Rabbi saying that he wanted his wife to die. The Rabbi was shocked and said: "G-d forbid! Why?" The man then related his long tale of suffering. He described how cruel his wife was to him, how she humiliated him, tormented him and maltreated him, to the point that the Rabbi had to agree with him - from the picture he painted, he really was living with a monster and not a wife. Once he'd finished his story, he repeated his request for the Rabbi's help to somehow make his wife die. He said that he simply couldn't carry on living like this.

The Rabbi asked him why he couldn't just get a divorce and then live happily alone. But he replied that divorce wouldn't be enough for him. He wouldn't be able to relax until he saw her in the grave since she had tormented him so badly. As long as he knew that she was in the world, he couldn't have any peace.

The Rabbi asked the rich miser to give him a few days to ponder the matter and then contact him again. Once the rich man left, the Rabbi prayed to Hashem for guidance. Hashem enlightened the Rabbi, and he understood that there must be some deficiency in the husband who had driven his wife to act so cruelly to him. The Rabbi decided to send one of his students to the man's home to try to discover what it was.

The Rabbi sent one of his faithful students, dressed as a beggar, to the rich man's house with instructions to enter and search for anything unusual. The student managed to enter at a time when the rich man was out. He heard his wife crying and cursing her husband, "That stingy, wicked man. He leaves me here without a penny and goes off to his business. If only he would say one nice thing to me, but even with words he's stingy. I'm going to make him suffer when he gets home. At least then I won't be the only one suffering."

The student came back to the Rabbi and told him what he had heard. The Rabbi, with his new perspective on the situation, came up with a plan. He called for the rich miser to come to him.

"Yes Rabbi. Do you have a solution for me?"

"Yes. I remembered the Talmud which says that the punishment for making a vow and not fulfilling it is that one will bury his wife. For most people this would be a punishment, but in your case, it will be the end of your problems. All you have to do is make a vow that you won't fulfill and your wife will die."

The rich man liked the idea.

"Okay. What vow should I make?"

"Well, we don't have a mikvah here in town. Why not vow to build us a big mikvah, built to the highest specifications, with every comfort and luxury? It would cost a fortune to actually do it. Don't do it, and she'll die."

"Okay, but how long will this take? Perhaps Hashem will give me a few years to fulfill such a big vow. I haven't got strength to wait that long. I can't bear my wife's cruelty any longer."

"Don't worry. You'll make the vow here in front of me and two other witnesses, which will make it impossible to annul. That, coupled with the fact that Hashem knows full well that you have no intention of fulfilling it, means that you should get the punishment almost immediately."

"Give me a date, Rabbi. Otherwise I can't take the pressure."

"Fine. I promise you that if you make the vow now, she will die within three weeks from today."

This satisfied the miser. With a joyous heart he vowed, in front of the Rabbi and two others, to build a huge mikvah, big enough to cater for the whole community, built to the highest rabbinical specifications. Then he went home.

"One minute," the Rabbi called to him. "There's one more thing I want you to do."

"Of course, Rabbi. What is it?"

"Well, since your wife has so little time left to live, I want you to put in every effort to make her last few weeks in this world as pleasant as possible. Buy her whatever she likes, give her plenty of money to spend, compliment her, praise her and generally fuss over her. What do you have to lose? Once she dies, all the money will come back to you anyway. As for the compliments, what do you care? Give them to her now; soon, she'll be gone and you'll have peace from her."

"No problem, Rabbi. I'll do all that happily. The very thought that I'll soon be rid of her gives me so much joy that I'll have no problem in altering my normal behavior to make her happy."

Two weeks passed. The rich man burst into the Rabbi's room with tears in his eyes.

"Rabbi! Please! I want to annul my vow."

The Rabbi looked at him and said gravely: "What do you mean? We specially made the vow in a way that it's impossible to annul. Why do you want to annul it? Don't you want your wife to die?"

"That's just it, Rabbi. I don't want her to die anymore. Since I made the vow, and then did what you told me - to do everything I could to make her happy - she's completely changed. She's so good to me. She's taking care of me, loves me, even prays for me. She's become like an angel. Suddenly I realized what a good wife she is, and I don't want to lose her."

"Well, we can't annul the vow now. If you don't want her to die your only option is to fulfill it. You'll really have to build the mikvah, exactly as you promised, with all the trimmings."

With no other choice, the rich miser started that very day to organize the building of the mikvah, and from that time on lived peacefully and lovingly with his wife.

Dear reader, I want you to understand. If you fulfill your role as a husband properly, there is no reason why won't have a peaceful and successful relationship with your wife. Just remember that you must be a man.

Sometimes couples come to me, but I find myself talking to two females. I can't make peace between two females in what's supposed to be a male-female relationship. The husband says: "She should make the first move. She should correct her behavior." And she, understandably, says: "No. He's the one who needs to change." There is no solution in such situations, apart from the husband learning to become a man.

This explains the Talmud in Kiddushin (82b) that says: "Happy is one who has male sons, and woe to one whose sons are females." It's a merit to have sons who behave as males and not as females.

The phenomenon of men losing their male characteristics stems from violating personal holiness. When men lust for sexual pleasure and satisfaction - in other words, when they want to take and receive - they lose their true male potency, which is their power to give. This then leads to their acquiring other female traits such as seeking honor, attention, empathy and the like. When a husband violates his personal holiness and lusts after his wife, he reverses roles with her. He puts her into the position of giving, and himself into the position of taking. This can only lead to him becoming miserable and weak. For further discussion of this point, refer to the chapter: "And their faces were towards one another."

In conclusion, we can say that there are three levels of husbands:

1. Truly male husbands – with one reading of this book such a husband will learn all he needs to and will be able and willing to put in into practice. He is already a giver, so it will come naturally to him.

2. A husband who has female characteristics, but is aware of this and wants to change. This book will serve as a comprehensive guide for him. If he learns it, reviews it once a month and tries to fulfill everything written in it, he will definitely merit becoming a man and achieve lasting peace in his home.

3. A husband who has such female characteristics that he cannot give up anything, including his desire to take. This book won't help him, until he realizes how far he has fallen and starts to pray every day that Hashem help him to become male again. The most important area for him to work on is his personal holiness, the most fundamental mitzvah for men. He must start to learn, pray, and stay as far away from sexual lust as he can, both outside and inside the home, as we'll see later in Chapter Six.

A reminder

Everyone, even "truly male husbands", should review this book at least once a month. I myself have reviewed these ideas countless times and have prayed at length for every point in this book. Even today, as a grandfather whose white hairs in my beard outnumber the black ones, not a day goes by without my praying for peace with my wife, that I should feel all her needs, not withhold anything from her, and not make comments to her. All these things must be reviewed and prayed for again and again.

I hereby bless every husband who assumes the task of learning this book diligently and reviewing it at least once a month, that he should merit true peace in his home, righteous children, happiness and riches and everything good in this world and the next, amen.

Chapter Five
Honor your Wife

Unlike a man, whose principal evil inclination is the lust for forbidden sexual relationships, a woman's principal evil inclination is the desire for honor. A woman longs for honor more than anything in the world, specifically from her husband, and she will go to any lengths to get it. This is what our Sages meant when they said that "Women are light-headed" – because when she is given honor and a few kind words, a woman can be swayed in any direction.

A woman's joy and vitality come from the honor she receives from her husband. Honor from other people in her world just doesn't satisfy her. If her husband, the most important person in her life, doesn't honor her, no matter what else she has in life, no matter how many other people like her and respect her, she will be miserable. A wife needs honor and positive attention like she needs air to breathe. A husband can be helpful, loyal and bring home plenty of money, which are all good things, but if he doesn't also give his wife respect and loving attention, she will feel miserable, hopeless and broken.

Many husbands feel they can't compliment their wives because they don't want to lie, thinking that no compliment is better than an insincere one. How can you tell your wife that she's beautiful, if she isn't? How can you say that she's well organized, when she isn't? This type of thinking is a mistake. Our sages teach us that there are many compliments that every husband can give to his wife, without exaggeration or phony flattery.

Her beauty

The story is told of Rabbi Elazar the son of Rabbi Shimon who once came across an extremely ugly man and commented to him about his unbecoming appearance. The man responded: "Go and tell the craftsmen who fashioned me, 'What an ugly vessel you made.'" Rabbi Elazar heard his rebuke and was deeply embarrassed. He was right – if this was how Hashem had created him, then this was his unique beauty.

So too, when a husband believes that Hashem created his wife to look as she does, it puts a new perspective on her looks and her 'beauty'. Being Hashem's handiwork means that she has the precise form and beauty that both expresses the nature of her soul and enables her to achieve all that she needs to in this world, which includes being attractive enough for her husband. If she is his wife, then her beauty is the precise measure of beauty that he requires.

Every husband who internalizes this concept can tell his wife, with full sincerity: "You're truly beautiful. I love the way you look." If she says: "You're just saying it", he can tell her: "When it comes to taste and attraction, everyone's different. To me, you're attractive and beautiful!" The more the husband believes it himself, the more his wife will too.

The Talmud in tractate Yevamot (62b) lists all the things that an unmarried man lacks: "A man without a wife dwells without joy, without blessing, without good, without walls and without peace. A man without a wife is not a man." This is an explicit statement in the Talmud. Based on this a husband can tell his wife, again with full sincerity: "You are the source of all the joy, all the blessings, and all the good in my life. Without you I wouldn't have any boundaries or peace of mind. I wouldn't be anything without you." According to this Talmudic teaching this is no exaggeration – this is the truth!

In Exodus (20:23), Hashem tells us that a ramp, and not stairs, must be used to ascend to the top of the altar in the Tabernacle. The reason for this being that walking up steps requires a very slight level of immodesty, which is avoided when walking up a ramp. This 'immodesty' would be felt only by the stones of the steps themselves, but nevertheless we are told to be mindful of this. We are forbidden to treat even the stones of the Altar with the slightest disrespect. Rashi comments on this: "Now if for these stones, which have no consciousness, and cannot become upset, the Torah says - since they serve a purpose, we must not treat them disrespectfully – all the more must we be careful to treat our fellow man with respect, for he is greatly affected by our behavior towards him." For our purposes here we can say, 'And all the more so for a wife, who is so sensitive and whose feelings are so easily hurt.'

The Torah says: "You should rejoice on your festivals," and our sages teach us that the 'rejoicing' referred to here is the consumption of sacrificial meat in honor of the festival. Women, however, are not obligated to bring sacrifices on the festivals. The woman's mitzvah of joy on the festival is actually incumbent upon her husband – *he* is responsible to make sure that she has a good time. His wife's happiness is *his* responsibility.

A husband needs to be constantly on the lookout for opportunities to lavish compliments and kind words on his wife. Her good looks, her cooking, her ideas, her hard work, how well she deals with the children, and her housekeeping all deserve praise on a regular basis. Telling her how good she looks in what she's wearing will always give her joy. The more and varied things that a husband finds to praise and compliment his wife about, the happier she'll be.

Why complain?

It's a woman's nature to talk about whatever's on her mind. So it's natural for a wife to tell her husband about her own shortcomings, and about what she feels she is missing in life, when these are on her mind. However, when complaining and negativity become her *only* topics of conversation, this is a sign that something is wrong and that she is suffering.

Many husbands feel that their wives complain too much with no justification. They feel that they are trying their best to be good husbands - they help out with the shopping, they help out at home, they smile, they try to be supportive, and so on. And they feel that if after all this their wives are still complaining, then it's a sign that their wives must have a problem. Some even complain to their wives: "Why do you complain so much all the time?"

This is a tremendous mistake. Not only is such a husband not showing any consideration or compassion to his unhappy wife, but he also makes her suffering worse by putting the blame on her. He lets her know that he is one hundred percent okay, so if she is unhappy, *she* must have some sort of problem. This is tragic, especially when a bit of empathy and a few kind words could have uplifted her from her deep, dark mood. If a wife is unhappy, it's the husband's problem, not hers.

In the previous chapter, we told the story about the rich man who came to the Rabbi of his city to complain about his 'awful' wife. The Rabbi advised him to make a vow without following through on it, and according to Kabbalistic teachings, it's only matter of weeks before she dies, once it is clear that he has no intention of fulfilling his vow. The Rabbi then suggested that since she doesn't have long to live now - why not make her last few weeks in this world as pleasant as possible? The rich miser went home and started treating her well - buying her presents, sitting with her, giving her lots of attention, and so on. To his great surprise, his wife started to pay him back in kind – speaking pleasantly to him, making him the meals that he liked, and so forth. She became an altogether different person. We learn an important lesson from this story: the miser's negative way of relating to his wife was the cause of her unpleasant behavior towards him. As soon as he started to honor her, to praise her and give to her, she transformed into a loving and sweet wife. She was his mirror. Shortcomings of a wife are rooted in the husband.

Rabbi Berland tells me: "We must constantly give our wives compliments, and we must pray that they will believe that we love them. As long as a man is not entirely pure in matters of *shmirat habrit* – personal holiness, he can love only himself and not his wife. So, we must pray that in the meanwhile, while we work on ourselves, that Hashem should make our wives believe that we truly love them."

When a husband makes negative comments to his wife, no matter how slight they may seem to him, and when he doesn't shower her with love, her mind runs wild with self-persecution and with thoughts that he doesn't love her. This is death itself for a wife. A wife who feels that her husband doesn't love her is liable to lose her mind from pain and sorrow. The moment she reaches the conclusion that her husband doesn't love her, she becomes full of anger, despondency and despair.

A husband should give his wife many, many compliments and *never* show her any anger, because anger will take her straight to the conclusion that he doesn't love her. He should also pray that she believe he loves her, and that she will interpret his every word, action and deed as signs of his love for her.

You have clothing, be our ruler (Isaiah 3)

The Zohar (Genesis, Ch.49) clearly describes the obligation of the husband to honor his wife, give her absolute rule in the home, and the extent to which he must shower her with words of love and honor:[1]

"In the beginning" – in the beginning of the Torah we are told: "And He brought her to Adam" – that Hashem brought Eve to Adam. From here we learn how the father and mother must behave with the bride. *"For until now the father and mother must do"* – until the wedding day the father and mother of the bride must buy her jewelry, prepare her and bring her to her groom under the chupah (marital canopy). *"Afterwards, he must go to her"* – afterwards her husband must go to her to unite with her. *"And the entire home belongs to her"* – because the running of the home is dependent on her. *"And he must take permission from her"* – he must ask her for permission to lie with her. *"And regarding this we have explained what it says"* – what is written about Jacob, *"And he encountered the place, and lay down there" (Genesis 28), that he asked permission first"* – that he first took permission from her and only then did he lie with her. *"From here we learn that one who wishes to bond with his wife needs to meet with her and sweeten her with words"* – that he must ask her permission and also make her happy with his words. *"And if not he must not go up to her"* – if he does not do this, he must not lie with her. *"In order that their wills will be as one, without force"* – so that their desires will be as one, with no pressure or force.

---

1. The words of the Zohar are in italics, followed by the commentary of the Matok Mi'Dvash

We see from the words of the Zohar that a husband who wants conjugal relations with his wife must first praise her and placate her. If he doesn't do this, he is forbidden to lie with her. If a man knows that he will not be able to praise and compliment his wife then he should not get married. If he cannot compliment his wife, he will never be able to lawfully unite with her.

It is clear from the above Zohar that the woman is the pillar of the home, and that the home is under her charge. The Zohar says further in this regard:

"And he took from the stones of the place and lay them at his head"(Genesis 28:11) – from here we learn that even if a King has a bed of gold, and beautiful quilts to lie on, but the Queen prepares for him a bed of stones, then he must leave his bed, the bed of gold, and lay in the bed that she has prepared, as it says, "And he lay down in that place,"(ibid.) meaning that he lay down on a bed of stones.

The home is the wife's dominion: however she wishes to run it, her husband must accept it. So would Rabbi Hirsh Leib, of blessed memory, relate in the name of his Rebbe, Rabbi Avraham Sternhartz, of blessed memory, that a man must realize that his wife is the General of the home, and he is a private. Just as a private in the army has to listen to and obey every command of his General, without argument or objection, so too must he listen to his wife. And just like in a real army, where a private has to leave his ego at the entrance to the base, so too a husband must leave his status at the door of his home. Outside the home, he may be highly intellectual and successful; he may be in charge of a large company or the head of a community; or he might even be the Commander-in-Chief or the President. But, when he walks through his front door of his house, he reverts to being a private and awaits orders.

The Zohar continues with a description of the types of praises and compliments a husband should give to his wife:

"Come and see what it says here: 'And Adam said, 'This is now... bone of my bones, and flesh of my flesh; to this shall be called Woman, because out of Man was this one taken.'"(Genesis 2:23) These were the sweet words that Adam said to his wife, to create affection with her and draw her to his will, to arouse her to love. See how sweet the words are that Adam said to Eve: 'You are the bone of my bones and the flesh of my flesh - how could I ever despise or forsake you, since the light that shines in you is the essence of my essence,' [He said this] in order to show her that they have a common bond that unites them and that there is nothing at all that separates them.

Once he had told her these words of love he started to praise he:, "To this shall be called 'Woman'" – his intention was to say that this is a woman whose equal cannot be found, this is the honor of my home, all other women compared to her are like monkeys compared to man, but she, Eve, shall be called 'Woman' the most perfect of all the created beings, only she is fitting to be called 'woman'.

All these are words of love and affection that Adam said to his wife, as it says also in Proverbs, the kinds of praises that a man must say to his wife to increase her feelings of love and affection: (Proverbs, 31:29) "Many daughters have achieved much, but you surpassed them all." We see that by telling her that she has merits above all other women, he increases her feelings of love and affection." (Zohar Genesis Ch.49 with explanation of the 'Matok Midvash'.)

This Zohar teaches the correct way for a husband to regard his wife. A husband must consider – if Adam, whose wife Eve had no competition for his love, felt it necessary to praise and compliment her and to tell her that she was the only one for him, that there was no other like her – how much more so must a husband nowadays lavish praise on his wife. A husband should compliment his wife as much as possible, and make her feel that she is the most beautiful woman in the world in his eyes, the glory of his home, and perfect in every way.

Honor

One of the clauses of the *Ketuba*, the official Jewish marriage contract that every husband signs before getting married, is an obligation to honor one's wife. This is the husband's solemn obligation that is not linked in any way with the wife's behavior towards him. Unless his wife is unfaithful or refuses to procreate, the obligation stands, no matter what else she does. The Talmud tells of Rabbi Chiya, whose wife would upset him tremendously, yet whenever he found something beautiful in the market he would buy it for her. His friend Rebbi asked him: "But doesn't she just give you constant sorrow?" Reb Chiya replied to him: "It's enough that she brings up the children and saves me from sin."

Maimonides, in his section on the Laws of Marriage (Ch.15. Law 19) writes: "And so the Sages commanded that a husband honor his wife more than himself, and love her as himself, and if he has money he must treat her to the best that he can afford. He must not make her fearful of him, but must speak to her in a pleasant manner, and not be negative or angry."

Although he brings in the next law that: "So too the Sages commanded that a wife should greatly honor her husband" - the obligation of the wife is not equivalent to that of the husband. Jewish law does not require a wife to sign a contract that obligates her to honor her husband.

The honor that a wife gives her husband is a consequence of the honor that he gives her. If he fulfills all of his obligations to her, she will automatically honor him in return. Maimonides was speaking of the ideal situation where there is mutual honor and respect that comes naturally when the husband honors his wife and she reciprocates in kind. What is unnatural, however, is a situation where a husband wants his wife to honor him.

This is unnatural because the true nature of man is to be a giver, and of woman to be a receiver. It's the husband who must honor his wife, not the other way around. A husband who seeks honor should understand that this is actually a female attribute.

Who's the man in the house?

Elijah the Prophet (Tanna D'bei Eliyahu Ch.15) teaches that: "A man must be humble in his Torah learning, in good deeds and in his fear of Heaven, with his father and mother and with his Rebbe and with his wife, with his children and the members of his household, with his neighbors and with those near and far, and even with non-Jews in the market, in order that he should be beloved above and pleasant below and accepted by all, and fill his days and years with a good name. For when a man is humble in Torah and good deeds, then his wife will fear him, and so too the members of his household, his neighbors and relatives, and even the non-Jews will fear him, as it states (Deuteronomy 28:10): 'And all the nations of the world will see that the name of the L-rd is called upon you, and they will be afraid of you'."

The "Shay LeMora" explains why it is that "the man who is humble in his fear of heaven... his wife will fear him," because the Divine Presence rests upon whoever is humble, and that is what causes her awe and respect of him. The opposite is also true. Whoever is arrogant and haughty is dishonored, as our sages tell us: (Talmud, tractate Bava Basra 98) "Whoever is arrogant – even the members of his household do not accept him." Rashi explains that the "members of his household" refers to his wife who will 'not accept him' but rather shame and humiliate him.

Elijah taught further: (*ibid.* Ch.4) "Our sages taught: be unassuming and humble to all men, and to the members of your household more than to anyone else." The Shay LeMora comments on this: "'Unassuming' means that he does not respond if they humiliate him or go against his will. Instead, he remains silent."

This is a critical message for those husbands who feel that their wives are obligated to honor them and object to these teachings, saying: "What is this?! Who's the man here?! My wife needs to honor *me*, to give in to *my* wishes, to be humble, to listen to what *I* say…" and so on. According to this Midrash we see that such husbands are making a huge mistake, because *they* are the ones who need to honor their wives, to be humble, to give in, and to not respond to insults. Whoever thinks that his wife needs to honor him should know that his thinking is that of a woman, not a man.

This explains the statement of our sages: (Talmud, tractate Niddah, 70) "What should a man do to merit male sons?" Why 'male sons' – if it would just say 'sons' we would understand that the intention is not for girls? So too in many of our prayers we request 'male sons'. Are there sons who aren't males? According to what we have just written this becomes clear – because there are men with female attributes, in particular, the desire for honor and respect. When we pray for 'male sons' we are praying that we should have sons with entirely male attributes. These are sons who will give and not look to receive.

From these Midrashic teachings it's clear that how a wife treats her husband depends on how he treats her and on how he relates to Hashem. If his wife does not fear him, it's clear that he does not fear Hashem enough. The words of our sages are the laws of nature itself, inherent in creation.

This also explains why the Sages did not obligate the wife to honor her husband. The honor a wife gives her husband is a consequence of his behavior. If he honors her and Hashem as he should, and is careful with personal holiness – then she will instinctively honor him.

But, if he is deserving of humiliation and affliction, then he will receive it via his wife. This is for his own good. Sin pollutes a person's blood, both physically and spiritually, and this 'polluted' blood must be purged. The best way is through humiliation. If a husband doesn't want to be humiliated by his wife, he may need to be wounded, G-d forbid, in order to get rid of the polluted blood in a physical manner. Therefore, a husband with emuna he accepts all the verbal abuse from his wife with love, just like King David did when he was cursed by Shimi ben Gera. When the latter cursed him and David's men wanted to punish him, he told them not to, saying that: "Hashem told him to curse me…"

When a husband has strong emuna he realizes that it is not his wife who is humiliating him, but Hashem, and he rejoices that Hashem is ridding him of his polluted blood. He also knows that he has to do two types of repentance – one for the sin that incurred the humiliation, and a second for the suffering he caused his wife, because she suffers when she's forced to get angry with him and humiliate him. She didn't do so of her own accord; Heaven compelled her to do so because of the husband's sins. This makes him responsible for her suffering.

I witnessed an example of this when I once served one of the great leaders of the Jewish community and I accompanied him home. On his arrival his wife started hurling abuse at him and shouting at him – and he began to cry. When I asked him to explain, he said that he was crying that his wife had to suffer because of him. Rather than complaining about her abuse of him and being angry at her for humiliating him in front of a stranger, instead he was upset and concerned that he had caused her such suffering!

Fulfilling obligations

When a wife prevents her husband from doing things that he likes to do, it's a sign that he's not fulfilling his obligations to her. Now, he's getting a taste of his own medicine. She'll hit him right where he's vulnerable. Even if he wants to learn Torah, she'll give him problems. This is her way of sending him a distress signal, letting him know that she is hurting. The message she wants to convey is: "Just as you are suffering now, you should know that I am also suffering - because of you." Her hidden cry is: "You don't pay me any attention. I'm missing things. I'm in pain. Things aren't good for me. Why should you have it good? You should also feel that something's wrong, you should also feel some pain."

Whenever a wife obstructs her husband in any way, it's for one of two reasons: either Hashem is using his wife as an agent to arouse him to correct some spiritual wrongdoing; or, Hashem is simply pointing out to him that he has not been treating his wife properly – she's not getting from him what he should be giving her, so she's not letting him do what he wants to do.

The most common reason that a wife obstructs her husband or humiliates him is his violations of personal holiness. A wife will oppose any husband commits misdeeds in this area, as it says: "I will make him a helper to match him (literally: against him)" (Genesis 2:18), and our Sages explain: "If he merits she is a 'helper', if he does not merit she is 'against him'."

The word used in Hebrew for merit, *zechut*, is rooted in the word *zach*, which denotes 'clear' or 'pure.' Therefore, one who 'merits' refers to one who is pure in personal holiness – his wife will help him, encourage him, support him, and so on. One who does not merit – meaning that he is not pure in personal holiness, G-d forbid - his wife will obstruct him in every way she can.

Hence, when a husband with emuna sees that his wife is preventing him from doing something, he searches for what he needs to correct in himself. He says to himself: "My wife is not the one holding me back here, it's Hashem, and I have to figure out what Hashem wants from me. Perhaps I have violated my personal holiness, perhaps I am not treating my wife well enough, or maybe I need to pray more to achieve my goal."

The bottom line is that he looks at everything through the lenses of emuna. Not only does he refrain from criticizing his wife, he does just the opposite. He honors, respects and comforts her. And if a husband humbles himself before Hashem in this test of faith by searching for the hint about what he must correct and by subsequently following-up with action, then his wife herself will let him do whatever he wanted to. His greatest enemy will transform into his greatest helper - because he returned to the status of 'merit'. This is what it says in Proverbs: (16:7) "When a man's ways please the L-rd, even his enemies will make peace with him." 'His enemies' refers to his wife, since the biggest obstacles a man faces often come from her. But it all depends on him – if he repents, and once again his ways "please the L-rd," then his wife will transform into his greatest supporter.

This phenomenon is one that every married man can testify to: when Hashem wants a wife to help her husband, she'll be understanding, supportive, encouraging, and amiable. And the minute Hashem wants her to be the opposite, she transforms into the cruelest enemy he has ever faced.

Husbands who witness this phenomenon can't believe the transformation that takes place. One day their home is like paradise – a happy haven of peace of love. The next day, and sometimes by the very same evening, their home has transformed into a battlefield of pain, bitterness and suffering, where you can slice the tension in the atmosphere with a knife. And then a few hours later, or a day or week later, it's back to paradise again.

This phenomenon comes to teach us that peace in the home, *shalom bayit*, is supernatural - it is a marvel of Divine Providence, a wonder which depends entirely on the spirituality of the husband.

To illuminate, and not to make comments

A very delicate and sensitive situation is when a husband has become more observant and his wife hasn't. Most husbands in this predicament fall straight into the trap of the Evil Inclination and make comments to their wives about their lack of observance. The husband, based on his new understanding and belief system, feels that he is justified in pointing out to his wife what she's doing wrong. Such a wife might find herself subjected to stress and insults from morning to night.

This is bad enough. No-one, including this husband, ever became observant because someone beat them with a stick, so his insults will achieve nothing. But together with all the comments, he also makes it clear to her that she no longer interests him as before. He now has Hashem and His Torah. He may stop taking her out and talking with her. Understandably, when she sees all this, especially when she sees how much he enjoys his Torah lessons, then his 'teshuva' becomes her number one enemy. For his teshuva is responsible for all the insults that she is suffering, and for her no longer being important to him.

Since she despises her husband, she despises everything associated with him. In this case, she construes that his teshuva is her enemy, so that any chance of her becoming more observant is lost. She will move further and further away, to the point that she is repulsed by anything to do with Torah observance, and even the little respect that she may have had for tradition will also disappear. In this regard, our sages have taught us that before every soul descends to this world it is made to swear an oath: "Be righteous, and do not be wicked", and the Chassidic masters explain this to mean: "Don't be wicked with your righteousness."

First, a husband must avoid making any comments to his wife at all, and certainly not in regards to Torah and mitzvot. He should never say to her: "You should be doing this", "You should be like this" or, "Why aren't you doing this?" Second, he should now honor, praise and respect her **more** than he ever did before. He should do everything he can to let her know how much he loves her and make her as happy as he can.

These two steps should guarantee that, not only will he not push her away by his teshuva, and it will not be a burden for her, but on the contrary - she will see that his repentance and religious observance have improved his character and his behavior toward her. He is now more considerate, loving and giving than he ever was. This will show her the true light and goodness of Torah and its way of life. After this, if he truly wants to bring her closer to Judaism, he should pray for her. Everything can be achieved through prayer, as it says: (Proverbs 21:1) "The heart of kings is in the hand of Hashem" – the same certainly applies to the heart of his wife.

The Talmud tells of Rebbe Meir who once had some wicked neighbors who caused many problems for the Jewish community. At the request of the community, Rebbe Meir prayed that they should die. His wife Bruria, when she heard of this, said to him:

"Why are you praying that they die? It says 'Sins will cease from the earth' (Psalms 104:35) and not 'Sinners'. Pray instead that they do teshuva."

Rebbe Meir prayed that the wicked men should do teshuva - and they did! From here our Sages learned that, although teshuva is seemingly dependent on the free will of the individual, even so, praying for someone else can help to stimulate their teshuva. If this is the case regarding truly wicked people, it certainly applies in our times when there are no truly wicked people – just people for whom the strain of exile has driven them to where they are. The husband should remember that his not-yet-observant wife is no more 'wicked' than he was. If he merited that the light of teshuva was shined upon him from Heaven, he should have mercy on his wife and pray that she should also merit to taste the good that he has now come to know.

This is true love for his wife. He prays for her with love and says to Hashem: "Master of the world, in Your mercy You have aroused me to do teshuva. All this light I have is certainly from you, since I was walking in darkness until you opened my eyes. Thank You so much. I beg You now – please! Arouse my wife to teshuva too. Open her heart and her eyes just like You did for me."

He should keep on praying for her, while honoring her and being careful to not make any comments. The rule is: Illuminate and don't make comments. The light that the husband shines on his wife comes from the love that he gives her, the joy that he shows her and the prayers that he prays for her.

Honor and be honored

A wife whose husband truly honors her won't go against him for very long. She will feel uncomfortable to oppose him when he is so considerate of her feelings, honors her and gives to her so much. After he is so kind to her, why should she fight him?

A husband should tell his wife that he loves her just the way she is, and that everything he has and achieves is in her merit. It is only with her support that he can go out to learn Torah. He would much rather stay at home and spend more time with her - just that for the good of the family he needs to go out to learn. These and any other words that will make her feel that she is the most important thing in his life, and comfort her that she shares all the merit of his Torah and mitzvot.

All this must be done sincerely. A husband should not expect that if he just smiles at his wife she will be putty in his hands. He might have to give on a one-sided basis and illuminate her life for a very long time until anything changes. In the meanwhile, she may continue with opposition and insults. He must be strong and not be discouraged. Illumination on his part must be a way of life from now on, no matter what. When she sees that he is sincere, eventually she will change, as it says: "When a man's ways please the L-rd, even his enemies will make peace with him."

Chapter Six
Facing each other

The Talmud (Bava Batra 99a) points out a contradiction between two verses that describe the cherubs that stood on top of the Ark of the Covenant[1]. In Exodus (25:20), the Bible states: "And the cherubim will be... with their faces towards one another," whereas in Chronicles II (3:13) the verse states that: "Their faces were towards the Sanctuary," – implying that they were facing away from each other.

The Talmud answers the contradiction by saying that the verse in Exodus refers to when the Jewish people are fulfilling Hashem's will, whereas the verse in Chronicles refers to when they are transgressing. When Israel fulfilled Hashem's will, the cherubs faced one another, like two lovers gazing into each other's eyes - a sign that Hashem Himself was looking lovingly upon His nation. When Israel transgressed, metaphorically turning their backs to Him, then the cherubs miraculously faced away from one another, a sign that Hashem had also turned His back to them. The cherubs served as an indicator of the nation's spirituality.

These cherubs had the form of a boy and girl, and from this teaching we can learn a fundamental principle regarding peace between husband and wife. When the Jewish people fulfilled Hashem's will, then Hashem made the cherubs lovingly face one

---

[1]. The ark that contained the tablets of stone with the Ten Commandments written on them, which was kept in the holiest room of the Temple

another; when the Jewish people transgressed, Hashem made the cherubs face away from one another. So too, when a husband and wife fulfill Hashem's will, Hashem brings them lovingly together; and if they transgress His will, then He turns them away from one another.

Just as the cherubs were an indicator of the nation's spiritual standing, so is peace in the home an indicator of the couple's - and specifically the husband's - spiritual standing. Peace in a home is like a certificate hanging on the living room wall, signed by Hashem, which declares that the husband is fulfilling Hashem's will - specifically, that he guards his personal holiness.

A good 'way' (Derech)

Rebbe Nachman in Likutei Moharan (II:87) writes that peace in the home depends entirely on the husband. He explains that when a husband is modest and guards his personal holiness, then he shines 224 spiritual lights to his wife (224 being the numerical equivalent of the Hebrew word for 'way' - 'Derech'), which she then in turn reflects back to him. His wife will be happy and will support him in all that he does. This is another meaning of the verse in Exodus regarding the cherubs: "And their faces were one towards the other," – that is, the husband illuminates his wife and she shines his light back on him.

But if the husband corrupts his 'way' by violating his personal holiness: "For all flesh had corrupted their *way* upon the earth," (Genesis 6:12), then he no longer illuminates his wife, and she will turn against him. As our Sages have taught: "If he does not merit – then she is against him."

This problematic body

The Zohar tells us that Adam did not benefit from the physical world at all since his very body was entirely spiritual. But this was only until he sinned...

"When the body of Adam came to the world, the sun and the moon of this world saw him, and their lights were obscured before his, just like the light of a candle in the daylight...When Adam sinned by eating from the Tree of Knowledge... this caused a blemish in all the worlds and they all descended from their previous levels. The supernal light that had previously shone upon him was darkened... He required a new body made of physical flesh and skin from this world, as it says: 'And the L-rd G-d made for Adam and his wife garments of skin and clothed them.' (Genesis 3:21). This was their physical body that could benefit from the physical lusts of the physical world" (Zohar, Parshat Kedoshim p.83 with the explanation of the 'Matok Midvash').

Only after the sin of the Tree of Knowledge were Adam and Eve clothed in garments of skin - physical bodies - that could benefit from the physical lusts of this world. The experience of sexual lust came about as a punishment – a physical darkness that was forced upon Adam because of his sin. Before his sin, his body was entirely pure and shone brighter than the sun and the moon. Until then, his bonding with Eve took place on an entirely spiritual level and was completely removed from lust and physical pleasure.

A wife's happiness and peace in the home are dependent entirely on the personal holiness of the husband. This holiness is twofold, referring to the day to day conduct of the husband with his wife, in other words, that he should treat her with love and respect. Second, his conduct with her on their days of union should also be loving, characterized by kindness and consideration for her needs, rather than by his own animal lusts.

A husband's personal holiness, or "Tikkun HaBrit", strongly and positively influences a wife's happiness. There are many spiritual levels to "Tikkun HaBrit", but the basic level is the husband adherence to religious law - "Halacha" - in all aspects of conjugal relations. Rebbe Nathan of Breslev writes: "The Jewish bond of wedlock according to our holy Torah is an aspect of personal holiness" (Hilchot Nachlot, 3). Adherence to the statutes of Jewish Law in this area (see Shulchan Aruch, Orach Chaim, ch. 240) is conducive to successful and gratifying conjugal relations.

A wife's dissatisfaction or any problems in marital peace that are connected to conjugal relations can almost always be traced to a husband's breach in personal holiness. By strengthening his "Tikkun HaBrit," he'll discover that his wife will be much more satisfied with him, as we're about to see.

Attention or lust

After the sin of the Tree of Knowledge, Hashem cursed Eve that she and all women after her would be subservient to their husbands, as it says: "And to your husband will be your desire, and he will rule over you," (Genesis 3:16). The meaning of this punishment is that a woman's vitality and joy come from her husband – from the honor and loving attention that she receives from him, as we have said in previous chapters.

One thing that prevents a husband from giving this love and attention to his wife is the lust for sex. When a husband lusts to be with his wife he stops giving and instead looks to receive. He stops being a source of vitality for her, and consequently no longer "rules over her". On the contrary, she now controls him, since she has what he lusts for. The Rebbe of Kotsk commented on the above verse and said: "'And to your husband will be your desire – and he will rule over you.' The husband rules over the wife only when she longs for him, and not the other way around." If she is a mere object of his appetite, she will rule over him, and such a home will collapse.

Such a home cannot last, due to the following spiritual rule: when a husband craves for his wife, he creates in her an exact opposite force – the feeling that she cannot bear him. Lust from the husband is met by repulsion from his wife – the stronger the lust, the stronger the repulsion, until there is no greater suffering for the wife than to be intimate with her own husband. She will not want him to even touch her. Such a wife comes to dread the day of her ritual immersion in the mikvah, feeling like a death row convict on the day of execution – the steps down into the mikvah are like the steps to the gallows. The husband feels that he is coming to give her love, and she feels that she's entering the depths of purgatory. He looks like the angel of death to her, a monster, and she is entirely repulsed by him.

Often husbands mistake their lust for their wives for love. The truth is that as long as a husband lusts for his wife, he cannot truly love her. Love is giving, but lust is selfish taking. One way to test love is by looking at what happens once any physical lusts have been satisfied. Does his 'longing' for his wife suddenly disappear? Do his excitement and 'love' for her disappear as if they never existed? Perhaps he even feels repulsed by her, and has no patience to talk with her any more. Does he go straight to sleep? If this is what happens, it seems fair to say that his contact with his wife is more for the purpose of fulfilling his own desires than it is for fulfilling her needs – the 'love' that he feels is really nothing other than 'lust'.

When husbands treat their wives in the same way that they treat inanimate objects that have neither soul nor feelings, their wives feel more dead than alive, like empty vessels.

Love or hatred

The Bible relates the story of Amnon and Tamar. Amnon had

a tremendous desire to be with his sister Tamar. After many unsuccessful attempts to entice her, he took her by force. Immediately after this incident the Bible tells us: "And Amnon hated her with a great hatred, for greater was the hatred that he hated her with than the love with which he loved her" (Samuel II Ch.13).

Our Sages learned from this story that love built on lust will in the end turn to hatred, for: "Any love that depends on a specific cause, when that cause is gone, the love is gone; but if it does not depend on a specific cause, it will never cease. What sort of love depended on a specific cause - the love of Amnon and Tamar. And what love did not depend on a specific cause - the love of David and Yonatan" (Ethics of the Fathers 5:19). The Meiri explains that Amnon loved Tamar merely for lustful gratification. Once he had his gratification, he couldn't stand her any longer.

When a husband craves for his wife, he will ultimately come to hate her. His lust for her constitutes a 'specific cause,' so as soon as it is not satiated, his love for her will cease. Once she no longer satiates him, he will come to hate her and complain about her.

As long as a husband is lustful he'll without a doubt develop a lust for infidelity as well. Even if he is not unfaithful in the most literal sense, he will definitely be unfaithful with his eyes and in his mind. He will gaze at other women and be desirous of their beauty. The evil inclination will constantly show him that other women are far more attractive and exciting than his wife, as King Solomon wrote in Proverbs (9:17): "Stolen waters are sweeter."

A man that looks at other women can't fully love his own wife. She'll always be angry with him, for it is written: "Lust breeds separation" (Proverbs 18:1). The Ben Ish Chai relates a story in this vein and tells that a Rabbi once asked one of his congregants how many wives he has. The confused man answered: "Dear

Rabbi, you know that I have only one wife." The Rabbi responded: "You are lying. In truth, you have many wives that you hide away in secret chambers. I can see that you often fantasize about other men's wives, and the thoughts of these women are embedded in your mind and heart. The latter are the secret chambers that I was referring to, where you hide these 'other wives.'" The man ashamedly admitted to the truth.

When a man thinks about other women - gazing at them and fantasizing about them - apart from being 'unfaithful' to his wife, he also transgresses many severe Torah prohibitions, since it is forbidden for a man to purposely gaze at women or think about them. Such a husband transgresses two of the Ten Commandments: "Do not commit adultery" and "Do not covet your neighbor's wife".

The Mitzvah of 'Her Time'

Loving, warm and affectionate treatment before physical union is of paramount importance to a wife. Rav Shlomo Wolbe, of blessed memory, wrote: "Physical intimacy is a powerful bribe, but a wife is not deceived by such a bribe. On the contrary, during physical contact she can sense, with pain, if there is not yet any spiritual closeness. For this we have to know – physical union is the peak of intimacy, but every peak has a journey that must be trod until one reaches it. Physical intimacy void of spiritual closeness is offensive to a woman. Women look only to spiritual intimacy and consideration – this is what they love. When she receives such treatment, then the wife herself will desire to also have physical intimacy. But if her husband does not show her true consideration and care, and constant closeness of mind and soul, then she will feel disgusted at the thought of physical intimacy with him. Physical closeness that does not flow from closeness of mind and soul is degrading and painful for a woman."

Rav Wolbe's above teaching is the foundation for successful conjugal relations. Spiritually, one's true love and respect of one's wife is very conducive to a good livelihood. True love is the result of a husband's concern for his wife and not for his own lustful drives, as well as his recognition of her as a cherished person and not as a mere vehicle to fulfill his desires.

A wife wants her husband to be with *her*. She is not merely a body, but a vibrant soul that thrives on intimacy, attention, communication, consideration, respect, and the love of two souls binding together. A husband that focuses on his own physical gratification doesn't provide his wife with *any* of the emotional and spiritual gratification that is the basis of her vitality.

The Hebrew term for the wife's conjugal rights – *onah* - translates literally as 'her time.' The true fulfillment of this obligation requires much more than the physical act alone. A husband only fulfills this mitzvah if he succeeds in making his wife feel that he truly cares for her and loves her. He accomplishes this by letting her know how much she means to him, by being compassionate to her, by listening to her, by praising her for all that she is and does, and by expressing his gratitude to her. These are the steps that lead up the mountain of intimacy. At the very peak is the physical union, and that itself must also be imbued with love and care for her and the desire to bond with her as a person, not just as a body.

The act of physical union doesn't fulfill an essential spiritual and emotional need of a wife, except when it serves as a means for her to experience her husband's love for her. If love is missing, there is nothing for her. She has no need or desire for the act itself, in the way that the husband does. Generally women are tired in the evening and pleased to rest from the toils of the day. Intimacy that will recharge her spiritual and emotional batteries is worth the effort. An empty animalistic act to relieve her husband's pent-up lust scores extremely low on her list of priorities. Her need is solely for the spiritual closeness that intimacy can bring about between them.

When a husband is lustful, or knows that he struggles with his personal holiness, whenever he approaches his wife for intimacy he should determine whether he is coming to fulfill 'her time' or '*his* time'. If he approaches his wife without any intention of expressing his love for her or wanting to make her happy, he is most likely coming to fulfill 'his time', which is not a mitzvah, and his wife will pick up on it. This can set off a negative cycle of events, as we will discuss in the next section. The more a husband focuses on giving to his wife, and guards his personal holiness to the best of his ability, the more Hashem will help him to fulfill this mitzvah properly and will help him to live in true peace and love with his wife.

In summary, physical proximity doesn't mean the type of togetherness that a wife longs for. A wife needs to be loved in her entirety – soul, mind, and body. If a husband is blemished in the area of personal holiness, he won't succeed in connecting with his wife's soul. But, the more he enhances his personal holiness, the more his wife will be enamored by him and long for him.

Vicious cycle

In the "Sefer HaMiddot" (Money 2:27) Rebbe Nachman writes:

"Whoever separates a man from his wife, meaning that he goes to the husband and beautifies his wife to him, and then goes to the wife and degrades her husband in her eyes, until they separate – he will lose his income."

We won't discuss why the one who separates between them will lose his income. Let's focus on the way he does it – by "beautifying" the wife to her husband. This doesn't logical – surely if he wants to separate them he should degrade the wife to her husband. He would tell him how ugly and simple she is, that she's not good enough for him, and then go to the wife and talk against her husband. How does beautifying the wife separate between them?

This can be understood according to the aforementioned spiritual rule. By beautifying the wife to her husband, the third party increases the husband's lust for her. Feeling his lust, the wife will be repulsed by him. The trouble-maker strengthens this sense of repulsion by telling the wife what a worthless husband he is. The husband becomes angry at her for refusing intimacy, and a vicious cycle is created. In this way, the trouble-maker sets the couple off on a downward spiral that may well end in separation and divorce.

Get out of Purgatory

From the many hours that I have spent listening to the sorrows, afflictions and pains of the people that come to me, both couples and individuals, I have noted one consistent recurring theme – the destruction of both individuals and families that results from a man having become a slave to his sexual lusts.

At the beginning of my journey, my teacher and spiritual guide Rabbi Eliezer Berland sent me to make peace between a couple. I went to the home and spoke to the wife of the man who was close to Rabbi Berland. She told me the truth – that her husband had an insatiable lust and that she was absolutely repulsed by him. She had been pushed to the edge and said that she was not willing to even consider continuing to live with him.

I returned to my Rabbi and told him, "There's nothing to do, the husband is so crazy with lust that his wife is not prepared to live with him anymore." "If that is the case," Rabbi Berland replied, "then you are right. There is nothing we can do."

Many husbands that contact me suffer from anxiety, confusion, and worries - some even to the point that they want to terminate their marriages and even their lives. From listening carefully to their stories I realize that they too have become slaves to their lust. It gives them no rest, and they don't know what to do with themselves. For many of them, it is a living hell. Their wives are repulsed by them. Those husbands that pursue their lusts in other ways become filled with remorse and self-hatred. I tell them that the only solution is to escape from their lust. They need to sleep by themselves, stop gazing lewdly at their wives, at other women, and at the media. They should devote hours to prayer, begging Hashem to save them from the prison of lust that they find themselves in. Immodest pictures should be taboo in their lives, and they should say "Tikkun Klali" every day and go to the mikva daily, or at least once a week. More than anything, they should seek Hashem's assistance in overcoming their urge for lust, especially by devoting extensive time to personal prayer.

Some husbands, who are not at all troubled by their lusts, have complained to me that their wives are refusing to be with them, hoping that I will justify their complaints and put their wives in their places. They expect me to blame their wives for not fulfilling their conjugal duties. To their great surprise, not only do I not justify their complaints, but instead I tell them clearly that if *they* don't get themselves out of *their* lowly lusts, their suffering will never end.

Escaping from lust is essential for peace in the home. Our Sages have called the guarding of personal holiness the 'guarding of the foundation.' Personal holiness is the foundation of faith and of every good character trait. If a man wants to have strong faith, humility, peace of mind and tranquility, if he wants to be joyous and patient with others, and especially with his wife – he needs to begin by guarding his personal holiness. This creates a space and a fertile ground in which he can develop all these other good traits. The only good and healthy way for husband and wife to live together is in the way described at the beginning of the Torah: "And to your husband will be your desire *(not the other way around)*, and he will rule over you." Someone who wants to merit peace in his home must escape this lust.

Holiness

In the Book of Kings II (Ch.4) we are told about the 'Shunamite' woman, who dedicated a room in her home for the prophet Elisha to sleep in whenever he would pass through her town. This is how she described Elisha to her husband: "And she said to her husband: behold now I know that it is a holy man of G-d who often passed by us."

The Talmud (tractate Berachot 10b) asks: "How did she know that he was holy?" Our two great sages Rav and Shmuel each give a different answer. One says that she never saw a fly on his table, while the other states that she never saw a nocturnal emission on his sheets. We can understand the latter opinion – this is a clear sign of his holiness. But the one who said that she never saw a fly on his table – how does this testify to his holiness? This opinion comes to teach us that flies do not come to a place of holiness. This explains why there were never any flies in the Holy Temple, even though animals were being slaughtered there all day long, and there was plenty of blood and fat around – but because there was no holier place in the world than the Temple, flies could not enter.

The Maharsha, a 17th Century CE commentator on the Talmud, explains that a man's dining table acts in place of the altar in the Holy Temple. Therefore, just like there were no flies in the Temple, so too flies could not come near to Elisha's table, which had the holiness of the altar.

The Rabbi who said that the Shunamite woman didn't see a fly on his table and the Rabbi who said that she didn't see a nocturnal emission on his bed really meant the same thing, because one goes with the other. The intention of both was the same: she saw something that testified to Elisha's personal holiness.

This explains what Rebbe Nachman writes in Sefer HaMiddot: (Love II:2) "The love of a wife for her husband can be recognized by the flies and mosquitoes in the home. Also, through their love it can be known if the strength of the evil inclination has been weakened or not."

The presence or absence of flies and mosquitoes in the home is indicative of the husband's holiness. The degree of his holiness in turn determines how much his wife will love him, as we said before: a wife only loves a husband who guards his personal holiness. And the degree of love between them will be indicative of whether the strength of the evil inclination has been weakened or not, because true love is only possible when the husband has weakened his passions and is not lustful.

Peace to the distanced

The Medrash (Beraishis Rabboh 54) on the verse: "*When a man's ways please the L-rd, even his enemies will make peace with him,*" (Proverbs 16:7) writes: "Rabbi Yochanan says: 'his enemies' – this refers to his wife. Rabbi Yosef the son of Levi says - this refers to the evil inclination. Said Rabbi Chiya: 'even his enemies will make peace with him' - this comes to include demons, flies and mosquitoes."

This Midrash summarizes everything that we have said until now. When Hashem helps a man to conquer his evil inclination for lust and attain personal holiness, this leads to him having true peace with his wife, and to there being no demons, flies or mosquitoes in his home.

The verse says: "When a man's ways please the L-rd." This is the prerequisite to his enemies making peace with him. We might think that it's possible to make peace with the evil inclination in other ways – through discussion and compromise. This is a mistake. The evil inclination is only willing to make peace once he has been knocked to the ground and conquered. There can be no negotiations with the evil inclination. Giving in to his requests only makes him want and demand more. As our Sages have taught: "A person does not die with even half his desires met."

King David himself made this mistake. When Hashem informed him that He was going to test him by tempting him with a forbidden sexual relationship, he immediately performed a conjugal act during the daytime, thinking that doing so would satisfy him and prevent him from craving a woman for the rest of the day. But our Sages warn: "A man possesses a small limb – when he satisfies it, it hungers for more; when he starves it, it is satisfied." In the end, King David stumbled.

Our Sages comment on the verse: (Deuteronomy 11:13) "To love the L-rd your G-d and to serve Him with all your heart," and say that we must serve G-d with both our inclinations, good and bad. If we subdue the evil inclination, we can then harness his great power to help us serve Hashem. This is true peace with the evil inclination.

The greatest punishment

Slavery to sexual lust is a terrible punishment, since someone trapped by it constantly longs for an illusory pleasure that can never be satisfied. If it is a punishment, then it must have been preceded by some sort of sin which has brought about a Divine decree, for the Gemara teaches that there are no afflictions without sin. And since arrogance is the cause of almost all the decrees that come upon man, when a man finds himself enslaved to his lusts, it is a sign that needs to humble himself.

Our Sages have explicitly taught that arrogance is the source of lust: "Whoever is arrogant will end up sinning with a married woman, as it says (Proverbs 6:26) 'A married woman will hunt the haughty soul,'" (Sotah 4b). If arrogance is the cause, then humility is the cure. Rebbe Nachman (Likutei Moharan I:130) uses this idea to explain the incident of Miriam and Aaron's slander of Moses. In the book of Numbers (12:1-3) we are told that Miriam and Aaron spoke about the 'Kushite' woman that Moses had married. Rashi explains that the term 'Kushite' means beautiful – Moses' wife Tzipporah was exceptionally beautiful. Miriam and Aaron had found out that Moses no longer had any physical contact with her, due to his very close prophetic relationship with Hashem. They found it hard to believe that he could separate from such a stunningly beautiful wife. In the very next verse, G-d testifies that: "The man Moses was very humble," (ibid. v.3) and Rebbe Nachman explains that this juxtaposition is no coincidence. G-d was providing the answer for Miriam and Aaron – Moses was able to separate from Tzipporah due to his extreme humility.

The Zohar (Leviticus 15b) teaches that the evil inclination and sexual lust can be considered one and the same thing. The evil inclination's primary focus is to get a man to violate his personal holiness - he is well aware that this is the gateway to hell. Arrogance opens the door to the evil inclination. This is the meaning of the Talmudic statement: *"Whoever is greater than his fellow, his evil inclination is greater than his,"* (Succah 52). When someone is 'great,' meaning arrogant, then his evil inclination will overpower him with sexual lust.

Don't destroy

We are not on the spiritual level to withdraw entirely from physical relations like Moses did. This is a level reserved only for unique individuals throughout the generations who received explicit instructions to do so. Our task is to keep as far away from lusts as we can, to be humble, to live with our wives according to Torah law and to do our very best to make our wives happy.[2]

One might ask, how did the wives of the great tzaddikim like Moses and Rabbi Shimon Bar Yochai agree to live with such husbands who had entirely withdrawn from the physical world? The answer is simple: these great righteous men gave their wives absolute respect, honor, and love, to the point where their wives felt no deficiency.

Only a person on the level of a prophet or a man of holy spirit – "ruach hakodesh" - is allowed to refrain from conjugal relations, and this is by Divine directive only. All others – which means all of us – must religiously perform our obligations to our wives as stipulated in Section 240 of The Code of Jewish Law, Oruch Chaim, which deals with the laws of marital intimacy.

Many young men in search of artificial holiness fail to fulfill their conjugal duties. By making their wives suffer, not only do they

---

2. A husband must know that his work on personal holiness is a private matter between him and Hashem. He should never say a word to his wife about holiness or separation, since she will only interpret this as an insult – that he doesn't love her or want to be with her.

fail to achieve true holiness but they destroy their own homes, Heaven forbid. On the other hand, in satisfying one's wife, a person is performing a wonderful mitzvah of Torah.

Let's get to work

Now we can understand why our Sages have taught that one who is not yet married cannot be called 'Adam' – a true man. A bachelor who lusts after women is in trouble, but may have little motivation to change - only he and Hashem know about it. But when a husband lusts for his wife, it destroys his relationship with her and makes his home into a battlefield of pain, anger and sorrow. He *has* to do something about it. When he conquers his lust, he merits the true status of 'Man'.

There is hope

Sometimes it may seem that we have little or no hope, G-d forbid, of achieving peace in our homes. If peace in our homes depends on overcoming our lusts and desires, what happens until we reach this level? This is the work of many years. Will our homes be battlefields until then? Will our children be sacrifices to arguments and conflict?

Here we have to know another important spiritual rule – Hashem leads a person according to his own particular spiritual level at a given time. As such, Hashem "does not come with complaints to his creations." Hashem hints to each and every one, on his level, what he needs to do now. If a person heeds the message and gets to work, then he has already succeeded.

The main thing is that a person should know where he stands and the direction in where he needs to be going. He should know that the test of lust is the primary test of life, and one of the main purposes of the descent of his soul to this world. To succeed in life he *must* escape it. He should not think for a moment that because the Torah permits his wife to him, he has permission to be lustful. Instead he must know that falling into lust will destroy his home.

He should pray every day for Divine assistance in guarding his eyes, knowing that with every forbidden gaze he transgresses many Torah prohibitions. Hashem desires that people pray for this every day. Without such a prayer, a person stumbles. He must pray and beg Hashem to free him from lust to the extent that he should have no desire for illusory pleasures.

When it is clear to a person what his task is, and he does it to the best of his abilities, then Hashem will have no complaints about him. Hashem won't have to give him harsh wake-up calls. Such a person progresses up the spiritual ladder until he achieves the peak of personal holiness. Then, he'll be successful in this world and in the next, since personal holiness is the source of all blessings – it is the gateway to heaven, to all blessings, and to true success in this life. This is why our Sages nicknamed personal holiness as 'guarding the foundation', and violation of it as 'violating the foundation' – to teach us that personal holiness is the foundation of everything.

Important warning!

A husband should know that all his efforts to perfect his *tikkun habrit*, or personal holiness, are a matter that should remain far from public knowledge, including his wife's. A husband should never tell his wife that he aspires for more holiness or abstinence from bodily pleasures, because she will likely misunderstand him. She'll think he doesn't love her and is looking for reasons to shirk his conjugal responsibilities. A wife doesn't want to pay the price of her husband's holiness. Personal prayer to Hashem while asking for true holiness and freedom from lewd thoughts and desires is the best way to seek holiness. This should be done inconspicuously as well.

If one strives for freedom from lust, the Yetzer (Evil Inclination) jumps in the act and tries to ruin things. The Yetzer says: "To be holy, you must refrain from the conjugal act!" He's a liar. One who fulfills his conjugal responsibilities to his wife is fulfilling several very important mitzvoth at the same time. By denying a wife her conjugal rights, the husband is not only guilty of severe violations of Torah, but he deeply saddens his wife. Saddening one's wife alone is *Onaat devorim*, a severe transgression of Torah (see "Abridged Laws of Onaat Devorim", Nafshi Tidom, chapter 9).

One cannot fathom the humiliation and insult a neglected wife feels. Hashem instills in a wife a yearning for her husband. Indeed, the more he attains personal holiness, the more she yearns for him. The physical bond is a vital complement to the emotional and spiritual bond between a husband and wife. For that reason, a husband must be careful about fulfilling his conjugal responsibilities in a loving and joyful manner. If not, then he'll have to account for a sad, frustrated, and vindictive wife who feels like dying, and who probably spends Shabbat and holidays crying.

A misguided husband who strives for holiness is liable to destroy his own marital peace. When he does, it shows that his efforts are not for the sake of holiness, for if he really was holy, he'd be sensitive to the needs of his wife and eager to perform all the mitzvoth of Torah. In his arrogance, the misguided "holy celibate" is none other than a cruel and inconsiderate person with warped fantasies about what the Torah really wants from a person.

The zealously misguided "holy celibate" tells his wife that he doesn't need the sexual act and that she brings him down because of her lusts. He accuses her of being an obstacle in his path to holiness. He injects her with the venom of guilt until she becomes totally frustrated and starts persecuting herself for the very desires that Hashem instilled in her! She's bewildered, for on one hand she longs for her husband. Not only that, the Code of Jewish Law requires her to dress up for - and look enticing to - her husband (see Even Ha'Ezer, Ch. 70, and many other places throughout the Code of Jewish Law). On the other hand, she now has feelings of guilt that she's in the wrong, for she thinks that she's obstructing her husband's service of Hashem. Such an unfortunate wife finds herself in a dangerous whirlpool of frustration and confusion. The result - the "holy celibate" ends up destroying his home, his marriage, and his wife's sanity with his own two hands.

The Yetzer has yet another ploy to trap the gullible, misguided husband that wants to be a holy celibate. He says: "Ask your wife politely to share in your aspirations of being a tzaddik. Surely she'd love to be the wife of a tzaddik! Ask her politely – for the sake of holiness, of course, to forego conjugal relations." G-d forbid! Such a request is a dire insult to a wife, a mere declaration in her eyes that her husband no longer loves her and no longer desires her. He is robbing her of what she longs for – a perfect union with her husband.

Rebbe Nachman of Breslev teaches (Likutei Moharan II:32) that the flawless union between an upright husband and an upright wife in this lowly material world is so lofty that it influences the union of Hashem's Holy Name in the upper worlds. The Divine Presence hovers between a worthy husband and wife (Gemara, tractate Sotah 17). As such, the lower union corresponds to the upper union.

A husband should therefore know that the Torah doesn't require celibacy, it requires holiness. One must be careful to fulfill one's conjugal responsibilities, what the Torah refers to as *Onah*. A wife should feel her husband's love for her and not his efforts at striving to be holy. Once again, a husband that desires to be truly holy in thought, speech, and deed should do so by way of extensive personal prayer. One should never be demonstrative about striving for holiness.

The mitzvah of Onah, or periodic conjugal relations, should be done with extreme joy. A husband should never be sad or depressed. On the contrary, he should be gentle, loving, considerate, and happy to be with her. His thoughts should be uplifted and he should desire to gratify his wife. Before conjugal relations, one should pray to Hashem and ask for assistance in fulfilling this mitzvah in the proper manner. Indeed, the more a husband nullifies his own lust, the more he can be patient and involved in fulfilling his wife's pleasure.

In summary, one can only attain true holiness by fulfilling one's conjugal responsibilities properly, and not by abstention. A husband's job is to overcome bodily lust, a spiritual level that anyone can attain (see Rebbe Nachman's Discourses, 17). Personal holiness, *shemirat habrit*, is the foundation of all blessings and the gate to success in this world and in the next.

Chapter Seven
The House of Prayer

The following story teaches us an important lesson in faith and peace in the home:

A certain young man returned to emuna from listening to tapes of my lectures, and soon began attending my lectures in person. He came to my talks for a long time, but didn't make much headway in terms of practical observance. There was just one thing that he connected to right away - personal prayer, what we call hitbodedut, or talking to Hashem in our own language.

Though it wasn't apparent on the outside, he soon became a real 'master of prayer'. He would engage in hitbodedut at every opportunity and could do so for a few hours straight. Although he was talking to Hashem every day, his observance of mitzvot was still lacking.

One night he came up to me and told me about a girl he had met. Although she didn't share his interest in Judaism, he nevertheless wanted to marry her.

I had known him for quite some time, and knew that he was moving slowly in the right direction. He now had his own tefillin and was learning a bit of Torah. I felt that a girl who was on the same path would be better for him, so I advised him against marrying this particular girl. I said to him: "Why should you enter yourself into such a difficult test of lack of communication and tension?"

He replied that although he did want to get stronger and continue on the path that he had started, he couldn't see himself ever marrying an orthodox girl. This girl seemed really right to him, and he hoped that it would be okay.

I didn't argue with him, and he married her.

This is your correction

Not many days transpired after the wedding before he came to me again, this time with a gloomy face, telling me all about the problems he was having with his new wife. They just weren't getting along. All she was interested in was mobile phones and having a good time, and these things didn't interest him much. He had a different perspective on life, a perspective of emuna, of prayer, and it was difficult for him to find any common ground for communication with her. He saw her as being superficial and 'empty.' His loved her less with each passing day.

"It seems like you were right, Rabbi," he said sheepishly. "What should I do? Divorce her?"

I gave him a big smile and told him: "No way my friend. Before you married her, I advised you against it. But now that you're married – that's it. There's no way back. This must be your soul correction. You know how to do hitbodedut. Get to work."

I told him what to pray for and how to work on his character traits – not to make even the slightest negative comment to his wife, to honor her, and give her whatever he can. I encouraged him and strengthened his resolve, over and over. "This is your wife. If Heaven allowed you to marry her, then she is your intended wife and this is your soul correction. It's up to you to use your power of prayer to solve any problems that arise."

That young man, who was in no way lazy when it came to personal prayer, went and started to work on himself in a most admirable manner. Every day, he engaged in hitbodedut for a few hours. He asked Hashem for help him in refraining from comments and criticism, in honoring his wife and making her happy, and in believing that this was all for the very best.

His vigorous efforts resulted in peaceful relations with her.

Moving up a level

A year and a half of peaceful married life passed. Then one night he came up to me again, this time with a new problem: "Dear Rabbi, thank G-d I have peace with my wife now. This is no longer a problem. I have no difficulty in coping with whatever she does to me. I only see Hashem. I never pay her back in kind. On the contrary, I'm only good to her – I lavish things on her without end. It's clear to me that all the suffering that I get from her is what is due me. As much as she complains and is never happy – I accept it all with love. As regards peace in the home everything is fine."

"The problem now is that I have such a strong desire to live a Torah life, to live in a Torah community – and my wife has no connection to Judaism at all, zilch. I don't say a word to her about this, but I wanted to ask you, dear Rabbi, maybe we really aren't suited, and the best thing would be to get a divorce after all?"

I looked at this young man with amazement. I had seen how far he had come since his marriage. Now he wanted to live a Torah life – something that before his marriage was far away from his aspirations. He had achieved a high level of emuna. To live with a wife who constantly complained and to accept it all with love was no small accomplishment. His personal growth was clear.

His whole manner expressed humility – he was shining - a delight to look at.

Our efforts are all for the best

Then, I understood what a tremendous lesson Hashem was teaching me. I had always believed that whatever Hashem did was for the good. But here it was so obvious – everything really is for the very best. I thought that by marrying this girl he had made the mistake of his life. Yet, he accepted the situation with emuna, looked for the messages that Hashem was sending him, and then faithfully set out to improve. The truth became apparent in all its glory: everything Hashem does is always for the best.

If not for the challenges of getting along with a difficult wife, he would never have prayed as he did, from the depths of his heart and at such length. Also, he wouldn't have worked on himself in the way that he did. The merit of those heartfelt prayers and his dedicated efforts to improve himself were what brought him in the end to long for a holier life – a true life of Torah.

Had he married a G-d-fearing girl, as I had thought he should, perhaps he would have done hitbodedut for one hour a day, but it most likely would have been without much warmth or passion. In terms of Judaism he would have probably crawled along at the slow pace that he was going at. Who knows if he might even have taken some steps backwards, as I have seen many times, when young couples' enthusiasm for spirituality wanes after the marriage.

The girl he married, being the way she was, gave him more of a boost for spirituality than the most zealous orthodox girl could have. In the area of emuna – the most important part of teshuva – he reached levels that few achieve. He totally corrected his character traits. He started off with a very angry disposition, and now he was the most patient and pleasant person you could meet. He accepted all of his wife's complaints with faith. He pampered her and honored her with no expectations of receiving anything in return. If not for the challenge of having such a wife, he would never have merited all this.

From here we see the wonders of Hashem's Providence. Common sense said that it was a big mistake for our young man to marry that woman. In reality, they faced many difficult challenges. Yet, when we look through the lenses of emuna, we see that once they were married – very good! By coping with the difficulties, he ultimately became closer to Judaism. His tribulations helped him to achieve character traits and faith that few merit to achieve.

This is a lesson for every situation in our lives. Although a person shouldn't seek difficult challenges or suffering, when he finds himself already in such a situation he should know that this is definitely for the best. With such an incentive to pray and work on his character traits and his faith, the fruits of his labor will accompany him forever.

A good ending

Back to the story: when he asked me what to do, to divorce her or not, I told him: "There's no such thing. You've worked beautifully on yourself - now you have a new project. You anyway do hitbodedut for a few hours every day, start to dedicate one hour to pray that your wife should do teshuva. She'll change. Don't think about anything else." He started praying for his wife for an hour every day, and soon enough she started to change in the desired direction. An hour of prayer every day for somebody else will definitely have an effect. They then happily continued on the path to religious observance together.

There are two essential lessons to take from this story:

The first lesson is that there are no mistakes in Divine Providence. When newly married couples start to experience difficulties, as inevitably happens, their minds race with all sorts of disturbing thoughts. Here are a few familiar examples:

* "Perhaps I made a mistake; perhaps this marriage wasn't 'made in heaven.'"

* "If only I hadn't gotten married. Why didn't I see that she had such a character and that she's not at all suited for me?"

* "That matchmaker! It's all her fault. She pressured me into it and now I'm stuck."

* "I felt sorry for her, and so I didn't want to say 'no,' but now what can I do?"

All such thoughts are both unproductive and untrue. Laying the blame for a marriage on a human being – whether it is the person himself, his wife, his parents, the matchmaker, or the Rabbi – is blasphemous.

Certainly, before a couple gets married they must ask questions and check, to the best of their ability that they seem compatible. Marriage is not a 'Welfare Bureau' – we don't get married because we feel sorry for someone, because it's not 'nice' to refuse or because the matchmaker is pushy. At the outset we must endeavor to set up a home that has every chance of success, where there will be peace and love, and where both sides want the children to be educated in the way of the Torah. A person should not deliberately enter into a situation where he can see that he will face difficulty and conflict.

After the marriage, however, there are no more questions and no one to blame. There are no mistakes in Providence. Hashem is the one who pairs up couples, so if the wedding took place, it was from Heaven. You got married? This must be your soul correction, your primary mission in life. Hashem wouldn't have allowed it, otherwise.

On the contrary, when problems arise only after the wedding, they are a sign that the husband has something to rectify, not that the marriage was a mistake. He needs to ask Hashem to show him what he needs to correct and then get to work. If he doesn't understand what he needs to work on, he should seek advice from a rabbi who will know how to advise him accordingly.

When problems arise after a wedding, or when the couple suddenly feels that they are just not compatible, this is further proof that their marriage is Hashem's will. Here's how: the wife didn't see that her fiancé was just not her type. The husband did not see that he didn't have anything in common with his bride-to-be. These are signs that Hashem wanted them to get married and so He brought about the circumstances that got them together.

Maybe Hashem led the wife to agree in a hurry, or made the husband give in to the pressure of the matchmaker. Whatever it was that took place - confusion, stress and 'mistakes' that led up to the wedding – are simply Hashem's fingerprints, indicating that this was what He wanted.

The second lesson that we learn from our story is that coping with adversity elevates a person. Without difficulties and challenges it's very hard for a person to grow, since by nature we all want everything to go smoothly in life, and to take it easy. We don't, and shouldn't, seek out problems. But when a challenge presents itself, we must realize that we are being given an opportunity to elevate ourselves. If we want what's best for us, we should pray for help and step up to the challenge. Throughout all generations the greatest people have been the ones who stood up to, and conquered, adversity.

Our duty is to strengthen our faith and know that whatever situation we find ourselves in, Hashem is the One who put us there. It's for our own good, because this is the pathway to the correction of our soul, our personal mission and challenge. If we step up to the challenge, we will most definitely grow and reach levels that we couldn't have otherwise achieved.

Peace in the home through prayer

True domestic peace can only be achieved through prayer. A person could learn all the books in the world about peace in the home and use all of the techniques that he found in them; without prayer, they won't help. Here's why:

First, peace in the home is not natural, but supernatural. Our Sages have taught: "Pairing a couple together is as difficult as splitting the Red Sea." Just like the splitting of the Red Sea was a supernatural miracle, the pairing of a man and his wife is a supernatural miracle also. A husband and wife are two opposites and naturally incompatible. To bring them together and have them live peacefully with one another requires a supernatural miracle, and that necessitates prayer. As it says in Likutei Moharan: (I:7) "Prayer is supernatural, because nature dictates that something should be a certain way, and prayer can change nature."

Second, the Evil Inclination tries to destroy marriages, and the only way we can combat him is through prayer. Rebbe Nachman teaches (Sichot HaRan, 263:)

"Regarding the matter of the young men, where it is very common that they have problems with their wives, and they separate from one another for some time, and sometimes they even separate entirely, G-d forbid. He [Rebbe Nachman] said that this was the work of the Satan, who invests all of his energy into this matter, to ruin the peace in the home of young couples, so that they can thereby be caught in his trap, G-d forbid. He waits in ambush to catch them by ruining the peace in their homes, which he causes through his strategies, to destroy the peace between them…"

The Evil Inclination focuses his energy onto destroying homes. Our Sages tell us: "If it wasn't for Hashem's help, he [man] could not beat him [the Evil Inclination]." He's a heavyweight opponent and to have any chance against him, we must rely on our heavyweight reinforcement, prayer.

Third, the only way to implement what we learn is through prayer. The Torah says: "And you should know this day and integrate it to your heart." (Deuteronomy 4:39). As long as knowledge isn't integrated into the heart, it doesn't affect a person. The place of character traits is the heart. We behave according to what we know in our hearts, not in our brains. And the only way to transfer and implant knowledge from our brains to our hearts is through prayer. Prayer and the heart go together, like our Sages have taught: "How do we serve Hashem with our hearts? Through prayer." Even if a husband knows all the theories and techniques of peace in the home, he can only implement them through prayer.

For example, husbands have a very strong evil inclination to make comments and criticize their wives. Avoiding this pitfall requires extensive prayer. Even if a husband would hear a thousand lectures on this point, they won't help him unless he turns to Hashem and requests: "Master of the World, help me to avoid making comments to my wife any more. Help me to refrain from criticizing her; and help me to compliment and praise her every day." All the lessons in this book, as well, can only be internalized through prayer.

Fourth, Rebbe Nachman taught that we need to pray for everything, down to a small button missing from a shirt. A person should first pray for whatever he wants or needs, however big or small, and only then take some practical action towards getting it. Without praying first he can fall into the trap of: "My strength and the might of my arm" (Deuteronomy, 8:17), attributing his achievement to himself. Without prayer, one is liable to think: "I don't need anybody's help. I know how to act. I know how to speak to people, how to pacify them and persuade them, and how to get what I want." This attitude leads to downfall, for the wisest of all men said: (Proverbs 16:18) "Pride goes before destruction and haughtiness of spirit before a fall."

Adel, the Baal Shem Tov's daughter, would repeat many times the prayer we recite on the departure of Shabbat that begins: "Master of the World," stressing the passage: "Open to us the gates of Divine assistance." Divine assistance is what we need more than anything. A person needs to ask Hashem to help him so that all his efforts should be successful, especially in regards to living peacefully with his wife.

The essence of peace in the home is prayer. Without Hashem's help a couple cannot achieve true peace and love. They won't be strong enough alone to conquer their differences, or to combat the Evil Inclination, who loves to destroy homes. The husband won't be able to implement whatever he learns without praying that Hashem open his heart and let the teachings sink in. And if for little things we must rely on Hashem, how much more so do we need to turn to Him for the most important element in our lives, namely peace in the home.

The power of an hour

A couple once came to see me and I assumed that they wanted me to help them achieve peace with one another. After a few minutes of talking with the wife, it was clear that she had no such intention. She had a different agenda – perhaps I could persuade her husband to finally release her and give her a '*Get*' – the Jewish writ of divorce.

This was a difficult case. In similar situations, it had been possible to placate the wife, to promise her that after I spoke to her husband there would be a change and that it was worth her while to give him one more chance. In this case the wife was adamant: there was nothing to talk about. They had already been to many Rabbis and counselors, to no avail. She wasn't open to hearing anything more about living peacefully together. Although he wanted to try again, she had only come to ask me to persuade her husband to grant her a 'get' and put an end to the long chapter of suffering that she had been through with him.

I saw that it would be a waste of time and energy to even try to talk to her. She didn't believe that her husband could change. I took him aside and said to him the following: "Listen here. Your wife is not prepared to hear of any more talk of peace in the home, she only wants a divorce. The only One who can help here is Hashem Himself. If you'll take my advice – accept upon yourself that from today, you will not let one day pass without one hour of personal prayer. For that entire hour focus on repenting for your sins, and beg Hashem to sway your wife's heart so she'll forgive you for all the wrongs you've done to her; and that she should believe that you love her; and that she should be willing to give married life another chance."

The husband accepted to do this, and kept his word. He started to do an hour of personal prayer every day with true self-sacrifice. He didn't let one day pass without an hour of personal prayer. Even when many obstacles and interferences meant that the whole day had gone by without the hour, he would stay up into the early hours of the morning – he would not go to bed until he had done his hour of prayer.

An amazing change

Two months passed. The wife wanted to see me again. I prayed that this time she should be willing to hear something about peace in the home, but I didn't get my hopes up.

As soon as she started talking I realized that I was witness to a miracle. She said: "I don't believe it. My husband has changed. He's working on himself. He had a terrible temper, really, he had no self-control at all; he would break things in the house. And now he gets through difficult situations with patience and calm. I don't believe that there can be such a huge change in a person. He responds to the grief I give him with love. I almost feel ashamed."

She was prepared to consider trying again. The whole situation had turned around after just two months of serious personal prayer.

I left the meeting and whoever saw me then must have thought that I'd gone crazy. I started to talk to myself excitedly about the power of personal prayer that I had been witness to. I said to myself: "Whoever does an hour of hitbodedut, what Heaven he has. In this world and the next, there's nothing that cannot be achieved by personal prayer."

Although I've seen many miracles that have come about through hitbodedut over the years, this one was especially tangible. Whoever hadn't seen the change in this woman can't really understand. The fate of this couple had been signed and sealed long before – things hadn't changed for years. Rabbis, counselors – nothing had helped until the husband accepted upon himself to do an hour of personal prayer every day. Only then, everything changed. Now she praises his good character traits and is ready to consider living together in peace.

When a person does an hour of personal prayer every day, his life can change from one extreme to the other.

Repentance – Teshuva

Sometimes it happens that all the guidance and advice about peace in the home just doesn't help. Couples come to me with serious problems, and it's senseless that they are having such difficulties.

Obviously when I see that a husband has bad character traits or doesn't treat his wife properly then I guide him accordingly. But in many cases both husband and wife are good people who are both trying and want to achieve peace together. Still, they just don't get along. They have no peace together and their lives are full of pain and suffering. So what's the problem here? Maybe they are just not a "match made in heaven"? Perhaps they simply aren't compatible?

No, the answer is that although they are definitely a "match made in heaven" and are perfectly suited for one another, "stern judgments" or *dinim* are resting on them and it is these that are ruining the peace between them. Let me explain.

Sweetening of judgments

Every day the Heavenly Court judges everyone for their behavior over the past twenty-four hours. Every thought, word and action is scrutinized. When a transgression is found, a "judgment" is ruled, and afflictions are sent to the person to arouse him to repent.

These afflictions can come from anything or anyone. King David wrote in Psalms: (119) "To fulfill Your decrees they stand until this day, for all are Your servants," which means that when there is a judgment on man, all of Hashem's creations can act as His messengers to execute this judgment. "To fulfill Your decrees they stand," when there is a judgment on man, then "all are Your servants" execute the judgment.

Often, this task is given to the members of one's household. They, and particularly one's wife, are chosen as the messengers to execute the judgment and deliver the afflictions. This is the true source of many of the domestic problems in the world. Logically, the situations cannot be understood. The husband says one word, and sparks off an atomic explosion. In reality, it wasn't what he said or didn't say, or the intonation of his voice, or anything else that he did. The explosion was coming to him anyway – it just needed something in this world to implement it.

No guidance or techniques will help in such situations, apart from teaching the husband to take time every day to "sweeten the judgments." This is achieved by taking a personal accounting every day of his behavior over the last twenty-four hours, and repenting for any wrongs that he did. By doing this, he removes (sweetens) any judgments that may have been decreed upon him. Judgments are like a stick of dynamite. Sparks still remain sparks, but with no outstanding judgments, there's nothing to explode. The perfect time to take such an accounting is during an hour of personal prayer.

Spiritual law forbids double jeopardy: "When there is judgment down below – there is no judgment up above." Therefore, when a man stands before Hashem and confesses his sins, expresses regret for them, and accepts upon himself not to return to them, then the Heavenly Court are not allowed to judge him for them. He won't be sent any afflictions, since these would be unwarranted.

Afflictions and tribulations are sent to arouse a person to repent - if he arouses himself, they become superfluous. When a man does an hour of hitbodedut every day and repents during that hour he sweetens any judgments that he may have incurred and saves himself from troubles, especially at home.

Our Sages said that: "If a husband and wife merit, then the Divine Presence is between them. If they do not merit, then fire consumes them." The husband and wife "merit" when they repent for their sins and are free of judgments. If they do not repent they will be sent afflictions to arouse them. If they still don't take the hint, then fire will consume them.

This teaching itself is alluded to in the Hebrew words for man and woman. The name for man in Hebrew is *Ish* which is made up of three letters. Two of the letters spell the Hebrew word for fire – *Aish* and the third is one of the letters of the Tetragrammaton, Hashem's ineffable name. The name for a woman in Hebrew is *Isha* which is also made up of the two letters that spell fire in Hebrew, *Aish*, and a different letter of the Tetragrammaton. The two letters of the Tetragrammaton put together spell a shorter name of G-d. When the couple "merits" the two letters of the Tetragrammaton come together and the Divine Presence dwells with them. When they do not "merit" the Divine Presence leaves them, the two letters of the Tetragrammaton are gone and what is left is fire on both sides. These spiritual fires combine and destroy their household.

There are particular sins that immediately drive away the Divine Presence. One of them is immodesty, for the Torah says: "And there should not be amongst you a profane thing, that He see no unclean thing in you, and turn away from you" (Deuteronomy 23:15). Hashem's presence cannot dwell in a home where there is lewdness.

The Divine Presence also only feels comfortable in a place of joy. Anger and joy don't go together. The "Raishit Chochmah" writes that: "Anger is the greatest cause for the departure of the Divine Presence from between a couple." These are two aspects where the couple must be especially careful. They, and in particular the husband, should try their best to ensure that their home be a place of modesty and joy.

To learn more about using the hour of personal prayer for personal accounting and repentance, the reader is recommended to listen to the CDs about this topic, a list of which can be found at the back of this book.

"I will make him a helper – against him"

Although unpleasant, it is actually a blessing that a man's afflictions are delivered to him in his own home, by his own wife.

Imagine if the messenger for his afflictions was his boss. The man might make some mistake at work and his boss would then explode at him, humiliating him in front of all his colleagues. The boss might even fire him. The shame would be incredible, and bosses are notoriously difficult to placate.

Suppose his neighbors would suddenly turn against him and stop talking to him. Life for him and his family would soon become unbearable. Should he move away, or change jobs every time there's conflict? Wherever he goes the decrees will follow him, until he repents.

When his wife is the agent of affliction, however painful it may be, he's much more fortunate. She is easier to placate than a boss, and she wants to live in peace with him. She wants him to stay, not to run away. And as soon as he repents, Hashem will return his home to a state of peace and love, and the past will be forgotten.

Another reason that suffering at home is a blessing is because it is the greatest catalyst for change. If a person suffers outside the home, but is safe within his own four walls, it's easier for him to avoid taking a proper accounting of his actions and making any necessary changes. But when he has no peace in his own home, he'll get to work. Living without peace in one's own home is unbearable.

Having the afflictions delivered, not just to his doorstep, but to his living room is therefore a great blessing. It's the easiest situation to remedy, and ensures that he will make an effort to improve. The husband will be the one who benefits the most when peace and love again reign in his home. Even when his wife is against him, she is still his greatest helper.

Every man has his hour

We began this section by discussing cases where 'judgments' were ruining couples domestic bliss. We said that the only way to deal with this was for the husband to do an hour of personal accounting and repentance during personal prayer.

Personal prayer is necessary for all husbands, even when the other techniques are working for them and peace with their wives is not a problem. This enhances personal growth and helps in all situations.

When a person suffers at the hands of others, it's easy to see them as the source of the trouble and blame them, thinking that if it wasn't for them, everything would be fine. The truth is that they are only agents, chosen by Hashem to carry out His decree. If not through them, then the suffering would have come through someone else. By "sweetening" the judgments every day, such suffering at the hands of others can be almost entirely avoided.

For a man to have peace in his home with his wife, peace with everyone else in his environment, and peace with himself, he needs a daily hour of personal prayer and self-evaluation. This will sweeten any judgments for him, and make suffering unwarranted.

This may sound too much for many people, as if I am saying that a husband must be perfectly righteous to achieve peace with his wife and others.

Once again, Hashem doesn't make senseless demands. When He sees a man trying his best to fulfill His will, and promptly admitting his errors, Hashem values his efforts tremendously. He is not angry with him, but on the contrary, takes great delight in him and will send him all the help he needs to achieve his goal of peace.

Chapter Eight
The way to a happy home

Rabbi Yosef Chaim, the "Ben Ish Chai", of blessed memory, tells the story of how Hashem decided where to build his Temple:

In a certain village lived two brothers who loved each other very much. Their father had given each of them a field as a source of income. One of them was successful and became very rich, though to his great sorrow, he did not have children. The other did not succeed financially and was quite destitute, but was blessed with a large family.

One night the poor brother awoke from his sleep and started to think how hard it must be for his rich brother, not having any children. He said to himself: "I may be destitute, but thank G-d I have children who bring me much joy. But my poor brother, since he has no children to gladden his heart, what can make him happy?" He thought about what he could do to cheer him, and decided: "I will take some of my grain every night and add it to his… perhaps the additional blessing and wealth will comfort him."

And so the poor brother began to get up every night to take to his brother's field half of the grain that he had harvested that day.

On that same night, the wealthy brother had also awoken from his sleep, and had contemplated the plight of his destitute brother. He said in his heart: "I am so rich, but I don't have any children to provide for, and my poor brother is so much in need of money…

I will take some of my grain harvest every night and add it to his." He too started to take half of the grain that he had harvested each day to his brother's field.

For quite a while, each brother brought the other half of his daily harvest, for both were unaware of each other's actions. Neither understood the next day how their own harvest wasn't diminished despite the fact that they had given half of their own grain away the night before.

One night, the poor brother decided to stay awake all night long in his field to discover what was happening. The rich brother decided to do the same thing. In the dark of night, the two brothers met and immediately understood what each had been doing for the other. They fell on each other's necks and cried with great emotion. When Hashem saw this beautiful sight, He decided that this place - where there was so much brotherly love - would be the place where His Divine Presence would rest. This is the place where the Holy Temple was subsequently built.

At the very same time, a completely opposite tale was taking place in another location. There were also two brothers, one rich without children, and one poor with a large family. The difference was that here, the brothers had a bitter hate for one another.

On the same night that the other brothers had awoken, these two brothers had also awoken from their slumber and had started thinking about one another. The poor brother thought to himself: "My rich brother – what does he need all his wealth for? Does he have children to support?" He decided to go each night and steal some of his brother's grain.

The rich brother said to himself: "It's enough for my brother that he is so blessed with children. It's not fair that he should have wealth as well." He, too, decided that he would go each night and steal some grain from his brother's field.

This occurred a few times, until the poor brother decided that he would wait in ambush for the thief. The rich brother had the same idea. The brothers met in the dark of night, understood what had been happening and viciously attacked one another. When Hashem saw this terrible thing he decided to remove His presence from that place. On that very site a temple for idol worship was built, which spread hatred, intolerance and conflict in the world.

It all depends on us. If we emulate the second pair of brothers, if we are inconsiderate, argue and fight, then Hashem will remove His presence from our homes, and they will become places of conflict and misery, G-d forbid. If we want the Divine Presence to dwell in our homes, then we must emulate the first pair of brothers. We need to think compassionately about our wives, think about their needs and what would bring them joy. We should fulfill their needs lovingly, even if this means sacrificing things that we desire. When Hashem sees us behaving in this way, He'll bestow His Holy Presence in our homes. Such homes are a *Mikdash Ma'at*, a miniature Holy Temple.

Heaven in this world

Hashem desires to dwell among us, as He says: "And they will make for me a Sanctuary and I will dwell in them," (Exodus 25:8). Hashem doesn't not say: "I will dwell in *it*," referring to the Sanctuary, but rather "in *them*" – in each and every one of us. Hashem's greatest joy is that every Jewish home should become a miniature Sanctuary where the Divine Presence can rest. Then, there would be no need to travel all the way from Haifa to the Western Wall to pray - one could simply go to a Jewish home where there is true peace between husband and wife, and place notes of prayer in the mailbox – literally.

A peaceful, loving home is the vessel that invokes every type of blessing in the world. Material success, good income, good health, spiritual fulfillment and growth, happiness – even the final redemption of the world – all depend on caring, loving homes.

Everyone functions better in a happy, supportive and loving environment. Such an environment produces emotionally healthy people, who are the most efficient, creative and productive members of society. A man with peace at home has a clear mind to focus on his studies, his work, his prayers, his personal growth, and on giving to others. In a home where there is no peace, almost everyone suffers from emotional problems.

What is also true, but is far less apparent, is that the future redemption of the world also depends on peace in the home, as we'll explain shortly, with Hashem's help.

The importance of guidance

From my many years of working with domestic peace problems, I have found a common denominator in virtually every case – the couple never received any proper premarital coaching.

The couples with problems are normal in every way. They have no intention to hurt or upset one another. Both husband and wife share the goal of a peaceful, loving and supportive relationship. What's missing is the practical know-how of how to achieve this. No-one ever taught them, and it may never have occurred to them that there was anything to learn.

Once people are open to learning about the differences between the sexes and how to live successfully together, peace is not far from coming. However, there are many men who object to learning the basics of successful marriage.

Some think that there's simply no need, and say: "What is there to learn? Did my parents learn about peace in the home? Am I so simple-minded that someone needs to explain to me how to live with a wife? Just like everyone else gets married and learns how to manage, so will I…"

In the case of living together with a roommate, where one man lives with another, then such an argument would be justified. A dose of common sense, some sensitivity and the willingness to compromise are enough for two men to live together peacefully. But marriage is about a man living his life in close quarters with a woman, who differs from him in every way. She sees the world differently than he does, reacts differently to situations, and has different priorities and values. Without an understanding of what makes a wife tick, a husband is bound to make big mistakes without even understanding what he's doing wrong.

There is a fundamental difference between a man and a woman. Few people appreciate how extreme this difference is. The evil inclination of a man is entirely different to the evil inclination of a woman. A man's way of thinking and his emotional attachment to certain things and not to others are so different from that of a woman. This topic requires in-depth learning.

If husbands would realize the tremendous difference between the spiritual and mental make-up of men and of women, they would certainly seek a capable person that could teach them how to successfully live with their wives.

This matter doesn't depend on intellect, but on learning. Just as a person would not expect to understand medicine without having studied for many years in medical school, so too a man cannot expect to understand his wife, to live with her successfully, or to treat her properly without having studied this issue.

Besides the difference between men and women, marriage also brings with it a whole package of new mitzvot for the husband to fulfill, and each of these requires much study, just like all other mitzvot of the Torah. For example, everyone knows that in order to put on Tefillin properly, a person needs instruction – how to put them on, when to put them on, what to do in different situations, and so on. Even if a person were to buy the most beautiful and kosher Tefillin in the world, if he'd put them on his forehead where no hair grows, as many people mistakenly do, he will not once fulfill the mitzvah of wearing Tefillin.

The mitzvah of Tefillin is one of the simplest mitzvot to fulfill, far easier than the many mitzvot involved in marriage. Yet, it requires extensive study in order to fulfill it properly. All the more so does a successful marriage require effort, learning, guidance, much prayer and Divine assistance.

The Torah Scholars

Evens great rabbis with vast knowledge in different branches of the Torah sometimes don't understand why they should need marital guidance, especially when those giving the guidance may be far less learned than they are in other areas of Torah knowledge.

The answer to these rabbis comes from the teaching of Ben Zoma in Ethics of the Fathers (Ch.4): "Who is the wise man? The one who learns from everyone, as it says: 'From all those who taught me, I became wise,'" (Psalms 119).

Imagine a person with a heart problem going to the world's leading expert on eye ailments. The latter would have no shame in referring this person on to the heart specialists who can help him, since he recognizes that his knowledge of heart complaints is very limited. No one would look down on him for this.

One might be an outstanding Talmud scholar but yet know little about how to live peacefully with his wife. He shouldn't be ashamed to consult a rabbinical expert in the field of marital peace, even though the latter might be less learned than him when it comes to the Talmud.

Arrogance is the main reason that a person is not willing to accept guidance and direction, or to invest effort in marital success. A person's arrogance makes him feel that everything is fine by him, and that others are the ones who need to change.

Almost all the problems of peace in the home stem from a lack of knowledge, meaning that if the couple would have had the know-how and proper guidance, the problems would never have occurred. Seeking this knowledge is a sign that a person desires to improve.

The perfection of creation

The purpose of creation can only be realized through peace in the home. It makes no difference what other mitzvot a person does in this world, or what other service of Hashem he engages in. Without peace in the home between a husband and his wife in this world, Hashem has not achieved the purpose for which He created the world, as I will explain.

At the creation of man it states: "And G-d created man in His image, in the image of G-d He created him, male and female He created them," (Genesis 1:27). From here we see that someone who is not married is not called "man", for it was only when male and female were united as one that they were called "man". A man without a woman, or a woman without a man, does not have the status of "man".

In a similar vein, the Zohar writes that: "Any form that does not contain both male and female aspects is not a supernal form. For the supernal form about which it was said: 'In the image of G-d he created him,' was both male and female." Where there is no unity of male and female, meaning that there is no love between them (the word for love in Hebrew has the same numerical value as the Hebrew word for one), then there is no Divine image.

The Zohar adds: "Wherever male and female are not found together in unity, Hashem does not bestow His Divine Presence or dwelling in that place." A man could be the most righteous person in the world, but as long as there is no unity between him and his wife – Hashem will not dwell in his home.

The Midrash writes: "Not a man without a woman, and not a woman without a man, and not both of them without the Divine Presence." A man without a woman or a woman without a man is nothing. What's more, both of them together but without the Divine Presence are also nothing. If they do not have peace in their home, the Divine Presence will not be between them. But, once they merit having peace in their home: "The Divine Presence rests between them" – only then can there be perfection.

Rabbi Moshe Cordovero, of blessed memory, writes: "It is a simple fact that the Divine Presence does not rest with a man who lives without a wife. The Divine Presence dwells in a household primarily by virtue of the wife."

From this short collection of teachings we can understand why creation cannot realize its purpose and reach perfection without peace in the home. The purpose of creation was Hashem's desire to have a "dwelling place in the lower worlds" – in other words, down here in this lowly world. Since He only rests His Divine Presence in this world in the homes of true unity and love, then peace in the home is a necessary element for the purpose of creation to be achieved.

"It is not good for man to be alone" (Genesis 2:18)

A man who does not marry certainly doesn't fulfill the purpose of creation. The Divine Presence rests only in a place where there is male and female. A bachelor, however righteous he may be, is unable to bring the Divine Presence down to this world. Therefore, many great Tzadikkim who were widowed late in their lives immediately re-married, despite the fact that they could have lived without a wife.

When his first wife died, Rebbe Nachman of Breslev, may his merit protect us, quickly remarried. He remarked that if not for embarrassment, he would have remarried immediately after the month of mourning for his first wife was over. Since the Torah says: "It is not good for man to be alone", he wanted to minimize the time that he had the status of "not good".

Even once a man is married, he has still not fulfilled his obligation in realizing the purpose of creation until he has peace in his home. The couples that live in conflict and dissension fail to fulfill the purpose of creation and blemish their own souls. The Divine Presence waits to descend upon them, but cannot. The conflict between them causes conflict and separation in the higher worlds, G-d forbid.

Only when a person marries and has true peace and harmony with his wife - not just a cease-fire or a lull in hostilities - can the world reach its perfection. Hashem will want to dwell in such a home. Their peace and love therefore invokes Hashem's Presence. This in turn brings blessings and abundance to the whole world, all in virtue of the wonderful husband and wife that dwell in peace with each other, just like the two brothers that we spoke about at the beginning of the chapter.

We conclude that every husband must become aware that he has to learn and invest effort to attain peace in his home. Even one who thinks that he has already achieved this should know that he may have no idea what true peace in the home means. As we said, we are not talking about a cease-fire or a peace-treaty. Peace in the home means absolute unity and love – where love equals one.

The need for guidance about how to achieve peace in the home is indisputable. Peace in the home is not like any other mitzvah – it is a mitzvah that the whole of creation depends on.

Loving-kindness

Psalm 89 states that: "The world is built by loving-kindness." If the home is a microcosm of the world then we can say also that: "The home is built by loving-kindness." In Ethics of the Fathers we are told that: "On three things the world stands: on Torah study, on the service [of G-d], and on loving-kindness." Acts of loving-kindness are what sustain both the home and the world.

A man can be the kindest person, helping widows and orphans, and being very charitable. But if he doesn't do acts of loving-kindness for his wife, then all his kindness to others is worth nothing. Loving-kindness to strangers that's coupled with neglect at home is not the type of loving-kindness that sustains the world.

The loving-kindness of a husband that sustains and builds the world is only that which he does *after* he has been kind to his wife. Once he has concerned himself with her needs so that she lacks nothing and is happy and content – if he then tends to the needs of others, there is no end to the reward.

A red carpet

A man who performs all kinds of loving-kindness outside the home but forgets about his wife faces a very difficult challenge. In his own eyes and in the eyes of almost everyone that knows him, he is a truly generous person. He is respected and honored in his community. People like him. They are happy to see him and want to be around him. He feels good about himself for all the kind acts that he does and from the positive feedback that he receives. As the Talmud says, the world stands in the merit of his good deeds.

When he comes home he expects to get the same warm and respectful treatment from his wife. He knows about all the good that he does and thinks that she should be grateful to be married to such a kind, thoughtful and well-liked husband. The reality that greets him is very different. His wife is full of anger, disdain, and complaints against him. She doesn't honor him in the slightest. His status outside the home doesn't impress her in the least.

Her complaints are totally justified. She should be first priority in his world, but she isn't. He spends his whole day doing favors for everyone else, but not for her. She doesn't understand why she comes last on his list of priorities. Why is she less than everyone else? Why does he do acts of kindness for everyone except for her? Why does he have time for complete strangers, but not for her?

Having learned the chapter "First Place," one readily understands the mistake that such a husband is making. But a naïve and unaware husband that's ignorant of the message of 'First Place' may think that he's justified in his behavior and expectations.

Suppose the story ends here, with both sides having complaints about each other. The husband complains that his wife doesn't honor him like everyone else does, and she complains that she's bottom rung in his life. But it doesn't end here. The wife's frustration grows from day to day. She constantly complains that he has no time for her and doesn't do things for her. He fails to understand and sees her as a selfish shrew that wants to stop him from doing all of his good deeds. This further drives his wife into deep emotional distress and into a downward cycle of despair.

The poor of your household come first

We have to think – why does that husband hold his wife last, as his lowest priority? Is he such a wicked, cruel person? No – he's simply forgotten an essential rule of loving-kindness, namely, that the poor of one's household come first. Rav Yosef elaborated on the verse: "If you lend money to My people, to the poor who are with you," (Exodus 22:24) and said: "Poor people or rich people – the poor come first; the poor of your city and the poor of another city – the poor of your city come first; the poor of your family and the poor of your city – the poor of your family come first." (Talmud, Bava Metsia 71)

If a person wants to give charity, lend money, or do any other act of loving-kindness, and there are many who are in need of such help - rich people, poor people, local people, those in his street, the members of his own household - he must start with the poor of his own home. If there is anything left over, he should give to the poor of his street, and work outwards from there.

One's first obligation is to one's own family. Only afterwards can he give to other needy people. When inspired to do kindness, one must remember that kindness begins at home with his own wife. Once he has been generous to her, he can use the opportunity to do even more kindness outside the home - in his street, in his neighborhood, or to the whole world – and he'll be blessed.

The litmus test of a man's character is how he behaves in his own home, behind closed doors. This is true of all his traits, and especially with the traits of kindness and generosity. If a person is not kind and generous with his wife it is a sign that whatever 'kindness' he does outside the home is false and insincere. It is a show that he puts on for ulterior motives. The test is specifically with his wife and not with his children, for there are many husbands who treat their children well, but don't treat their wives properly. This is a big mistake, since such behavior shows his wife that he doesn't love her, only his children.

Rav Chaim Vital, of blessed memory, the principal disciple of the AriZal wrote:

"There are people who do kindness with everyone, but not with the members of their own homes, and they think to themselves that when they arrive in the World of Truth, the gates of the Garden of Eden will be opened for them. Woe to them and woe to their souls, for they do not realize that all their acts of kindness are vanity."

A man who's first charitable at home with his wife and only afterwards does favors for others merits the title of a truly charitable person. His acts of loving-kindness will contribute to the building of the world, since they first contributed to the building of his own home.

Gratitude

In the Book of Exodus, Hashem commanded Moses to command Aaron to smite the sand with Aaron's rod, and out would swarm millions of lice – the third of the ten plagues that Hashem brought upon Egypt. The question that is asked is why did this plague have to come about through Aaron and not through Moses? Rashi answers: "It was not fitting for the sand to be smitten by Moses, since it protected him when he killed the Egyptian taskmaster and buried him in the sand. Therefore, Aaron was the one to smite it."

This is the extent of gratitude that Hashem expects from us. Sand is an inanimate object and did not consciously choose to help Moses. By nature, things can be buried in sand. What's more, the 'kindness' that the sand did for Moses was more than sixty years previously. That notwithstanding, Hashem wanted Moses to remember how the sand had 'helped' him, and be grateful to it. Not just to the few cubits of sand that he used, but to all the sand in the world. Turning the sand into lice would be ungrateful on Moses' behalf, so Aaron had to be the one to initiate this plague.

If this is the extent of gratitude that we need to show to inanimate objects that have benefited us in some way, how much more so must we be grateful to a fellow human being who has benefited us! Sand doesn't have feelings but a person does. We should all the more be grateful to a wife, who does so much for us, and who is especially sensitive and emotional.

An ingrate has no connection with Hashem. Our sages said that whoever denies the kindness that his friend has done for him will ultimately deny Hashem's loving-kindness. To learn to be grateful to Hashem, one must first learn to be grateful to "sand", just like Moses. Before a person can acknowledge and be grateful for the loving-kindness of Hashem, he must first learn to acknowledge and be grateful for the loving-kindness that he receives from his friends, his wife, and even the benefits that he derives from inanimate objects. Without gratitude to the agents of Hashem's kindness, he will never be able to be grateful to Hashem Himself, the true source of loving-kindness.

It is therefore forbidden to treat anything that has benefited or served us in any way with disrespect. Even to tread on clothes is not allowed, to help us develop our sense of gratitude. And certainly we must very careful to honor a fellow human that has done anything in the slightest for us. Rebbe Nachman writes in Sefer HaMidot (Benefitting from others): "Somebody that you benefitted from once, don't shame him." Though it is forbidden to shame anyone, it is far worse to shame a person who has been kind to us, since this shows such a lack of gratitude.

Homework

Gratitude takes time and effort to develop. One way to do this is to buy a notebook and write in it all the kindnesses that one's wife does and has done for him. If a man would write only a fraction of the kindnesses that his wife has done for him, the book will soon be filled. To record everything that she has ever done would fill up many books. After having done this, he needs to regularly review the list and add to it. Then he can approach his wife and express his gratitude to her for all that she has done and does for him.

A "gratitude notebook" is a good practice to remember and recognize everyone who has been kind to us, our parents, teachers, friends and even strangers. By recording their kindness in writing, we develop our sense of gratitude and are more likely to express our thanks to them. One can then go on to contemplate the benefits one has had from animate and inanimate objects, to think about how they contribute to his life and well-being. In this way, a person can make gratitude second nature, and gratitude brings us to joy. When we see the half of the cup that's full, rather than focusing on the half of the cup that's empty, we become closer to emuna and to Hashem. The simple exercise of expressing gratitude can change a person's entire perspective in life.

First, gratitude begins at home, with one's wife. This is the area where the evil inclination works his hardest to make a man see only the negative. She, more than anyone, deserves his gratitude, for no-one does as many kindnesses for a man as his wife does.

A husband must let his wife know that he is cognizant of all the acts of kindness that she does for him. When a wife sees that her husband appreciates all that she does for him, thanking and praising her profusely, she derives the strength to continue. She will look favorably on her husband and will want to do more for him, because it is a pleasure to do things for someone who is truly grateful and knows how to express his gratitude.

Learning to smile

When a husband records and regularly reviews all the things that his wife does for him, then when she makes some mistakes or exhibits some character flaws, as we all inevitably do, they won't matter. Compared to all the kindnesses that she does, a mistake or blemish is nothing in the eyes of a grateful and appreciative husband. He focuses on all that she does do and how much he needs to thank her and reciprocate her kindness in every way that he can. The more he contemplates all that she does for him, the more he will love her, and the more he loves her and does for her, the more she will reciprocate this love and continue giving.

When a wife feels appreciated, she feels fulfillment from her efforts and has the strength to continue with her difficult task. Nothing is worse than the feeling that no one acknowledges or values our hard work. With no positive reinforcement, a person eventually stops working altogether, saying to himself: "No one is acknowledging or valuing my work anyway. What's the point of carrying on?" If a husband is an ingrate and doesn't acknowledge all the kindnesses that his wife does for him, she will soon stop giving to him, and the relationship will turn from sweet to sour.

Yuck! Ingrate!

Nothing is more despicable than an ingrate. Our sages teach that it is forbidden to do any kindness for someone who is ungrateful. Indeed, they say that the favors one does for such a person are tantamount to idolatry!

Why were our sages so stringent in this matter? Simple: the root of ingratitude is arrogance – the mother of all sin. An arrogant person feels that he deserves everything, that everyone owes him, and that others should even be glad for the privilege of serving him.

When you tell such a person that he needs to thank his wife for all she does for him, he says: "What? I have to thank her? What for? She should thank me for putting up with her." Such was the attitude of the wicked Haman, who declared himself a deity and said that everyone had to bow down to him and serve him. Whoever extends kindness to an arrogant person resembles someone that is serving an idol.

Ultimately, he will deny Hashem's loving-kindness

A man who does not recognize the loving-kindness that others do for him will definitely deny the loving-kindness of Hashem. A person who is kind to another is only the agent through which Hashem does kindness with him. If the recipient doesn't acknowledge the kindness being done for him by a fellow human being, how can he possibly discern its true source and be grateful to Hashem? In other words, if he doesn't acknowledge the agent, how will he ever remember the sender?

The Talmud in tractate Sotah says regarding the period before the final redemption: "The face of the generation will resemble the face of a dog." The accepted interpretation of this statement is that it teaches us about suffering. A dog bites the stick that hits it without looking at the person that wields the stick. In like manner, people will fight with those who hurt them without searching for the One who really sent them their afflictions.

According to what our Sages have taught us regarding an ingrate, namely, that someone who does not acknowledge the kindnesses of his friend will in the end deny the kindnesses of Hashem, we can understand the abovementioned Gemara passage in another way. When you stretch out a stick with a big steak on the end to a dog, he won't even see the stick, because he is so enamored by the steak. He won't notice the person stretching out the stick to him. In the same way, men will be so focused on and absorbed in their desires that they won't notice who or what it is providing their needs. They won't see the stick. They will be so absorbed in fulfilling their lusts that they will have no time to thank The Master of the Universe that provides for them.

Ungratefulness to one's wife is a repetition of Adam's mistake. Hashem questioned him: "Did you eat from the tree that I told you not to eat from (Genesis 3:11)?" Adam then answered: "The woman You gave me, she gave me to eat, and I ate." Rashi states that here, Adam denied Hashem's kindness to him, of giving him a wife to help him. As soon as he stumbled he blamed both his wife and Hashem. He said to Hashem: "The wife you gave me is guilty, and You are guilty for giving me such a wife." The Baal HaTurim writes that Adam repaid good with bad.

When a wife feels that her husband doesn't value her and all that she does, she understandably has complaints against him. If he'd hear her complaints and mend his ways, then he'd restore peace in the home. But in the majority of cases, when someone has never learned to be grateful, he doesn't understand what his wife wants from him. He doesn't understand what she's missing, and then puts her down, telling her that she is arrogant for wanting people to praise her all the time. He gives her guilty feelings that result in her utter discontent.

Such a wife may feel that death would be better than life, since at least her suffering would end with death. As it is, with her husband saying such things to her, it is as if he is shooting arrows into her and killing her anew, time after time. Such disparagement is like plunging a knife in her heart, and every time she remembers what he said, the knife goes in again. This could happen hundreds of times a day – a knife in the heart. "What have I done to him? Why does he say those things to me?" The world of such an unfortunate wife is dark and miserable.

Gratitude to Hashem

Arrogance is the root of ingratitude. It is also the root of anger, stress and depression. An arrogant person feels that everything and everyone should behave in accordance with his wishes. He thinks that Hashem owes him something and gets stressed whenever He doesn't give him precisely what he wants. As soon as something doesn't go exactly according to his plans, he gets agitated. He harbors anger against Hashem and this leads him to depression. Rebbe Nachman writes clearly in "Sichot HaRan" that when people are depressed, it's as if they're angry with Hashem for not giving them what they wanted. Such folks harbor complaints against Hashem, even if they don't openly express them. Depression indicates a person's grievances with Hashem.

The ingrate's feeling that Hashem owes him something stems from his feeling that everyone else owes him. From childhood, the ingrate took for granted all that his parents did for him. Now, he thinks that his wife owes him all that she does. From his perspective, there is nothing to be grateful for. On the contrary, since he is owed everything, he has the right to complain when others don't give him what he deserves.

If only a husband would know that no one owes him anything and that he deserves nothing at all in this world, he would be grateful for any tiny favor. This is humility, and working to achieve peace in the home means working to achieve humility.

When a husband dedicates time every day to contemplate the kindnesses that his wife does for him, in his attempt to increase his feelings of appreciation and gratitude, he comes closer to Hashem and closer to humility. A humble husband constantly expresses his gratitude to his wife and lets her know that he appreciates and recognizes everything she does for him. He in turn thanks Hashem, acknowledging the true source of his good fortune, thanking and praising Him for the blessing of such a good wife and for all the other blessings in his life.

The home is the true testing ground of a husband's character. Outside the home, it's easy to put on an act. A person's true colors come out when he is alone with his wife and children. Humility, the crown and root of all good character traits, begins at home, with one's wife. It is expressed by being grateful to her and by honoring and respecting her. The home is the best testimony to other good character traits as well.

The perfection of creation therefore depends on peace in the home. When we strive for peace in the home, we are truly working to change ourselves into humble, appreciative, happy and giving people. When we achieve this, our homes become suitable dwellings for the Divine Presence.

Chapter Nine
How great is peace!

Rabbi Shimon the son of Chalafta taught: "The vessel for blessings is peace, for it says, (Psalms 29) 'Hashem will give strength unto His nation, Hashem will bless His nation with peace'" (Midrash Rabba 21).

Only someone who has peace in his home can truly succeed in life. Hashem's blessings, the source of all success, both physical and spiritual, including income, health, children's education, comfort, joy, wisdom and understanding, require a vessel of peace. In other words, these blessings can be maintained only in an environment of a peaceful home.

True peace starts at home by living peacefully with one's wife. A man who doesn't strive for peace with his wife, the person closest to him in the world, can't say that he lives peacefully with other people.

Many make a mistake in thinking that they have peace with everyone, but their home life is a different story. They even use this fact to justify themselves – since they get along fine with everyone else, their wife must certainly be responsible for their problems at home.

If a person lives in peace with strangers but not with his own wife, then he is the culprit. If he's honest with himself, he'll see that he's kind to those who really deserve nothing. Casual acquaintances haven't given him a tiny fraction of the kindnesses that his wife has, yet with them he's patient, polite, considerate, compromising and all smiles, even when he's not in a good mood. But when he comes home to his wife - the closest person to him in the world, who does incessant loving-kindnesses for him, and with whom he has the greatest obligation to live in peace – his behavior is far from loving and considerate.

He has little patience for her. He's too tired to talk to her or to listen to her. He doesn't smile if he's not in the mood and makes no effort to make her happy or to give her a good feeling about herself. He's less willing to compromise with her than he is with a stranger, and demands that she should show him proper respect. If he'd behave with her like he behaves with other people, he'd enjoy a peaceful relationship with her too and she'd be happy as a lark.

A man without peace at home can't boast that he has peace outside the home. On the contrary, he should be ashamed, for this indicates that he is a hypocrite. The peaceful person that he appears to be outside the home is just a ploy to obtain approval and honor. It has nothing to do with him being a truly peaceful person, and certainly doesn't qualify him as a vessel worthy of Divine blessings.

Homework

The true measure of a person's character is how he behaves at home with his wife. The home is the primary place for the fulfillment of all the commandments between ourselves and our fellow man: "Love your neighbor as yourself," to judge others favorably, to empathize, to be considerate, to make others happy, and to concede one's own wishes for the sake of peace, and so on.

Only someone who merits peaces at home merits the "peace" that is the spiritual vessel for all blessings.

A home without peace is a home without blessings. During the time we wrote this chapter, a rich couple came to me for counseling. Both husband and wife earned high salaries, and from a superficial glance, it seemed like they had everything. The wife began to relate her long saga of suffering. Her well-liked and well-respected husband was an entirely different person behind closed doors. He constantly belittled her and tormented her, so much that she felt she could die from the suffering. Their big income was just an illusion. They were both deeply in debt, and whatever they earned simply disappeared.

The wife begged me in tears: "Help me, help me… I have no one to turn to, to tell the truth to. My husband is well known and well respected. People won't believe that my husband, with his 'wonderful character' behaves at home like he does. I can't live like this. We have no blessings. Every day something else goes wrong - one day the car, then the refrigerator. All our money gets spent on repairmen and medical bills…"

Despite their huge income, the couple was in debt and miserable, simply because the husband didn't treat his wife properly. They lacked the thing they needed most - the vessel for containing blessings – peace.

A husband who lives peacefully with his wife will see blessings in whatever he does and will not lack for anything.

Our Sages say that: "A man must always be careful with his wife's honor, since blessing in a man's home is by virtue of his wife." (Yalkut Shimoni, Lech-Lecha). Even though the quote brought at the beginning of the chapter says that peace is the only vessel for blessings, there is no contradiction. The peace that is the vessel for blessings is the peace between a man and his wife.

The source of all good

Our Sages also taught that: "When a husband and wife merit – the Divine presence dwells between them." (Talmud Sotah, 17) When a man has peace in his home, the Divine presence accompanies him and protects him from the pitfalls of this world. He has success and blessing in everything he does. Without peace in his home, he is exposed to all dangers, and doomed to darkness and failure, for: "When they do not merit, a fire consumes them (ibid)." Without *shalom bayit*, he can't succeed, for Hashem is not with him.

Peace in the home is the source of all of Hashem's blessings, which we need in order to bring ourselves and the world as a whole to perfection. Peace in the home is not a luxury or an added extra, something to make our lives more comfortable or enjoyable. It's the most important factor in a man's individual life, and in the perfection of the entire world.

Marital peace is the most important and precious asset we have. We need to devote all our energy to achieving it and be willing to pay any price to obtain it. We can't afford to live without it.

Above everything else

Hashem places peace between husband and wife above everything else – even above His own honor. We learn this from the case of the "Sotah" – the wayward wife. The husband of a woman who secluded herself with another man suspects her of infidelity and brings her to a priest in the Holy Temple. The latter would inscribe the biblical passage dealing with the "Sotah" onto a parchment, which was then immersed in a jug of fresh spring water until the writing was dissolved. The wife would then drink some of this water and it would test her innocence or guilt.

The passage written on this parchment contained the Tetragrammaton, Hashem's ineffable four letter name, which it is forbidden to erase. Yet, here the parchment was purposefully immersed in water until the writing had all been washed off. Hashem commands us to erase His name in order to prove the innocence of a wife and make peace between her and her husband. There is no other situation where this is allowed.

This is even more incredible when we consider that Hashem Himself observes the laws of the Torah. "From where do we know that Hashem visits the sick? Genesis states (18:1) 'And Hashem appeared to him [Abraham, after his circumcision] in the plains of Mamre.' From where do we know that He buries the dead? As it says in Deuteronomy (34:6) 'And He buried him [Moses] in the valley'" (Braishit Rabbah 8). But, when a couple's relationship is hanging in the balance, Hashem commands us to transgress a severe prohibition of the Torah – to erase His name, to teach us how important it is to Him that husband and wife live in peace.

"How great is peace, for Hashem says to erase in water The Name that is written in holiness, in order to make peace between a man and his wife." (Vayikra Rabba 9)

No loss, all gain

For the sake of peace, Hashem is willing to forego His honor, even though the whole world was created only for His honor, as it says in Isaiah: (43:7) "Everything which is called by My name and for My honor I created it, formed it and made it." Hashem wants us to know that His greatest honor is a couple's peaceful marriage.

Even though Hashem forgoes His honor to make peace between a man and his wife, this way His honor is actually increased. This is an expression of Hashem's magnificent humility, which makes us love and respect Him all the more. We learn an essential principle from this, namely, that when we concede something to make peace, we never lose, but only gain.

The benefits of maintaining peace are twofold – you obtain peace, the vessel for all blessings, and you also often preserve whatever you were willing to concede. But, if a person is obstinate and unwilling to concede something for the sake of peace, his loss will be double - no peace and therefore no vessel for Divine blessings, plus the loss of whatever one was unwilling to concede as well.

Let's see some real-life examples:

Who is the King of Glory?

A man who's not willing to concede his honor for the sake of peace with his wife might succeed momentarily, but in the long term he'll suffer greatly for it. His losses will outweigh his gains. Since it's impossible to have a peaceful relationship when a husband is fussy about his honor, once the peace is gone, he'll suffer greater humiliation than whatever his wife would have given him.

The greatest humiliation is when others know that a man's home is a battleground. If he tries to blame his wife, people will nonetheless look at him pitifully. Who is he is trying to humiliate, the mother of his children and the foundation of his home? She's the woman he pledged to honor, love and care for. Why is he destroying his own home, for his conceived honor?

One can't hide a lack of peace in the home. Eventually, the wife will break down and confide in one of her friends, or in her mother. The neighbors will hear things or will just see the miserable couple's faces. Not only will people look down at the husband, but his wife and children will lose respect for him, since he is responsible for this shameful situation. He is a source of embarrassment to them.

By forfeiting peace with his wife to preserve his honor, he ends up disgracing himself and his family beyond his worst nightmares. He becomes a living example of what our Sages say, that whoever chases honor – honor eludes him.

When a man places peace before anything else, including his own honor, then although he may lose face occasionally in the short term, in the long term he merits true honor - peace in his home. Everyone respects a person with self-control who concedes to others for the sake of peace. The Gemara praises such a person: "Who are shamed but do not shame, who hear their disgrace and do not respond, about them it says (Judges 5:31), 'And His beloved ones are like the sun coming out in its strength' (Talmud Shabbos 88)."

We are taught that he who is honorable is the one who honors others. The Torah is not impressed by someone whom others honor, but only by someone who honors other people. Such a person is truly honorable. His wife and children will respect him, since they see in him the calming image of a man with good character traits and inner strength. These qualities give him an aura of authority and royalty.

A person who is willing to forego his own honor for the sake of peace, eventually gains both peace and honor. "Whoever flees from honor – honor pursues him."

Peace is priceless

When a man is exacting about every penny that his wife spends and quarrels with her whenever he feels she spent unnecessarily, he'll say goodbye to both *shalom bayit* and his income. Without peace, the household's income is negatively affected.

Someone that moans about a few pennies could ultimately lose thousands. If a husband would realize what blessings a peaceful relationship invokes, he wouldn't ruin his marital peace for any amount of money in the world, and certainly not for a few pennies.

When a man is easygoing about his wife's spending, and doesn't comment or complain even when he sees that she could have saved money here or there, he will have a constant influx of blessings and will lack nothing. Our Sages say: "Honor your wives in order to become rich." By being flexible in money matters for the sake of peace, a husband attains both peace and more money. By virtue of peace's blessing, he'll succeed in everything he does.

Mercy or cruelty?

A mother has had a trying afternoon with her rowdy children. They were rude to her, wild, and disobedient. By the time her husband comes home, she's lost her composure. She's shouting at them, calling them names, and waving a threatening palm at the most insolent one. Her husband, who hasn't had to deal with them all day long, is horrified. He runs up and grabs hold of her hand before she has a chance to bring it down on her son. "What's the matter with you? Calm down, for goodness sake. What crime have they committed?" There's a showdown, with "merciful Daddy" and the kid's on one side and Mommy the wicked witch on the other. It seems that Mommy loses, but in reality everyone has lost.

The husband understandably wanted to protect his children, but this shouldn't have been at the expense of his wife. Why not pity her? Maybe the kids were really insufferable, and had pushed her too far. Even if she has an uncontrollable temper, he should be compassionate with her and try his best to help with. But more so, in his attempt to protect his children from their mother's anger, he actually causes them far more damage than her anger ever would have. She may have called them names or even smacked them, but by siding with them, he ruins the peace in his home. The turbulent and unhappy home that he's now left with does more damage to a child's emotional health than anything else.

A husband that shows restraint and doesn't correct or challenge his wife in her moments of anger with the children gains on many levels.

First, he preserves the peace with his wife. When children grow up in a home where there is peace and love, where they see and feel that Mommy and Daddy are an inseparable entity, they derive a love of life and tremendous inner strength to cope with whatever difficulties they may face. A peaceful home is a basis to build on for their future married lives and the greatest guarantee of emotionally healthy children. With peace in the home, even a mother's greatest mistakes in raising the children won't hurt them at all.

On the other hand, when children grow up in a home where there is no peace between their parents, they develop emotional problems. They have difficulty in coping with life and are likely to fail miserably in their own marriages. So when a "merciful" father protects his children from their mother's rage at the expense of his peace with her, he actually damages them far more than he protects them. Destroying the peace in his home is like taking a sledgehammer to their souls.

Second, by supporting her rather than criticizing, a husband gains his wife's trust and calms her down. She regains her composure and joy, regrets her behavior, and soon makes amends with the children.

Children are not that deeply affected by their mother's anger because they innately know that she is emotional and acts on her feelings. They know she angers easily but is also quick to be appeased, and then smothers them with love. This is in sharp contrast to the anger of a father, which affects them far more deeply.

But, when a husband comments to his wife about her behavior with the children, she feels deeply insulted. Why doesn't he understand her and stand by her side? And if her husband and children join together against her, she has no motivation to improve her behavior. On the contrary, she gets even angrier with the children, since she blames them for her being insulted by her husband and for causing strife in her home.

From a purely practical point of view, the only way to successfully deal with any problems that arise is in the way of peace. Where there's love and peace, there is Divine assistance and peace of mind, and one can deal effectively with a problem.

By putting peace with his wife as his number one priority, a man merits Divine assistance and inner tranquility. Hashem will help him to understand the root of problems that arise, and show him the way to correct them. But, if a husband is willing to give up peace to protect his children, or for any other reason, he will never solve the problems that arise, because Hashem will not be with him and his own mind will be unsettled and confused.

How great is peace! No matter how difficult a problem, one's first priority should be solidifying the peace with his wife. Hashem will then dwell in his home. He and his wife merit Divine assistance, enabling them to overcome all difficulties and solve all problems in a peaceful, loving and effective way.

Dear parents: Peace!

Another very common and trying situation is where a wife has complaints against her mother-in-law, and tells her husband all about them. Here too, the husband must remember that the most important thing for him is to keep the peace with his wife. Although it's painful for him to hear her talk negatively about his parents, he must overcome the pain and agree with her. He should give her the feeling that he understands her and stands by her side.

It may seem that he is compromising his parents' honor for the sake of peace with his wife, but this is not so. The greatest honor for his parents is their son's peaceful, successful home. His love and peace with his wife will make it easier to appease her, and to bring back the peace between her and his parents. When she feels that her husband is firmly by her side, the things that upset her lose their sting. If she still has complaints against her mother-in-law, she'll feel that it's not fair to fight with a husband who is so good to her. She won't want to sacrifice such wonderful *shalom bayit*, so she'll find a way to reconcile herself with his parents.

If the husband puts his parents' honor before peace with his wife, he will lose both. Parents suffer greatly when their children fail in their relationships. The principal honor of one's parents is to avoid causing them sorry and anguish (Talmud Yoma, 86). When parents learn that their son had a fight with his wife, they are saddened deeply. They get no consolation from the fact that the fight was for their honor. Sensible parents are happy to forego their honor, if doing so will enable their son or daughter to live in peace with his or her spouse.

A woman by nature is highly emotional. If she has sorrow from her mother-in-law, it's very hard for her to make a balanced and objective appraisal of the situation. The responsibility to keep the peace lies with her husband, who is able to see such situations with less emotionality. He must remember that the greatest honor for his parents is having a son with a tranquil marriage and peaceful home.

Stand by her

Jewish law states (Maimonides, Laws of Marriage 17) that certain women frequently hate one another, such as a bride and her mother-in-law; and a bride and her sisters-in-law. A wife's complaints against her mother or sisters-in-law are therefore expected. Her husband must first stand by her side, and only then try to mediate between them and find a peaceful solution.

If a husband doesn't stand behind his wife and show her that he understands her, but instead backs up his mother or sister, he destroys his relationship with his wife. She is supposed to come first in his life, so now she's bitterly affronted. Her anger with him will take a long time to abate, because she feels that he abandoned her and rebelled against her. He is left now with no marital peace and no peace with his parents.

Peace comes before everything else. Only through peace is it possible to find solutions to the difficulties that arise in married life. In every situation a husband must reassure his wife that she comes before everyone and everything else and that he will never let anything or anyone come between them.

All its ways are peace

Another common and sensitive situation is where the wife transgresses the Torah, and it seems that she needs to be told so and even reprimanded. Even here, peace comes first. As long as there is peace, Hashem will be patient with her, for the Midrash says (Bamidbar Rabbah 11):

"Great is peace, for it is equivalent to everything else, as we say 'He who makes peace...', and only afterwards 'and creates everything.'" Rabbi Elazar, the son of Rabbi Eliezer Hakappar, says that even if the Jewish people serve idols, but have peace amongst them, Hashem says that the Satan cannot touch them, as it says: (Hoshea 4:17) "Ephraim is joined to idols: let him alone." But once they were divided what does it say about them? "Their heart is divided; now they shall be found guilty (ibid, 10:2)." Such is the value that Hashem places on us living peacefully with one another.

In such tricky situations, the first obligation is to keep the peace. Once this is accomplished, one can address problems in the proper manner through prayer, pleasantness, and love. When a husband showers his wife with love, even when she has transgressed, and prays for her – this itself will bring her back to the good. Our Sages taught us this when they said: "Love the creations and bring them close to the Torah." The husband is assured that in the merit of keeping the peace, Hashem will be patient with whatever transgressions are being done, and will assist his wife to return to Him.

Wanting the best

Peace comes first even when there are differences of opinion in matters of principle. A husband who momentarily compromises his convictions and/or aspirations to preserve the peace will ultimately attain both – the peace and his convictions and aspirations.

By realizing our ambitions through peaceful means, we truly attain them. Although it sometimes appears that a person makes gains through power, strife and arguments, achievements earned at someone else's expense are worthless and short-lived. Indeed, they'll all be outweighed by the long term losses.

The obstacle

Even when a husband wants to grow in his religious observance and his wife stands in his way, peace comes first, for it's the husband's first obligation. In such a situation, he should actually do everything he can to show her more love and improve the relationship in every way. If he keeps the peace and lives happily with his wife, she'll be open to his influence. Through prayer, patience and respectful discussion, he'll be able to make spiritual progress and uplift her as well.

No matter how inspired he may be, and however excited he is to pass on his inspiration to his wife, he must be careful to keep the peace. The husband must avoid commenting to her about anything that she may be doing that's not in line with the law and refrain from trying to force his opinions onto her. He should even be willing to concede some of his ambitions for the time being, for the sake of peace with her.

A husband must be patient even if he has to concede some goals for a long duration. This long way will end up being the shortest way to a life of happiness and peace. The short way of forcing the other person to immediately accept one's views, ends ups as a long way that never leads to a happy ending.

In the course of the years that I've been counseling on marital issues, I've seen this clearly hundreds of times. Here's one case:

A student who had been getting stronger and stronger in Torah and mitzvoth approached me with a strange request: "Dear Rabbi, bless me that I should get divorced from my wife!"

I knew him well, and knew that he had a good wife. I was shocked and asked him: "Why? What for? What great fault have you found in your wife?"

He answered me: "Look Rabbi, I've become very strong and want to live an Orthodox life in every way, and my wife just doesn't understand me at all. She doesn't want to change and doesn't commit herself to religious law. We argue constantly. For example, I am trying to educate the children in the ways of the Torah and she doesn't support this. I want my wife to go to Torah lectures, and she doesn't agree to. In short – however I try to strengthen her, it doesn't work. She is an obstacle to my progress, in the way I want to serve Hashem. I don't see any option except to divorce her and pray that I will find a wife whose wishes and ambitions are the same as mine."

I asked him: "My son, do you have emuna?"

"Of course," he replied.

"So if you have emuna, why should you divorce your wife? Emuna is prayer – every day, pray for ten minutes and ask Hashem to instill in your wife's heart the desire to comply with your way and be a help for you. In the meanwhile, don't make any comments to her and don't try to influence her in any way. Just show her a happy face and act lovingly with her, and I promise you that in a short time she will get stronger by herself and will even outshine you in the service of Hashem."

He replied: "But dear Rabbi, she just doesn't want to repent, she just wants this material world. A woman should follow her husband! She's simply not my true wife, otherwise she would be getting stronger with me."

I said to him: "In my opinion, you're being impatient. You must believe that all the obstacles that you have are from Heaven, to stimulate your prayer for each gain in spirituality. It's Heaven that's restricting you, so that you'll make gradual growth and not go too far too quickly. You think that your wife is obstructing you? Hashem is the one obstructing you for your own good, so that you should achieve each step of growth through extensive prayer and gradual progress. The progress may be slow, but it will be healthy. Whatever we attain without prayers and without proper preparation is very damaging."

"Our Sages said: 'When a man's ways please Hashem, even his enemies make peace with him,' whereas 'his enemies' refers to his wife. You say that you are a man of faith? Then believe that if Hashem wants you to attain something, He will give it to you, and no-one in the world can stop you. You think that your wife is your obstacle, but the truth is that you don't yet have the spiritual preparation to live the way you want to. You need more work. Our Sages say: (Avot 2:4) 'Nullify your will before His will, so that He will nullify the will of others before yours.' If you truly nullified yourself to Hashem's will, He would nullify your wife's will to yours, for this is an explicit rule of nature as expressed in the Mishnah. It's forbidden for you to think that your wife is holding you back, because there is no such thing that someone – apart from Hashem – can hold you back, since there is nothing but Him."

I tried to speak to his heart in this way, but he wasn't interested. He wanted to blaze ahead and lead an orthodox life with an orthodox wife. In his mind, there was no chance that his wife would ever repent. He began the divorce proceedings.

I was greatly distressed by this and tried once more to stop him from taking this hasty step. I pleaded with him: "Isn't it a pity to lose such a good wife? You've built a home together and have been through a lot together. You have children together. All in all, she's a good woman who doesn't stop you from doing what you want. She doesn't interfere in your life. You learn, pray, visit the graves of righteous men, and so on. Your only problem is that she isn't getting stronger, that your path doesn't inspire her. In that case, pray for her! Surely you should be grateful to her for all the good she has done for you and love her for it. You should pray that your path should inspire her too, and this will also have an effect on your children, that they will also be inspired also." He didn't want to listen.

I thought in my heart: "This man is entirely selfish. He just wants to fulfill his own wishes and desires and doesn't care at all about his wife and children. I'm sure that one day he will pay for his arrogance."

I tried one more time to influence him: "At least think about the children, they will be greatly hurt if you get a divorce, and you'll lose them completely. For them it's a terrible insult that you're divorcing their mother and going to marry another woman. Listen to me: instead of praying for a divorce and finding a wife who fits your new agenda, pray for your wife and children, and lavish her with love. Don't get divorced in any circumstances. It may seem to you that you are conceding on things, but in reality you will merit much more if you accept Hashem's Providence and keep the peace."

He wanted a divorce, and nothing else.

The truth comes to light

The young man began to pray fervently and at length for a divorce from his wife and for finding a new wife to his taste. He trekked to graves of righteous men to pray for this. And, as the Gemara says: "In the way that a man wants to go, he is led." Hashem definitely did not want this divorce to take place, but didn't tamper with the young man's free will. After a few months he came to me joyously to announce that that he was divorced and had come to invite me to his wedding.

"Dear Rabbi," he said emotionally, "You won't believe what a righteous wife I have found. Her only wish is that I should learn Torah and get stronger in serving Hashem. She has a good income and her own apartment. Hashem has given me a perfect wife, exactly what I wanted, and from now on I can progress in serving Hashem as I should. You see, dear Rabbi, I did a good thing by getting divorced."

Two years passed had from the wedding when his new wife knocked on my door. As soon as she walked in, she burst into tears: "Dear Rabbi, I can't live with this man any longer. I'm so sorry."

"What's happened?" I asked.

She told me: "Dear Rabbi, you know that my only wish is for my husband be a servant of Hashem, that he should truly spend day and night in serving Him. I am prepared to support him and give my all for this. But this husband, Hashem should forgive me, is simply a loafer. He doesn't get up for prayers. He wakes up late and mopes around aimlessly. He doesn't learn anything, doesn't do hitbodedut, doesn't go to the graves of the righteous – this is not what I wanted."

"This is not new," the young wife sobbed. "After the wedding I realized that he was not what I thought, but I didn't say anything. I tried to accept with emuna that this must be my correction, to work on my character traits, to judge him favorably, to restrain myself, and to pray for him."

"For two years I have suffered so much. I've tried everything – to encourage him, to shout at him, to threaten him that if he doesn't start to move, to go to pray, to learn, that I will divorce him. Occasionally, he promises that he'll change, but he never keeps his promises. I've already spoken with him many times about divorce, and now I simply can't bear life with him anymore. I have to get divorced from him."

I wanted to give this student one more chance, even though I saw that there was almost no hope of saving this relationship. I asked his wife to wait a bit longer before making her final decision, and told her to send her husband to me for instruction.

He came and I explained the situation to him, that if he didn't want to lose this wife as well he had to accept upon himself some resolutions, and I gave him a few instructions and plans of action. But he didn't do anything. This continued for a short while longer until his wife came back to me and told me that she wanted an immediate divorce. She could stomach no more of him.

A great gulf

At this point, I agreed with her. There was no need for her to continue suffering. She was a mature lady who had been serving Hashem for many years. She was actually a very righteous lady who didn't need a husband to inspire her or help her grow.

Before she married him, she had had a very full and interesting life. She had worked in outreach and had many ongoing projects.

The only reason she had for getting married was to support a husband in his service of Hashem. Otherwise, she had no reason to exchange her many activities for the yoke of running a home, cooking, cleaning, and so on. If her husband didn't serve Hashem, she had no reason to serve him.

A few weeks later they were divorced.

The entire episode became clear as daylight. That student had never been a true servant of Hashem. He therefore couldn't influence and inspire his first wife. The obstacles that he had faced in his first marriage were all for his good, to help him make real growth and attain true closeness to Hashem. Had he stayed with his first wife and accepted the challenges, then he would have progressed in serving Hashem, step by step. His progress may have been slow, but it would have been true and sincere, commensurate with the spiritual vessels that he had, and he would have succeeded in life.

The young man failed to accept his situation with emuna. Instead he rebelled against his good wife and children and married a woman who was far above his level. He had no obstacles at all from her in serving Hashem. On the contrary, compared to her, he needed inspiring.

There are no mistakes

There are no mistakes or coincidences in a man's life. Everything is under Hashem's exact Providence, and He does everything for man's good. In this case, Hashem knew full well that this student's motivation was very low, so He gave him many obstacles to stimulate true spiritual growth.

All he had to do was try a bit harder each time, while praying for strength and inspiration. As such, he would have come closer to Hashem. At every level, he would have yearned and prayed to take another step forward, and so he would have progressed. But he stubbornly insisted that he didn't want any obstacles, so Hashem gave him what he wanted. And as soon as the obstacles were gone, so was his motivation and inspiration.

Here's another detail of Providence: Hashem knew how low his level of spirituality was, so He gave him his first wife whose spiritual level was even lower than his. In this way, she could look up to him, and he would have had someone else to inspire, which would have helped him grow. But when he stubbornly insisted that she wasn't good enough, he got a wife whose spiritual level was far higher than his.

She disdained him, and when he felt the great gulf that separated them, he lost all his self-confidence. He began to persecute himself, and in the end persecuted her as well, belittling her to protect his shattered ego. He couldn't stand to see her burning for Hashem, when he could hardly get himself out of bed. The wheel turned full circle – now he was the one trying to prevent his spouse from serving Hashem.

Holy Constriction

The young man didn't understand that the purpose of marriage is having someone who constricts him. This constriction then stimulates his yearning, motivation and prayer. The Zohar teaches that Hashem punished Nadav and Avihu, the son of Aaron the High Priest, because they didn't want to be constricted, and therefore didn't marry. They wanted to serve Hashem with no barriers or restrictions. When they attempted to overstep their level, He burnt them alive in front of all Israel. Hashem wants a person's service within the context of constrictions. Growth means overcoming obstacles by desire, longing and prayer.

The difference between Nadav and Avihu and the student of our story is that the former truly burned for Hashem with all their hearts, so their lack of constriction caused them to burn in their own uncontrolled flame of enthusiasm, in sanctification of Hashem's Holy Name. But, our student didn't burn for Hashem at all. His only 'burning' was to prove himself better than others by finding fault in them. When he was faced with someone who was obviously far superior to himself, he fell into despair.

The light in the Torah

Had he merited the true light of the Torah, whose: "Ways are ways of pleasantness and all its paths are peaceful" (Proverbs 3:17), he would have learned the good character traits of peace, love, humility and concession. He would have valued his first wife who had done him so many kindnesses and brought up his children. He would have waited for her patiently, showered her with love and warmth, supported her, judged her favorably and prayed for her.

Does a spark of inspiration justify a husband's animosity toward his wife? The true light of Torah doesn't turn a person into a heartless ingrate. The first wife didn't deserve such degrading treatment, especially since she didn't prevent him from doing anything that he wanted to do. It wasn't her fault that she wasn't inspired by him.

Since he only made negative comments to her, belittled and upset her, in the end he made her despise Judaism altogether. He showed her a Torah of darkness, anger, severity and afflictions. Understandably, she didn't want anything to do with such a "Torah", which is actually not Torah at all. Not only did he not bring her closer to his twisted path, but he pushed her and his children further away, to the point that they may never be willing to look at or listen to a religious person again.

The young man ended up with nothing. He lost his first wife and children, and succeeded in estranging them entirely from Judaism because of his cruel and arrogant behavior. He also lost his second wife, because she saw through his false façade and couldn't stomach him.

Unfortunately, some people learn the hard way. Hashem personally guides each individual. If the young man would have been careful to keep the peace, even though it appeared that this would have been at the expense of his ambitions – he would only have gained in the end. He would have achieved his ambitions at the right time and at the right pace, and his wife would also have come close in the end. His entire family could have been saved.

No short cuts

There are no short cuts on the path of truth, and no place for illusions. The best measure of whether or not a person is on the true path is peace. There are many verses in the Bible that connect peace and truth: "Love truth and peace" (Zechariah 8:19), is one example. If that student had truly reached the spiritual level that he thought he had, then his wife would have transformed into his helper. He would have lived happily with her and his children.

How much pain and sorrow he could have saved, if only he had gone in the way of peace! Many others, in situations similar to his, who did follow the long path of truth and peace, ultimately attained both happiness and togetherness with their wives, while living a beautiful Torah lifestyle.

Here too, we have many examples.

This against that

Another student of mine was also already married when he started to connect with Torah. At first, he wasn't guided in the way of peace. The rabbis who taught him then told him that he had to be strong with his wife, rebuke her, and tell her that if she wouldn't start observing the Sabbath and other mitzvoth, he would divorce her. He soon found himself at a crossroads where he had to make the decision – either continue with his *teshuva* (repentance) process and lose his wife and children, or forget about his aspiration of being an observant Jew.

In contrast to the previous student, this man was very attached to his family and couldn't bear the thought of losing them. So, in place of giving up on them, he decided to give up on Torah and mitzvoth instead. He stopped keeping the Sabbath and returned to his secular lifestyle.

One day, he bought a cassette tape of mine. My words spoke to his heart, and he wanted to meet me. But, he remembered what the rabbis in the past had said to him and he thought: "Why should I go to him? He'll tell me that I have to give up my wife and children, and I haven't got the strength to go through that nightmare again…"

Even so, since he felt that there was something different here, a different light, so he wanted to meet me and he came to the Yeshiva.

"The Rabbi is learning now," they told him, "It's impossible to disturb him."

"I'm not moving from here until the Rabbi blesses me," he replied. Meanwhile I heard the disturbance and asked what was going on. "There's a man here insisting to come in to see you."

"So let him come." He man came in and told me that he had bought a tape of mine at an intersection and was greatly aroused by what I said, so he wanted to meet me personally. I spoke to him for a while and invited him to accompany me to one of my lectures so we could talk on the way. This was the beginning of a strong relationship between the two of us, and he started to regularly listen to tapes and seek my advice in all sorts of areas.

At this point, he still did not observe the Sabbath or any other mitzvoth. My way is not to pressure anybody, so I never spoke to him about this. I simply enquired about his life, his business, his challenges, and his home. Gradually, I taught him emuna, to speak with Hashem, and to make extensive use of personal prayer. One day, he himself turned to me and told me that he really wanted to keep the Sabbath, but his wife won't hear about it. She still had a bitter taste in her mouth from the last round.

He told me the whole story of the first time that he made teshuva and how the rabbis had told him that he had to divorce his wife if she didn't keep the Sabbath and become observant. He wasn't willing to lose his family and therefore shed his observance altogether. Now, he felt that the same story might repeat itself. He was terrified that a scenario could develop where he would want to observe the Sabbath again, his wife would fail to comply, and that I would tell him to divorce her.

"Dear Rabbi," he said, choked with emotion and with tears in his eyes, "I so much want to return in complete repentance and keep the mitzvoth, but I can't lose my wife and children. What can I do?"

"Divorce?" I said, "Of course not!"

He stopped crying and looked at me with eyes full of surprise, as if he couldn't believe it. "What? I don't need to get divorced?"

"Of course not. On the contrary, love your wife. Don't say a word to her about keeping the Sabbath. And don't make any comments to her about keeping a kosher home either. Just live your life without it having to obligate or disturb her in any way."

"Also", I added, "you must compensate her in all sorts of ways. Speak to her lovingly, compliment her, and buy her jewelry. Do everything you can to make sure she doesn't feel that your teshuva affects her. She shouldn't feel any competition from your observance. On the contrary, she should feel that it is only turning you into a more loving, devoted, and attentive husband."

He argued: "That's not what the rabbis told me the first time. They told me that it was a terrible thing, that if she broke the Sabbath, I had to break off from her."

"G-d forbid," I told him. "What has she done to you that you should throw her away like that? You love her, don't you? Is that the way to behave to someone you love? On the contrary, if you love her, wait for her and pray for her. Didn't Hashem wait a long time for you until you were aroused to repent? Now you can also wait for her."

I can't begin to describe the young man's excitement when he heard my approach, based on the rationale of emuna and peace. A feeling of tremendous joy replaced all his worries. He shouted: "There's hope! I can repent and still live in peace with my wife! I'll pray for her, and Hashem will bring her close, and we'll live together lovingly in the way of Jewish couples. How good Hashem is! How beautiful and sweet the Torah is!" He ran to thank Hashem and started praying that Hashem should help him to start anew and honor his wife, that she would accept his actions, and in the end join him in observing the mitzvoth.

And so it was. He returned to observing the Sabbath and keeping the mitzvoth. He told his wife about my lectures and gave her tapes. She also felt that there was a different light here, a different approach. Once she understood it, she loved it, especially when she saw how her husband began to treat her with absolute respect, devotion, and no comments or criticism. She began to attend my lectures, to listen to tapes, and to seek advice from me. Gradually, she too adopted the light of emuna and Torah. To this day, they are living together happily in the way of the Torah, educating their children in the way of the Torah, and are grateful to me for saving their lives, both physically and spiritually.

The Wise man's eyes are in his head (Ecclesiastes 2:14)

Advice that didn't place peace above all else almost destroyed this man's family and his religious observance. What did the rabbis accomplish with their stringency?

Proper guidance that puts peace before everything else brings people closer to Torah and mitzvoth.

A principle that permeates Torah says that "a wise man's eyes are in his head." In each situation we need to carefully consider what our goal is, and then plan the best course of action to achieve it. Being stubborn and dogmatic rarely gets us anywhere, and it indicates a lack of forethought and peace of mind. The Gemara requires a person to breach the Sabbath in order to save someone's life (see tractate Yoma 85), and says: "Break one Sabbath for him, so that he will keep many Sabbaths." This rule exemplifies our approach.

To destroy the peace and the relationship on the pretext of observing the Sabbath would have led to none of them observing any Sabbaths, ever. Such dogmatic insistence comes from a lack of careful thought, and a lack of adherence to the words of our Sages that peace comes before everything else. Patience ultimately brings success.

From these stories, which are just two examples out of thousands of instances, we can learn the message of this chapter. Keeping the peace is the key to life in general and married life in particular. Only through peace is it possible to merit true progress in life, in Torah, and in the service of Hashem.

Approaching married life

Men who want to merit peace in their homes must be convinced that peace is the greatest and most important commodity in the world. If they seek guidance with this mindset, then they are assured that they'll succeed. But, if they believe that there is anything more important than peace, they won't succeed. No book, lecture, or guidance will help anyone that doesn't first seek peace.

One should learn this book with the knowledge and belief that peace in the home comes before everything else. Then the reader is assured that through his reading he will attain everything that he needs, because this book contains a comprehensive guide to peace in the home and the correction of all character traits.

Chapter Ten
The true test

The main tests of emuna occur at home. Our wives humiliate us and our children don't listen to us. Periodically, we have to deal with health, education, or money problems. The only way to successfully weather all these storms is emuna.

The challenges of married life force us to live with and work on our emuna more than any other challenges that we face. Therefore, the correction and perfection of our character only really begins once we get married.

Single life is easy. If you don't get along with someone, stay out of their way. Why work on emuna and think that Hashem wants to tell you something, when you can simply avoid the person? But when you're married, you can't just walk out of the house – you have to face the challenges. And the way you cope with each test gives you a precise measurement of the strength of your emuna. Seeing our true level of emuna can be a big catalyst for change.

When a single person is insulted, he can return the abuse without it making much difference to his life. He can also put on a show of being humble and respond politely, even though on the inside he may be fuming and cursing under his breath. But, when a man is humiliated by his wife or children in his own home, he reveals his true character. The way he reacts has long-reaching repercussions. If he has a temper, it surfaces. If he hurts anyone, verbally or physically, he has to sit with them at breakfast the next morning. He'll soon understand that without serious work on his emuna, he'll never have peace in his home.

A single man must take care of himself only, whereas a married man must be constantly giving. He needs to pay attention to his wife; listen to her; understand her; and inspire, comfort and encourage her. To do all this, he needs a tranquil and contented soul – something that's only possible with strong emuna.

A single man can put on a show of being sociable and joyous, but a married man needs to have true inner joy. Anything less and he won't be able to create a joyous and relaxed atmosphere in the home. True joy is a by-product of strong emuna.

Relationships outside the home often work on the principal of, "You scratch my back and I'll scratch yours." Everyone acts to maximize his own personal gain. At home though, there must be genuine giving, without ulterior motives. And at home there are no masks. A man behaves according to his true character. If he lacks emuna, his actions will bear witness and he'll get into trouble. Sooner or later, he'll have to work on strengthening his emuna.

Peace commensurate with emuna

Since peace in the home depends on the strength of one's emuna, only when a man gets married does he truly start to strengthen emuna.

Every challenge at home is a test of emuna. All the difficulties, whether with one's spouse, the children, the neighbors, the in-laws – all are tests of faith. The way to approach them all is with humility, with prayer, and by applying the three stages of emuna that we'll outline below, with Hashem's help.

Happy with their lot in life

Rabbi Mani once came before Rabbi Isaac the son of Elyashiv and said to him: "My wife doesn't find favor in my eyes, because she isn't beautiful." Rabbi Isaac asked for her name, which was Hannah, and he said: "Let Hannah be beautiful." She became beautiful. Weeks later, Rabbi Mani told Rabbi Isaac that he was once more dissatisfied with his wife. Since she had become beautiful, she had become arrogant. Rabbi Isaac said: "If so, let Hannah return to her ugliness," and she returned to how she had looked before.

From the fact that Rabbi Mani was then happy with his wife once she'd returned to her original state, we learn that Hashem knows what's best for us. Belief that whatever Hashem does is for our good is called belief in Divine Providence. Whoever has this is constantly happy with his lot in life. Thoughts of what he's missing don't bother him, because he knows that Hashem has given him, and will give him, exactly what he needs to achieve his purpose in life.

On the other hand, when a man lacks faith, he's full of complaints. He blames his wife and others for his problems, thinking that they are the source of his suffering, and doesn't take any steps to correct himself. He's jealous of others and takes no joy in what he does have. He's miserable, and scores 'zero' on all his tests of emuna.

Get out of the house

This section will discuss a test of emuna that most readers will never face. Even so, it shouldn't be skipped, because it explains fundamental principles for life in general, and for married life in particular. These are principals that every married couple should know, and those who are not yet married should also learn them as part of their preparation for married life.

The main tests of emuna are at home. When we consistently fail these tests, we can get ourselves into extremely difficult situations. One such situation, a phenomenon of modern times, is that of women evicting their husbands from the home, often using civil law to do so.

A husband whose wife has thrown him out of the house must know that although it seems that his eviction was unjust, it's nonetheless from Hashem. Everything Hashem does is justified.

Hashem is the one who really evicted him from his home. If his behavior was damaging himself and the members of his family, it's better for him to be out of the house rather than to do further damage. Even if he feels that his behavior was acceptable, Hashem doesn't do anything without a purpose.

Such occurrences don't happen overnight. They are preceded by extreme friction and countless arguments between his wife and himself. Had he worked on his emuna, the situation wouldn't have deteriorated to this point. He would have been aroused by Hashem's wake-up calls long ago, and repair whatever needed repairing.

At this point, the evicted husband must implement the three levels of emuna:

The first level is knowing that everything comes from Hashem. He has to fully believe that Hashem is the one who evicted him from his home, and not think any more about it. There is no place for self-flagellation or for blaming others. Anger, revenge, depression and self-pity are all anti-emuna dark-side emotions. With emuna there's only one thought – "this is what Hashem wants."

The second level is knowing that Hashem does everything for the best. He should believe that Hashem evicted him from his home for his own ultimate good and for the good of his wife and children. It's a great kindness to remove a man from the whirlpool that has trapped him and give him a time-out to ponder and to try to rectify the situation.

Reality speaks for itself. He and his wife were on a collision course. He hadn't listened to the hints that Hashem had sent him through his wife's complaints. Since he and his wife failed to deal with their problems effectively, Hashem stepped in and separated them for the time being. Hashem can't evict the wife and mother from the home; that's neither proper nor practical. So, the husband was the one who was evicted. This break in tension gives him and his wife the peace and space that they need to think, to do some serious introspection, to take counsel, understand, learn and to correct their lives. In truth, Hashem has done them a great kindness.

The third level of emuna is asking: "What does Hashem want from me?" Now, free of the pressures and tension of the home, the husband can work on himself. He can learn what his mistakes were and look for the root of the problems. He can pray about the situation and fix whatever needs fixing. If he truly repents, then the one who truly evicted him – Hashem – will send him back home again.

One must deal with problems while they are still small. Especially with difficulties in *shalom bayit*, one must immediately apply the three levels of emuna and not wait for a crisis. That way, small problems don't mushroom into major crises. The husband will save himself, his wife and his children tons of anguish and grief.

Everything's fine with me

Sometimes a husband feels that he's behaving fine at home and doing his best. He therefore dismisses his wife's complaints. His self-appraisal is meaningless; his wife's feelings are what counts. Her happiness is his responsibility. If she isn't happy then he must find out why and do something about it.

An engineer can work hard all day to fix an engine. He may change all the parts and feel that he's done everything he should to ensure its smooth functioning. But if the engine still doesn't work, he hasn't done his job. By the same token, if a wife is unhappy, her husband still has a job to do.

Take the hints

It's difficult for an evicted husband to accept his lot with emuna. But the fact that he reached the point of eviction is a sign that he's been far from emuna.

Hashem always starts off with gentle hints. If we don't pay attention, the hints get louder. If we're still not aroused, we get a slap. A man who got to the stage of being evicted already had many slaps. With emuna, he would have looked for the message that Hashem was sending him via the arguments with his wife and her complaints. He would have listened carefully to his wife's words, tried to get to the root of the problem, and then done something about it. He would've prevented the situation from deteriorating.

It's clear that he didn't pay attention to the hints and now finds himself on the wrong side of the front door. All is not lost, though. If he now accepts the situation with emuna, he's already taken the first step back home.

The only problem is lack of emuna

When someone without emuna goes through such a crisis, he gets entangled in a web of mistakes and misery. He may blame his wife and go around angry, thinking how to take revenge. Or he may be very broken-hearted and longing for his wife and children, and harbor feelings of misery, loneliness, and self-pity.

With emuna, he would understand that his current situation is entirely for his own good. If he loves his wife, he should make the most of the time that Hashem has given him. He must learn how to avoid upsetting her in the future; how to listen to her, how to honor her; and how to make her happy.

Lack of peace in the home greatly damages children's inner strength and self-confidence - their two main tools in life. An evicted father's love for his children should therefore motivate him to improve himself so that when he returns home he won't repeat the mistakes that destroyed his home previously.

Irresponsible advice

In situations like this, many irresponsible advisors join in along the way – family members, friends, acquaintances - each with his or her warped ideas as to how the evicted husband should behave. One urges him to divorce his wife, the second to stop sending her money. His mother tells him: "You're too good for her. She's taking advantage of your good heart." All this bad advice leads to one thing only - the destruction of a home that could have been saved, had they followed the path of emuna.

The only true advice for him is to start, from now, to act like a human being. He should be good to his wife and not expect anything in return. He must send her money and make sure that she and the children are not lacking anything. He must maintain contact with the children, comfort them and tell them to listen to their mother. The worst possible thing to do would be to upset his wife, or to use the children as weapons against her.

A new start

True, one's difficult situation is due to one's own big mistakes. But once the mistake is made, one can start to follow the path of emuna, and to rectify the situation. If the husband now strengthens himself with faith and doesn't get discouraged, he will clearly see Hashem's kind hand of providence, and begin to understand how this situation is for his ultimate good.

An amazing gift

The evicted husband now has the time and the quiet that he needs to contemplate and fix whatever needs repair.

Sometimes it's debts that trigger problems in the home. He now has the opportunity to quietly seek a solution to his debt problems.

A negative character trait often destroys domestic peace. Maybe he has a quick temper, or is lazy, stingy or ungrateful. Now, he has the time to work on himself and correct these traits.

If he has a serious problem like addiction to drugs, alcohol, or gambling, or if he is violent, now he has the free time he needs to seek help and to try to uproot these problems.

With emuna, the evicted husband is undaunted. He sees the current predicament as a golden opportunity to improve his life and the life of his family. He uses his time the best way he can, and he prays hard and long that Hashem should help him to rectify whatever needs rectification.

When Hashem sees that he's doing his part, his wife will too, and this will give her hope. The evicted husband won't have to make any effort to return home, because the wife herself will chase after him to return. When he does return home, and continues to devote serious effort to self-improvement, their relationship will be infinitely better. He'll then see that the "tragedy" was actually an amazing gift from Hashem, an opportunity to make a brand new start.

At the right time

It's very important that the husband not be impatient and try to return home too soon. Instead, he should believe that Hashem will know when he's ready to return, and will send him a sign. In the meanwhile, he must continue to make the most of this opportunity. That way, when he does return home it will be with his wife's wholehearted agreement.

Even if he thinks that he needs to be at home to deal with certain urgent problems, such as debts and payments, he mustn't return home for these purposes. He should deal with them from wherever he is. Debts and other pressures place a strain on even the best of relationships. Hashem evicted him because He knew that the husband could only effectively deal with his problems outside the home in a quiet environment. He needs to accept this lovingly.

"I'm guilty."

Often, it seems that others are at least partially to blame in such situations. His in-laws slandered him to his wife, encouraged her to throw him out and supported her in the process. His wife's divorced friends did the same. It often seems that the whole community plotted against him.

No matter what, a person with emuna doesn't blame anyone for his problems with his wife. Had his wife been happy, she wouldn't have told her problems to anyone else, especially her parents. A happy wife is one who knows that she can turn to her husband for everything, and who is confident that she will get his full support. Such a wife isn't interested in other people's advice. Her husband is her father, mother and best friend all rolled into one. She knows that he is always there, by her side, ready to listen to her, understand her and support her. When a wife feels that her husband is her best friend in the world, nothing and no one can separate them.

But, when a husband behaves like a state's attorney whenever his wife tells him anything, interrogating her, pointing out her faults and making her feel guilty, it doesn't take much to convince her that she'd be happier without him.

When a wife needs to pour her heart out to her friends, it's a sign that she doesn't feel comfortable telling her husband everything. When she needs her parents' support, it's a sign that she doesn't feel sufficiently supported by her husband, and when she spends hour upon hour on the telephone, it's a sign that she doesn't have her husband's listening ear.

Reading that a wife's happiness and peace in the home all depend on the husband may induce feelings of guilt and depression in some of our readers. This is not our intention, G-d forbid. Even if you did make many mistakes, depression, despair and self-persecution aren't the way to improve things. The way forward is to learn what mistakes you made and then make a new start. Commit to mending your old ways and pray to Hashem to help you grow, repair the relationship with your wife and bring peace and love to your home.

A recovery plan

I will now present a recovery plan for an evicted husband, which outlines how he needs to behave in order to successfully pass this test with emuna. This plan works for all trying situations in life.

First, the husband must stop any negative behavior towards his wife. If until now he's been stingy, tight-fisted and cruel, from now on he must give to his wife with an open hand. He should give her more than she needs and even send her presents. If he can speak to her, he should assure her that he takes full responsibility for the situation and is doing everything he can to remedy it. If he can speak to the children he should reassure them that he hasn't abandoned them, and never would, and explain to them that he needs to be away from home for the time being to sort certain things out. He should tell them that he has every intention of returning home and encourage them to listen to their mother and help her. In short, he should act like a responsible gentleman.

Here's our 4-stage plan:

1. **Emuna**: Once his negative behavior has stopped, the first stage in his work on himself is to pray for emuna. He should pray that he be able to accept that this was from Hashem, and what He wanted. Such belief leaves no room for blame - whether of himself or of others - nor for anger, depression or despair. When this belief is firmly in place, he is ready to progress to the next level.

2. **Learning**: Learn the rules of peace in the home by carefully studying this book and by listening to lectures by the author on this topic. The focus should be on learning what mistakes were made with his wife and how he should avoid them in the future.

3. **Soul searching and repentance**: Designate a time every day to pray about the situation, and to ask Hashem to forgive him for the pain he caused his wife and children. One should assess in detail exactly what he's done wrong according to what he's learned, and ask Hashem to instill in his wife's heart a willingness to forgive him and to give him another chance. He needs to put as much effort as he can into these prayers.

4. **Internalization**: One must internalize what he's learned. This means reviewing over and over the points where he was making mistakes, and the new approach that he needs to adopt. He also needs to pray for each point, namely, that Hashem help liberate him from his old negative behavior patterns, and also help him to adopt the new, positive ones.

For example: one of the fundamental rules of peace in the home is to never make any negative comments to one's wife. Fulfilling this requires extensive prayer. Man has a natural tendency to comment to everyone in his environment about whatever mistakes he sees them make, and to point out whatever flaws he thinks they have. Husbands often think that they have an obligation to point out their wife's flaws and mistakes, to help them grow. Such comments don't correct anything. All they do is destroy a wife's self-confidence and bring her to the conclusion that her husband doesn't love her. This causes a wife terrible suffering, because her deepest need is to feel that she is perfect in her husband's eyes.

Therefore, the husband must pray in the following manner:

"Master of the World, thank You for removing me from my home and for giving me the opportunity to correct my mistakes. Please, dear G-d, help me to stand up to the tests in my home. You've taught me that it's forbidden to make any comments to my wife, but I find it so hard to fulfill this. Every time I see my wife making a mistake or doing anything that I don't like, my heart fills with arrogance and I want to tell her what I feel she's doing wrong.

This makes me feel superior, that I'm better than her. I behave cruelly and make unfair comments to her. Sometimes I do this without even realizing. Until now, I've always justified myself that it's correct to make these comments to her.

"Please, Hashem. Have mercy on me and on my wife and my children and grant me wisdom and understanding to know that comments only destroy, and don't fix anything. Help me to realize that every comment that I make to my wife is an insult that deeply hurts her; And that what I am doing is destroying her self-confidence and positive self-image. My comments bring her to tears, and we fight and argue. This destroys the peace in our home which hurts the children too.

"Master of the World, have mercy on me and give me the spiritual and mental strength not to make any comments to my wife about anything, ever, in any place or under any circumstances.

"Help me understand and remember that my wife is my mirror and that any shortcomings that I see in her are really mine. Help me realize that even the things that she really does need to change won't be changed through my comments and rebukes, but only by me giving her more honor and love. Help me identify the root of the problem in myself and pray to You to help me fix it. Help me believe that the more love I give to my wife and the more I honor her, the more she'll change for the good, but only when I refrain from making comments.

"Please, help me to overcome my evil inclination to comment and criticize. Help me rid myself of this cruel trait of seeing my wife's shortcomings and mistakes and commenting to her about them. Help me see all the good she does and her genuine beauty. Help me to sincerely value her, to honor her, to support her and to praise her. Let me prefer to throw myself into a fiery furnace, rather than shame my wife."

In this manner he should pray for all of the fundamental points of peace in the home outlined in this book.

The "exiled" husband should work on the above four stages for an extended period, and meanwhile do whatever he can for his wife without expecting any acknowledgement or appreciation from her. He must be patient. When the time is right, Hashem will arrange for his safe return home.

The crucial point of this test is to avoid forcing the issue and to believe that Hashem will decide when it's time for the husband to return home. Despite his efforts, even if from her side things are only getting worse, he mustn't be discouraged. He should just do his part with emuna and keep going, praying and being good to her. If he truly does all that he can, eventually his wife will herself ask him to return home and they will have peace. Their life together won't be like it was previously; it will be completely new, as if they just got married.

To conclude this section, it's important to stress some of the points that we have learned, which are applicable to all situations in life:

1. Deal with problems while they are still small and don't wait for a crisis.

2. The only way to deal with problems is by applying the three levels of emuna.

3. With emuna we see how even the greatest crisis is for our ultimate good.

Divorce

This section should also be read by everyone and not just by those entertaining thoughts of divorce or currently in the process. Even those already divorced should not skip it, since they can learn here how to continue their lives from this moment on.

We asked one of the elders of this generation how he explains the great number of divorces in our times. He answered: "It seems to me that this is a spoiled generation that doesn't understand that married life requires hard work and effort, so for every small problem they run to the Rabbinate for a divorce.

"We also had many problems, arguments, misunderstandings and the like, like any young couple, but it never occurred to us to get divorced because of them. Instead, we were ready to put in every effort to make our marriage succeed. Thank G-d, we managed to overcome all the obstacles and merited raising a righteous generation. We've married off our children and grandchildren. We even have great-grandchildren now, and get much pleasure from all of them. If we hadn't been willing to bear the difficult times and hadn't put in all the effort that we did to establish our marriage, we would have lost all of this good."

From his words, we can learn to correct our false assumptions that peace in the home is something that comes naturally to some people. This isn't true at all. Even righteous people with good characters go through difficult times in their married lives. They also have differences of opinion and arguments. They too must learn how to concede, compromise, and keep the peace between themselves.

When a couple understands that marriage doesn't begin and end with the euphoria of the marriage canopy and are willing to learn and work on themselves, then there is no reason for them to ever get divorced. The problems only start when one or other of the couple, or both of them, are not prepared to listen to what they need to correct, and aren't prepared to put in the effort and hard work that's needed to achieve peace with their spouse.

The eyes of emuna

Man was created in order to attain emuna. To help him achieve this goal, Hashem sends him a series of tests during life which present him with the opportunity to develop his emuna. The biggest of these is his home life with his wife and children.

The root cause of all divorce is a lack of emuna. Instead of solving problems in the correct way through prayer and repentance, people think that they can solve them by getting a divorce. In this way, they hope to avoid future suffering. The truth is that they will just replace one set of problems with another. The suffering that a man had from his problems at home will be replaced by the great suffering of divorce, which is both harder to bear and slower to heal.

A husband's mistakes reveal his lack of emuna. If the Heavenly court has ruled that a man is due twenty units of suffering, no matter where he goes in the world, he'll get those twenty units, unless he repents. No advice will help, because what's required of him is repentance. If he repents, he will then merit peace in his home. If he doesn't, he won't. Divorce is not the solution. On the contrary, if he gets divorced with the hope of escaping his afflictions, he will only suffer more. Rebbe Nachman of Breslev, of blessed memory, taught that when a person isn't prepared to suffer a little, he'll ultimately suffer a lot. We can't hide from - or outsmart - Hashem.

Proper guidance

As long as a couple is still married, it's possible - with proper guidance - to solve any and all problems, no matter how difficult they may be.

Tens of thousands of couples can testify to the healing power of proper marriage guidance based on emuna. Many of these were couples who had already registered for divorce and had a date set for the proceedings to begin. Heaven directed them to books and tapes about peace in the home that were based on emuna and Divine Providence, and their lives changed from one extreme to the other. They achieved peace in their homes and were happier together than they'd ever been.

The power of emuna-oriented guidance is so great that every time a couple come to me saying that they want to get divorced, I don't even let them finish their stories. I ask them to listen to the lectures about peace in the home and to learn this book, and only afterwards come back to me if they still have problems.

They don't come back. Why? Once a husband understands the rules of peace in the home and what his role is, he sees that there's no place for his previous complaints. He sees what his mistakes were and knows what he has to do differently. He doesn't need to ask for advice or guidance anymore, because he knows the secrets of peace in the home. Many of these couples told me: "If only we'd have received this guidance a few years ago, it would have saved us so much misery, arguments and suffering."

Wounds of the heart

A couple considering divorce must know what troubles await them. The following are a just a few of the problems that people who get divorced commonly experience:

There are those who can't forget about their partner and overcome the longing they have for them. This prevents them from moving on and from forging new relationships. Many times, a couple is desperate to get divorced and think of nothing else, and then as soon as it happens, they realize that being single isn't so easy. The experience of being a divorcee is often more difficult to cope with than the problems they faced when they were married.

One divorced woman said to me: "I looked forward to getting my "get" (Jewish writ of divorce) with the same fervor that the Jewish people wait for the redemption. But once I got it I felt a terrible pain, such an emptiness, as if they'd cut off one of my limbs." This is really how it is. The Torah calls the divorce document a "writ of severance," referring to its function which is to split the couple, who were one soul, apart. That hurts.

Furthermore, the state of being single often doesn't end so quickly, because people aren't waiting in line to marry divorcees. It's very difficult to find a new partner, especially with the heavy baggage of children and debts. Those who experience such difficulties after their divorce - though they may not admit it - often regret the hasty step that they took.

Remove anger from your heart

There are those who are full of anger and hatred towards their old partner. Their hearts still burn from the hurt and pain they experienced, and they can't forgive and forget.

As long as one of the sides harbors pain or anger in his or her heart, neither of them can live peacefully. The one who's angry has no peace because of the anger and hatred that festers inside, and the other one has no peace because of the ex's harsh judgments. Neither of them has any rest until they placate and forgive one another, so how did divorce help? What they needed to do as a married couple – in other words, to make up and forgive one another – is still their task after their divorce. Now, though, it's much harder.

As a married couple they had every reason to reconcile and to continue their married life together. There's a workable template for this – apologize and make amends. Flowers or a gift with a note expressing one's regret and love do wonders. But now they're divorced, old wounds simply remain open.

The end of the arguments, or just the beginning?

Divorce seems to be the end of all the arguments. In reality, it doesn't end the arguments at all. On the contrary, divorce is just the beginning of a long and bitter argument that will be drawn out for the rest of one's lifetime.

This is especially true when the divorced couple has children. There is no end to the problems that arise; had they remained together, these wouldn't have been issues at all.

Every family occasion turns into a nightmare. At every birthday, bar-mitzvah, and wedding there are arguments about which side should host the party and who should come to it. Expressions such as: "If he comes, I'm not coming," and: "Make sure not to bring 'her' with you," are all too common. Bickering becomes a matter of routine. Whoever was involved in the arguments that led to the divorce continues to react according to the residue of pain that they still harbor in their hearts. All this comes together to make a pressure-cooker of anger, threats, tears and curses, as each person stubbornly fights to hold his position, feeling that the other one is specifically out to hurt and spite him.

Whenever a divorced couple meets, as they often need to, old memories return and old wounds reopen. When a divorcee sees his or her old partner happy with his or her new family, feelings of jealousy, hatred and revenge prevail.

The relationship with the children is a very complex one and is a constant cause of arguments. There are claims of: "Why doesn't he visit the children, he doesn't care about them," or the opposite:

"He's visiting too much; he's trying to turn the children against me." Sometimes the father is not allowed to visit the children at all, or has to limit his visits to particular hours during the week, and even these can only be in the presence of a social worker. There are the issues of supporting the family, court rulings and many other sorrows.

A divorced couple has difficulty coping with their children's emotional, social, educational or physical problems. Each one blames the other and places the responsibility on the other. Had they still been together, they would have focused their energies on finding a solution and helping the child, rather than on blame. Their joint strength and effort would've made it much easier to solve the problem.

In short – the solution which they thought would make their lives easier only ends up making their lives more difficult and more complicated than ever.

The true solution

A couple considering divorce needs to make an honest and responsible accounting of their situation. They must consider that their children will be the first sacrifices on the altar of their 'solution'. They require sound counsel and advice. Are they willing to seek guidance based on emuna, if they haven't done so already, and to give their marriage another chance? Others in their same predicament have managed to repair their relationship, and to go on to live a life of happiness and peace through such guidance. So many people have been spared so much suffering. This can happen for them, too.

Lack of knowledge

Divorce is often the result of the husband not knowing the rules of peace in the home. A husband needn't do anything extreme like hit his wife, G-d forbid, or raise his voice against her in order to ruin the relationship. He can even be helpful and supportive, but if he criticizes his wife and makes negative comments to her, this is enough to make her despise her life with him.

Someone who understands a woman's nature knows that refraining from snide remarks and negative comments is the first rule of peace in the home. A husband who doesn't know this simple but important fact of life will never have peace with his wife, no matter how good he is in other ways. No woman can bear to hear negative comments, especially from her husband.

A woman hopes that her husband will enlighten her life – give her attention, support, love and honor. She yearns that he'll cherish her and make her feel that she is everything he could ever want. If she doesn't get this – and even gets the opposite - there'll be no reason at all for her to want to stay married.

A wife who's criticized by her husband will long to rid herself of him. Even though she may have had children with him and they may have had some good times together, and despite the fact that deep down she's terrified of divorce, she simply won't be able to bear the suffering of more constant criticism and negative comments.

Her husband will most probably not understand why she's so upset and desperate for divorce. If he would have been aware of the nature of women and the rules of peace in the home, it would be as clear as a bell.

Lust

Many divorces are the result of the husband's lust, which entices him to abandon the wife of his youth and his children for a new woman. The evil inclination paints a portrait in his imagination of the beautiful, enchanting and euphoric life that will be his when he goes off with the new 'love' that he's found. It will surely be like living in the Garden of Eden. What the evil inclination doesn't tell him is that once he does abandon his family and go after the 'new' love, the 'Garden of Eden' that he expected will turn out to be a fiery furnace of purgatory.

If he begins a relationship with this other woman while he's still married, he'll get a taste of the hell that awaits him: his home will be full of tension and arguments and his children will start to show the signs of the emotional problems that are in store. The Heavenly court is infuriated by such behavior, as the Midrash says: "The G-d of these people despises immorality." He can expect severe punishments on his body, soul and possessions.

If the unfaithful husband goes on to divorce his wife and marry this other woman, the image of paradise will soon crumble before his eyes. The sweetness and understanding she showed him will disappear and be replaced by her true character. Now that she has no rival, she has no need to put on a show. Lo and behold, she's a woman like all others. She wants respect, pampering, attention, love and honor. When she's upset, she shouts and insults him. The romance is gone, substituted by her constant complaining that he doesn't give her enough. If he couldn't live peacefully with his first wife, he'll do no better with this one.

Now, his situation is far worse. With his first wife, had he put in effort to make the relationship work and prayed for help, Divine assistance would have been instantly forthcoming. But Hashem's not interested to help him have peace with this new wife. The pain that he caused his first wife arouses such a severe accusation against him in Heaven that he'll never again be left to enjoy a minute of peace, not in this world or the next.

Note that a husband needn't arrive at such extreme levels of betrayal to ruin the peace with his wife. Marriage is founded on absolute faithfulness. Any and all friendly relationships with other women, however innocent they may seem, damage the relationship with one's wife. When faithfulness is lost, everything else collapses.

Who's the trouble-maker?

Sometimes divorce appears to the result of a relative's meddling that made trouble between the couple. It really makes no difference what the apparent reason or cause was. The bottom line is (except in rare cases) that the husband is at fault. If he would live with the emuna that there are no tribulations without prior transgressions, he would repent. This, coupled with learning the rules of peace in the home, would assure him of peace with his wife. Consequently, the people who until now had fueled the crisis between the husband and wife would then either turn around and support them or would fade out of their lives.

Spiritual crisis

Divorce plunges the soul into a deep trauma that requires a long recovery time. Hurt feelings, a sense of failure and painful disappointment about the hopes and dreams for the future that have been shattered fill the divorced person's heart. We frequently encounter divorcees who still carry their pain around with them wherever they go – years after the divorce, their wound still hasn't healed.

The Talmud therefore states that when a man divorces his first wife, the altar sheds tears for them (Gittin 90). It's a tragedy when the soul's deepest connection is severed and broken.

It's not too late

A man should do everything possible, and concede whatever he needs to, in order to save his marriage and avoid divorce.

A man who didn't get this book in time and is already divorced shouldn't think that he has no hope and no way to start anew - not at all. He, too, needs to walk the path of emuna. If he does, it will help him correct the past and prepare him for a new, brighter future.

I would say to him: "Perhaps you've given up on your life, but Hashem hasn't. He has a beautiful future laid out for you – if you follow the path of emuna.

"If you believe that you ruined things, then believe that you can fix them again. True, until today you made lots of mistakes. You were destructive, both to yourself and to others. But now you're different; you recognize where you went wrong. Put the past behind you and make a new start. Learn to live with faith and prepare yourself for a new life and a new path that awaits you."

Look forward

A divorcee needs to look ahead. This is the only way that he will be able to cope with life and build himself anew. Though he's been through a trauma and still must deal with problems from the past, he must focus on what Hashem wants from him now. As long as he's still alive, Hashem has a purpose for him in this world.

This is a rule for all situations – whatever has happened has happened. Once we've repented and done our best to rectify, we must leave the past behind us and move on. We focus on our next step and how we can continue the journey of our life from this point on with emuna, as Hashem wants.

Forgiveness

As long as a divorced couple harbors resentment or bitterness in their hearts against one another, they won't be able to move forward and rebuild their lives. Sins between man and his fellow man are more severe than sins between man and G-d. The latter are relatively easy to fix by confession, regret and a resolution to not repeat the act. But the former are harder to correct. We are required to appease the person we wronged and to go to great lengths to gain their forgiveness. Until we do, the black cloud of the pain we caused them hangs over our head, darkening our lives.

It's essential that the couple fully forgive one another. If the husband hurt his wife he must do everything he can to appease her and gain her forgiveness. She should not be stubborn and not forgive him, even though she was the one wronged, since harboring resentment will only hold her back and prolong everyone's agony.

If you ask: "If she was the one wronged, why should she forgive? And why should her agony continue? She's justified in her anger." The answer is that not forgiving someone shows a lack of emuna. If the husband or wife who hurt their partner now shows true remorse and asks forgiveness, it's time to let go of the pain and to forgive.

Our suffering in life comes directly from Hashem, to arouse us to repent or to atone for our sins. Suffering is never random or happenstance. The person who brought about the suffering was only an agent - chosen, because of his or her sins, to be the rod that Hashem uses to beat us.

The pain we receive is what we're due according to Hashem's precise calculations. We had it coming in one way or another. When we're not willing to forgive the agent, we are in effect saying that the afflictions came from him or her and not from Hashem. This is heresy. If the agent asks our forgiveness, we should grant it.

Learning from the past

A divorced man must accept that what happened until now was Hashem's will and all for the best. He should focus on the present and future and ask himself: "Now that I'm already divorced, what does Hashem want from me? That I should be broken? That I should go around with thoughts of hatred, despair or self-persecution? Or does he want me to put the past behind me, and to start a new chapter in my life, a chapter of emuna and closeness to Him?"

Once he realizes that he still has a life to lead, he can learn from the past to make decisions for the future. He can learn where he went wrong and how he needs to behave now, in order to avoid falling into the same traps. His intent should be on living his life in the way that Hashem wants him to. He may want to return to his first wife, but should not set this as his goal.

He should repent for his mistakes, which involves confessing them to Hashem, asking for His forgiveness and making a resolution to not repeat them. He should also pray to Hashem that his ex-wife forgive him for the wrongs he did to her.

Once he has done all this he can pray in the following manner:

"Master of the World, if my ex-wife and I still have a joint mission, help us reconcile and live in peace and love. And if our correction together is complete, have mercy on us that we should each find a new partner and live lives of emuna, through which we will merit happiness, peace and tranquility."

The children's future

One extremely difficult problem that divorced couples sometimes face is when the children are put in the custody of the father or mother, who then doesn't take proper care of them, whether physically - as in cases of neglect or abuse - or spiritually, when the parent has abandoned religion and is giving the child an education that goes against the wishes of the other partner.

This is a very painful situation; it's understandable that the other partner is distraught with worry and tension. But this is not the way to help the children. We must never let a crisis defeat us.

A frightening incident occurred in the Ukraine at the time of the Cantonist decrees. This decree involved the conscription of young Jewish children into the Russian army for a service of no less than twenty-five years. Children as young as five years old, who knew nothing beyond their mother's apron, were snatched from their homes to the army camps, where they lived in very harsh conditions under the care of heartless Russian soldiers. In most cases, they never saw their parents again and disappeared into Russian society.

The parents did everything in their power to hide their children from the Tsar's soldiers, or send them away. But the soldiers would sweep through towns unannounced, and always manage to seize several children. The terrified children were cruelly snatched from their parents, who were screaming for mercy, and placed into sealed wagons specially made for this purpose. The cries and bangs of the children on the walls of the wagons, and the supplications and cries of the heartbroken parents fell on cold hearts. The pain of these scenes was indescribable.

On one of these occasions a woman, whose son had just been taken away, ran to the synagogue and opened the Holy Ark. She started screaming for Hashem's mercy before the Torah scrolls. She cried so hard that she fell down and died.

The event caused a big stir. When it was told to Rabbi Natan of Breslev, of blessed memory, who prayed tirelessly to nullify this decree, he said: "If she would have come to me, I would have advised her to strengthen herself and to fix a time every day to pray to Hashem that she should succeed in bringing back her son. In the merit of her pure heartfelt prayers not just her son, but many other Jewish children would also have returned home."

Even in such a painful and difficult crisis, where an innocent Jewish child is snatched away, we cannot allow ourselves to become overwhelmed and defeated. We must safeguard our peace of mind and believe that there's no problem that doesn't have a solution through prayer. With consistent prayer it's possible to change any decree.

Life goes on

No matter how difficult one's problems may be, a person mustn't let his problems defeat him. In the above story, the woman's hysterical sorrow brought about her own death, which meant that even if her son had returned home he wouldn't have had a mother to look after him.

A man should designate an hour every day to pray for help with his problems and then be happy the rest of the day. This is the only way to both continue living. and to make progress toward solving the problems. We can't let problems bring our lives to a halt.

When children are not in a father's custody and he suspects that they are not receiving proper care, he must say to himself: "I'm doing all that I can for my children. I'm providing for them financially, I'm visiting as much as I can and I'm giving them attention and love. Apart from praying for them, which I do every day, I can't do any more. I cannot control their mother's behavior." He should pray for their health, success and happiness every day for a fixed amount of time,. and then turn his attention to other things. Waging wars with lawyers and the like will only make the situation worse.

Prayer is the only advice for such a father, and his prayers will help more than anything else. I know many people who came from broken homes who turned out to be successful, happy, capable people in the merit of the prayers of one of their parents. With prayer we can achieve anything. A divorcee should entrust his children into Hashem's hands and pray to Him, saying:

"Master of the World, even if the children were still under my care, I would need to pray for Your mercy that they should grow up properly. And now that they aren't in my care, I'm placing them in Your hands. I believe that wherever they are, You are watching over them. Please have mercy on them and instill in their hearts to follow the right path. Keep them away from bad friends. Give them good friends and bring them close to You. Let them find favor and grace in Your eyes and in the eyes of all who see them. Fill their hearts with pure and simple emuna, and help them to grow up with good character traits and to lead upright, righteous lives."

Emuna is the cure for all sorrows, whether before the decree or after it. Happy is the one who lives his life with perfect faith.

Chapter Eleven
A man of valor

Rebbe Nachman of Breslev teaches (Likutei Moharan II:7) that one who desires to accept the challenge of making a living for his dependants must be a man of valor, and not the opposite, what's called in Yiddish a "shlemazel." He must have a measure of government over his own domain, since livelihood comes from the sphere of *malchut*, or monarchy.

Therefore, in order to receive a livelihood, one must have a measure of government in order to have a spiritual connection to the sphere of *Malchut*. One must especially exhibit kingliness at the time of a meal, for this invokes livelihood (see Gemara, tractate Zevachim 102).

Therefore, when a husband girds himself in strength and accepts the challenge of making a living for his wife according to his commitment in the *Ketuba* (marriage contract), then he is granted a measure of government, as the Torah says: "He shall govern over you," (Breishit 3:16). So, his measure of government invokes the blessing of income (Likutei Moharan II:7).

We can conclude from our holy Rebbe Nachman's teachings that in order to make a living for his family, one must be a man of valor. He shouldn't be lazy or a slouch, nor sad and depressed. He shouldn't rub his hands in despair or place the burden of livelihood on his wife. He should realize that the responsibility of making a living rests on his shoulders. He should believe in himself, and vigorously make every practical and spiritual effort to make a living.

Assuming responsibility

The obligation and responsibility of making a living is the husband's. A wife should have no business with - or worry about - livelihood issues. A Jewish bridegroom assumes this obligation and responsibility the moment he signs the Ketuba, for in it the husband commits to: "work for, honor, feed, provide for, and clothe" his wife. In other words, anything that's connected with making a living such as food, clothes, and shelter is solely the responsibility of the husband. He must fulfill all of her needs and she has no obligations in the area of making a living.

Rebbe Nachman's message is that only after a husband girds himself in strength, can he accept the responsibility of making a living. Once he governs, then he attaches himself to the spiritual sphere of monarchy (Malchut), and then he can provide for her. But if he shirks his responsibilities and acts like a helpless pauper, then he won't have his share of government and his connection to the sphere of monarchy, and he'll fail to invoke the blessing of a decent income.

When a husband boldly accepts the challenge of making a living for his wife and assumes complete responsibility thereof, he is already invoking the blessing of an adequate income. Such a husband acts like the governor of his own family unit. This is the measure of government that connects him to the sphere of Malchut and invokes a good income.

It's your problem

A husband should never collar his wife with the responsibility of making a living, nor should he involve her with the problems and worries of making a living. He should give to her in a generous and magnanimous manner; if he can't, it's his problem and he should take care of it. If he owes money, he should make every effort to pay his debts without upsetting her or involving her in any way, for it's not her problem! It's his problem! She married him on the basis of **his** signed and solemn commitment, and he's the one that's not fulfilling it.

A husband cannot use his outstanding debts as an excuse for not providing his wife's needs. He can't say: "First I'll repay the loans and then I'll provide for you." The duty to provide for her comes before repaying the loans.

The light of a wife's soul

Rebbe Nachman of Breslev also teaches that income is generated from the illumination of a wife's soul (Likutei Moharan I:69), for: "Money comes to a person by virtue of the wife (see Zohar, Tazria 52)."

A happy and joyous wife has an illuminated soul which serves as a spiritual catalyst for her husband's income. Therefore, there is no greater mistake than saddening or constricting the wife, arguing with her about money, or withholding her needs. When a wife can't buy what she needs or use money as she sees fit, the illumination of her soul is dulled and income is constricted.

A husband that argues with a wife about money axes the very limb that he sits upon. By saving a few cents, he loses hundreds and possibly thousands of dollars. By dulling her soul's illumination, he loses the income that her soul's illumination generates. Even if he thinks he's saving thousands of dollars by limiting her spending, his income problems will only increase.

The way to better his financial position is to be a man of valor and to do his job of making a living. This entails extensive prayer to Hashem and mending his ways, in addition to any necessary practical effort. He must assume the responsibility of his obligations in any necessary manner, without expecting her assistance or understanding. On the contrary, the husband must make his wife happy, buy her presents, and give her money to spend and fulfill her needs. By doing so, her soul will radiate and he will reap the benefits of an adequate income.

A bride's jewels

Our Sages said: "One should always be careful with a wife's honor, for the blessing in one's household is by virtue of the wife, for it is written (Breishit, ch. 12): 'And Abram benefited because of her.' Raba said to the townspeople of Mehoza: 'Honor your wives so that you'll become wealthy.'"

Maybe someone will say: "I don't need wealth and I don't feel like honoring my wife!" In that respect, the Gemara says that three things bring a person to poverty, one of which is when a wife curses her husband to his face. Raba comments that she curses him because he has money but he's too stingy to buy her jewelry (see tractate Shabbat, 62).

The above-mentioned Gemara passage teaches that for a woman, jewelry is not a luxury - it's a needed element for the health of her soul. Without it, she feels a deep distress. Otherwise, it's impossible to understand why a wife would curse a husband simply because he doesn't buy her jewelry. We also learn that if a husband doesn't honor his wife enough to buy her jewelry, he not only forfeits the blessing of wealth, but he also falls into poverty.

A person might continue to argue with the Gemara, and maintain that he doesn't need to buy his wife jewelry if he can't afford to. "Afford to" is a matter of priorities. Many men don't have spare cash, but if they really want something (the new digital camera, the ipod, tickets to the NBA, or whatever) they find the ways and means. If a husband moves his wife to the top of his priorities, he'll undoubtedly find the ways and means to provide her with her needs, in this case, jewelry.

Don't be petty

Rebbe Nachman of Breslev says that a constricted mind – which in money matters means pettiness – is a reason people fall into debt. Therefore, one should not be petty with one's wife, and certainly not demand a detailed report for every cent she spends. This won't help his financial situation one bit.

On the contrary, to escape debt one must generously give money to his wife and avoid arguments and criticism about how much she spends. When a husband opens his heart and his wallet to his wife – giving her a good feeling and trusting her judgment to use money as she sees fit – then Hashem will open the gates of Divine abundance for the husband, so that he'll be able to give to his wife.

Forget about money

A husband should forget about the money the very instant he gives it to his wife. It shouldn't matter to him what she does with it. He shouldn't argue with her about the way she spent it. If he doesn't have the money she needs, then he should be a man of valor and take the proper steps (in material and spiritual efforts) to attain what she needs. Providing for her is his solemn commitment, and his problem – not hers.

Go to work

The first words that a husband commits to in the Ketuba, the Jewish marital contact, is *b'siyata d'shmaya*, which means "with Hashem's help." Emuna – the pure and complete faith in Hashem – is what's needed to rely on Hashem's help. Without emuna, a husband is hard-pressed to meet all his obligations to his wife. Therefore, emuna is the first of a husband's commitments. His second commitment is go to work. This is explicit in the Ketuba, to shut the mouths of the lazy false-believers who roll their eyes, shrug their shoulders, and say: "Hashem will provide." When the wives of these "holy" deadbeats complain that they have no money, the husbands scold them and say: "Don't you have any trust in Hashem? Where's your emuna?"

Our sages foresaw the phenomena of the pseudo-holy lazy husband and therefore made him sign a written commitment (which is an integral part of the Ketuba) to go to work. It's his job to go to work and make a living, not hers. It's not his job to teach her faith and trust in Hashem, nor to lecture her about emuna. If our sages would have wanted to put the burden of livelihood on a wife's faith, then they wouldn't have required the husband to make a signed commitment of going to work.

Don't argue, dear reader, with the fact that many of our sages lived in utter poverty. Know full well that they lived within their means and didn't owe a cent in the world. Indeed, they were happy with their lot in life. One who is happy with his lot in life conveys the feeling to his wife that they lack nothing.

Proper management

Here's a story that teaches the proper approach to making a living:

A man asked for my advice in the area of his *shalom bayit*. He told me that his wife had complained incessantly about their inadequate livelihood. I asked him how he reacts to her complaints. He said that he tells her to strengthen her faith and trust in Hashem. He then told me that she responds with even more anger.

I explained to him that his words are no consolation to his wife. Instead, he's the one that should strengthen *his* emuna and trust, and do everything in his power - including more prayer and tangible efforts - to solve the problem.

"You give your wife the feeling that income is her worry," I explained. "By telling her that she needs to strengthen her faith, you're conveying the message that your financial problems are her fault. That gives her feelings of guilt and frustration which she releases on you. Instead, you should assure her and place all the responsibility on your shoulders."

Many husbands, by blaming their income problems on their wives, not only sadden them but insult them. According to the terms of the Ketuba, it's the husband's sole responsibility to feed, provide for, and clothe his wife.

Remember, the Torah in Parshat Breishit says that: "You shall eat bread by the sweat of your brow." This is the curse of having to work hard in order to make a living. But, this curse was said to Adam, not to Eve. He's the one that has to work in order to make a living.

Our sages say that a wife is like a yoke on her husband's neck. This means that making a living is his responsibility. They could have said that marriage is a yoke on a couple's neck, but they didn't, because it's not a wife's responsibility – even in part - to earn an income for her family. Even if the wife is a woman of valor who contributes to making a living or is even the sole provider, whenever a financial problem arises, the husband must meet the challenge and solve the problem.

Once, a rabbinical student approached Rabbi Ben-Tzion Abba Shaul, of saintly and blessed memory. The student claimed that he couldn't afford to buy his wife a new dress because he devoted all his time to Torah study. "In that case," said the rabbi, "close your Gemara, go get a job, and buy your wife what she needs. This is your solemn obligation according to the terms of your Ketuba." We see from here just how serious a husband's obligation to provide for his wife is.

A husband should never give his wife the feeling that he's incapable of making a living. He should never say no. If his wife asks for something, he should promise to do his utmost to fulfill her request. In that case, Hashem will provide for him. A wife looks to her husband, and the husband should look to Hashem.

The "Shevet Mussar" writes: "Don't mention anything to your family about your financial straits, for they can't support you." A wife doesn't have the emotional and spiritual wherewithal to cope with her husband's financial problems, since it's not her responsibility to make a living. Since income is a husband's concern, he should listen to her complaints, for it's his job to support her, and not the other way around.

In Hebrew, "to marry" and "to carry" is the same word: *la'sset*. When a husband marries a wife, it's his job to carry the wife, which means making a living and supporting her. Our sages say: "A man marries (play on words, and carries) a women," and not the other way around. From experience, when a husband burdens his wife with financial woes, in addition to the problems already at hand, he'll have to contend with his wife's anger, complaints, and frustration making his dilemma all the worse. Her having to contend with financial problems breaks her and saddens her no end.

As for money management, a husband has three alternatives: One, he can manage the money. Two, they manage the money together. Three, he lets her manage the money. The first two alternatives often lead to bickering and to disagreements, since the husband oversees and frequently criticizes his wife's expenditures. Also, if anything is lacking, then the wife blames the husband. But, when the husband gives free financial reign to his wife, he wins four times over: First, he shows her that he trusts her, and this gives her a wonderful feeling of security. Second, she has no complaints that he's holding back anything from her. Third, if his income is limited, she'll readily be more understanding of their situation. And fourth, they'll save the wear-and-tear of arguments about money.

Don't be stingy

One of the worst traits a person can have – and a guaranteed destroyer of peace in the home - is stinginess. Stingy people love money to the extent that their hearts are sealed to the needs of their loved ones. Stingy people are cruel. Since they have no mercy or pity on their fellow man, they refuse to give charity. Even worse, they're unaware that they're cruel, and justify their own stinginess. Their lust for money blinds them, just as the Torah says. No one likes stingy people. The disdain that most folks have for stingy people certainly doesn't add blessings to a stingy person's life.

That's mine!

Stinginess is a gross exhibition of a lack of emuna, since the stingy person trusts no one but himself. This type of heresy manifests itself in two ways:

First, when a stingy person has money, he thinks that the money was acquired by his own prowess. That's why he thinks that the money is his alone and he therefore wants to keep it for himself. He doesn't realize that Hashem gave him the money not only for himself, but for his dependents as well. Hashem can easily give the money to someone else at Divine discretion.

The stingy person doesn't realize that as long as Hashem wants him to have money – as much as he uses – Hashem will replenish it. For that reason, he won't lose a cent by donating to charity or by spending his money fulfilling mitzvoth. On the other hand, if for some reason Hashem doesn't want him to have money, a thousand iron-clad safes won't prevent him from parting with his money.

Second, when a stingy person doesn't have money, he thinks that he is no longer responsible to provide for or to see to the needs of his loved ones. In his spiritual blindness, he doesn't realize that Hashem is watching his every move. Since Hashem runs the world in a measure-for-measure fashion, He repays generosity with generosity. The miser's stinginess is therefore a deadly boomerang.

Misers can be divided into several categories: There are those who are stingy with strangers but generous with their own kin. At the other end of the spectrum, there are the demonstrative misers who are magnanimous with the whole world (especially when it brings them prestige and recognition), but stingy with their own kin.

Then there are misers who are stingy with everyone except for themselves. Finally, there are misers who are even stingy with themselves and can't stomach parting with a cent. In the end, they leave everything they've hoarded to someone else.

A good husband

One of the worst types of stinginess is a husband's stinginess in regard to his wife and children. He neither sees nor feels their needs. This is absolute cruelty. Every household expenditure is a waste that triggers his wrath. Such a husband is virtually impossible to live with.

Nothing saddens a woman like a stingy husband. By nature, a woman needs her husband to shine his light on her; in practical terms, this means giving her money. Even the understanding wife of a poverty-stricken husband that has nothing to give finds life unbearable; but it's even worse when the husband has money, but fails to give any to his wife. A husband's magnanimous attitude toward outsiders but stinginess with his wife is like a bitter living death for her.

If the husband would believe in the Gemara's words that honoring his wife would lead to wealth, then he'd certainly honor her by purchasing clothes and jewelry for her. The better she feels, the more her soul shines; the more her soul shines, the bigger the blessing of abundance that he reaps. Rather than being angry at her for spending money (since anger destroys income), he should be happy that she's happy and therefore let her spend the money on what she needs. By honoring her, he'll see enhanced blessings of income.

The Gemara gives solid advice to a husband (see tractate Chulin 84): "A man should always eat and drink below his means, dress according to his means, and honor his wife beyond his means."

Marriage is the one of the only mitzvoth in the Torah that requires a person to spend more than he can afford. Our sages emphasize how considerate Hashem is of what we earn. Hashem limits us in the amount we're allowed to spend even on such lofty mitzvoth as charity (no more than 20% of our income). Yet, when it comes to our wives, we're required to spend more than we can afford! This shows how important it is to Hashem that we honor our wives.

A lack of funds does not exempt a person from honoring his wife. On the contrary – he should increase his prayers, work overtime, take a side job, or do anything honest to provide for his wife.

If a person has a genuine desire to honor his wife and provide for his family, Hashem will surely help him and provide him with the wherewithal to do so. With other mitzvoth, Hashem won't necessarily do the same. Why? Suppose a person asks Hashem for two million dollars to build a Yeshiva. The Torah doesn't require a lone person to build a Yeshiva. Yet, the Torah requires a person to honor his wife. Hashem readily gives us the ability to fulfill the mitzvoth that we're required to fulfill.

Don't show your wife empty pockets and don't plead poverty. Tell her: "Certainly, sweetheart, I'll get you what you want. I won't spare any effort, with Hashem's loving help!" When Hashem sees that a husband is sincere, He'll readily help him to honor his wife.

Chapter Twelve
A Garden of Eden

I have added here a selection of topics from my previous Hebrew book on peace in the home: "The Primordial Garden of Eden."

Difficult times

There are times when severe judgments weaken a person's spiritual strength to cope with day-to-day life. Examples of this are illness, debts, problems at work, or arguments and friction with other people. These are times when a spouse must have extra patience and be even more helpful and supportive. Trying times test the couple's dedication to one another and their emuna. The one experiencing the difficulties is tested to see if he or she believes that everything is for the good and if they will strengthen themselves with joy, emuna, prayer and repentance. Their partner is tested to see if they act with kindness, mercy and extra patience.

The times when a woman is ritually impure or pregnant are periods of special difficulty. Another very stressful period for a woman is the time in-between marriage and the bearing of her first child. The longer it takes, the more distressed she becomes. We see this by our Matriarch Rachel who said to Jacob: "Give me children, and if not, I am dead" (Genesis 30:1). Nachmanides explains that she hoped that Jacob, out of his love for her, would fast and wear sackcloth and ashes and pray at great length that she merit having children, so that she shouldn't die in her sorrow.

In such a situation a husband must give extra attention to his wife, join her in her suffering, encourage her, strengthen her and pray long and hard for her. Elkanah, the father of the prophet Samuel, was the perfect example of this. While his wife was still barren he comforted her saying: "Aren't I better to you than ten sons?" (Samuel I 1:8), and Rashi explains: "I give you more love than I give to the ten sons that Peninah[1] has borne me." The Metsudat David explains: "I love you the same as if you'd given me ten sons." But when Jacob answered Rachel saying: "Am I in G-d's place, having withheld children from you?" (Genesis 30:2), and didn't pray for her, Hashem rebuked him saying: "Is this the way to answer a woman in distress? By your life, your children [the other tribes] will in the future all stand before her son [Yosef]" (Midrash Rabbah).

There are also times that are particularly ripe for arguments. The Chida, of blessed memory, writes: "Friday afternoon, before the Sabbath commences, is a dangerous time for arguments between husbands, wives and the servants. The 'dark side' works very hard to stir up arguments at this time. A man with fear of heaven should quash his evil inclination and not let himself be provoked into any argument or strictness. On the contrary, he should seek only peace."

The following is a good tip for preventing arguments: whenever you want to ask something from your spouse, first look and see if she is currently busy, because interrupting her will cause friction. A wife should not ask her husband for help when he is in a hurry to leave. A husband shouldn't ask his wife to prepare him some food while she is busy feeding the children. Only ask for things at an appropriate time.

Don't start a conversation with your spouse when he or she is in a rush to get out. You may want to talk for a while, but your partner,

---

1. Elkanah's other wife

feeling pressured to leave, is likely to get angry for being delayed. Leave it for another time when he or she has more time.

The first year of marriage

The Torah commands us: "When a man takes a new wife he shall not go out to war, neither shall he be charged with any thing; he shall be free for his house for one year and shall cheer the wife that he has taken" (Deuteronomy 24:5). The first year of marriage is the foundation upon which the couple's entire married life is built, because: "everything goes according to the beginning". Therefore, the Torah commands that a newly-married man be "free for his house" for this year, to cheer his new wife. This is the time for the couple to forge a spiritual and loving bond with one another. The better the husband is to his new wife and the happier he makes her, the stronger the bond between them will be. If the husband is successful, he can create a bond of love, unity, friendship and clinging to his wife that will last a lifetime.

In order to succeed, he must know how to honor his wife and make her happy. When the husband is aware of the things that upset her, he can avoid doing them. He should never make snide remarks to her and to never get angry with her. Mistakes in the first year, when the couple's bond isn't yet strong, can cause damage that lasts a lifetime.

Even a learned man with good character traits must learn what makes women happy and what upsets them, if he is to succeed in his first year of marriage. Rabbi Ben-Tzion Abba Shaul, of blessed memory, writes: "There are young men who, right after the wedding, realize that their wives are not behaving as they would like them to, and think it correct to bombard their new wives with all the ethical teachings that they heard and learnt in their Yeshivas." This is not the way.

The Chinuch writes: "We are commanded that the groom should rejoice with his wife for one year. That's to say, he shouldn't leave the city to go out to war, and should not live somewhere without her for any other purpose. Rather, he should stay with her one whole year from the wedding day. The reason for this commandment is that Hashem desired that His world be populated by upright creations, the children of male and female couples who would unite in a moral manner, since immorality is despicable to Him.

Therefore, Hashem commanded us to dwell with our own special woman for one whole uninterrupted year from the time we marry her. Through this we become accustomed to her, attach our desire to her and imprint her image and her deeds on our heart. By the end of this year, it becomes natural for us to look upon other women and their deeds as something foreign to us. In this way, a man is kept away from strange women and turns his thoughts to the woman who is right for him. The children she bears him will be kosher and the world will be pleasing to Hashem."

In the first year, a couple should not host many guests. They should certainly not entertain other young couples, because this always leads to comparisons between the husbands and wives – something that could seriously disturb their still-fragile relationship.

Some tips for a newlywed husband: pick up the telephone at least once a day and ask your wife what she's up to and how she's feeling. Doing this shows that you're thinking of her, and will make her feel happy and cared for. Rabbi Ben-Tzion Abba Shaul, of blessed memory, said that in the first year of marriage, a husband should always bring a present when he comes home, even if it's just a small sweet that his wife likes. With this he fulfills the positive command to: "cheer the wife that he has taken."

If someone angered you, or you're worried about something, don't take it home with you. If you do, you'll upset your wife. Rather, take a few moments outside to collect yourself and put it behind you. You can even pray to Hashem to help you leave your problems outside the home. Then, walk in smiling. These are good practices to keep up for as long as a person is married.

Know the difference

The Talmud states: "Women are a different nation." Women have a different character than men and want different things than men want. Men who don't appreciate this relate to their wives as they do to other men. This is a direct route to arguments and grief.

When a wife makes a mistake, whether in the running of the home or in relation to her husband, and her husband sees that she doesn't acknowledge the mistake or admit to it, he gets angry with her, thinking that she's the only wife who behaves like this. In truth, all women do this.

When Joseph was born, Rachel said: "G-d has gathered up my shame" (Genesis 30:23). The simple meaning is that Rachel no longer had to suffer the shame of being barren, but Rashi says that there was another intention: "Because as long as a woman doesn't have a child she has no-one to lay the blame on for her mistakes. But once she has a son, she lays the blame on him. When her husband asks: 'Who broke the plate?' she says: 'Your son did.'"

A wife's greatest need and hope is to be cherished by her husband. She therefore has a deep inner fear that she isn't. This hidden fear prevents her from admitting to her mistakes and makes her want to lay the blame on others. For her, admitting to a fault is tantamount to admitting that she's blemished and undeserving of her husband's love.

The need to feel cherished by their husbands is the reason why women can't bear negative comments or complaints from their husbands. Husbands who rebuke their wives and point out their mistakes and faults cause them untold suffering, because by doing this they reinforce their wife's fear that she is not cherished.

This need to feel cherished also explains why women are so particular about their honor. When a husband honors his wife, it's a sign that he cherishes her. Honor is the source of a woman's vibrancy and joy. Every slight to her honor drains her of her vibrancy and joy. This is why it's so hard for a woman to forgive any violation of her honor. The pain goes very deep and stays with her for a long time. Husbands don't understand why their wives can't just turn the page and forget about the past, as they would have done.

So many arguments in the home stem from the wife's need to feel loved and cherished. A husband must know that this need is part of the nature that Hashem has implanted in a woman - she can't choose to be any other way.. Knowing this, he will have compassion for his wife, understand her pain, judge her favorably and give her what she truly needs.

The essence of woman

Rabbi Ben-Tzion Abba Shaul, of blessed memory, writes: "Don't think that men and women were created with the same characteristics; there is a fundamental difference between them. Knowing this will save you much unnecessary anger. The main force at work in a woman is her feelings, whereas in a man, it's his intellect. This difference separates them in everything they do. Buying clothes is a good example. Husbands are amazed at how their wives make such a great deal about it, but a wife's appearance is tremendously important to her."

The Midrash states: "A woman wants a decorated home and beautiful clothes more than she wants to eat fattened calves." Women have different preferences to men. Men need to recognize this reality, understand their wives and respect their wishes. A wife loves to have a beautifully decorated home. Interior decoration, home layout, the furniture and its arrangement, pictures and decorations – these all mean a lot to her. When the husband doesn't interfere and just praises his wife's good taste, she takes great satisfaction in her home and is motivated to continue taking good care of it. This in turn brings tranquility to all the members of the household. On a deeper level, the manner in which a wife decorates the home represent an adornment of the Divine Presence, since the home of a happy wife is likened to a sanctuary of the Divine Presence.

Women don't function well with time-frame limitations. A study showed that it's common for women to be up to forty-five minutes late for appointments. A husband who's not aware of this will be drawn into many unnecessary arguments. When his wife is late he will get angry and grumble: "How long does it take you to get ready? You're always late!" But when a husband understands that this is simply her nature, he makes sure to always fix an earlier time for his wife. A man can 'freshen up' in next to no time; a woman needs much longer. A husband mustn't complain about how long it takes his wife to get ready. The female characteristic of working slowly and thoroughly is mentioned as early as our teacher the Meiri, a Medieval Talmudic commentator. He wrote: "Women work very slowly" and even the prophet Isaiah (32:9) referred to women as being "Leisurely".

Many women, especially in the first stages of marriage, are very attached to their parental home. It seems to the young husband that she doesn't want to be alone with him, but this is not so. This is simply her nature. The Torah says: "Therefore a man will forsake his father and his mother and cleave to his wife" (Genesis

2:24) - it does not say that a woman will forsake her parents. A husband should never try to distance his wife from her parents or argue with her about her wanting to be with them. Attempts to distance her from her parents can cause great damage to his relationship with her and destroy the peace in their home. On the contrary, he should do his best to forge good relations with his in-laws. This will enhance peace, love and unity between him and his wife. If her parents are far from Torah and mitzva observance, he should consult a competent Rabbi with outreach experience about how to act.

A wife cannot bear any comments about her cooking. This is an enormously sensitive issue for her. When a husband interferes and comments about his wife's cooking, he drains her of all the vitality and joy that she naturally feels when preparing food for her family.

A husband must understand, accept and make peace with the fact that his wife's G-d-given nature is different to his own.

The husband cheers the wife

The Torah commands: "And he shall cheer the wife that he has taken" (Deuteronomy 24:5). But the Torah does not command the wife to cheer her new husband. It also does not state that the husband should rejoice "with" his wife. Rashi comments: "One who explains that he should rejoice with his wife is mistaken." The mitzva is for the husband to 'cheer' his wife, not to rejoice together with her.

This mitzvah teaches us that a wife's happiness comes from her husband. We see that a woman can have everything - success, beauty, wealth, popularity, power, prestige and influence - but if her husband doesn't value and cherish her, she is miserable. This is because her joy depends entirely on the degree that he cherishes her. On the other hand, we can find simple women who aren't very successful, bright or beautiful. But if their husbands value and cherish them, they feel like they're floating on air.

The "Me'am Loez" writes on the verse in Ruth (1:9): *The L-rd grant you that you may find rest, each of you in the house of her husband*: "From here our Sages have said that a wife finds gratification only in her husband's home. Even a daughter that enjoys a wealth of clothes, jewelry and food in her father's home won't be gratified outside her husband's home. Therefore, Naomi didn't say to her daughters-in-law: 'And may you find rest each one in the house of her father', but: 'in the house of her husband', because that is the place of a woman's true contentment."

A wife is compared to the moon and a husband to the sun. The moon has no light of its own; it shines commensurate to the light that it receives from the sun. So too a wife only 'shines' commensurate with the light that she receives from her husband. Therefore, a husband must shine a warm light of love and joy towards his wife in order to illuminate her. If he is in darkness and depression, and needs someone else to shine light onto him, he won't be able to illuminate his wife. It's essential that a husband acquire the trait of joy.

The "Sefer Charedim" writes that the mitzva of making one's wife happy continues throughout our lives. Many times, by making his wife happy, a husband revives her spirit; our Sages say that it's as if he sustains an entire world.

Dear husbands - your wives have no one in the world but you. Their vitality and joy depend on you. Shower them with love and honor, and make them feel that their happiness is your top priority in life. Only then will they be happy. And to the degree that you make your wife happy, you in turn will receive happiness and blessing from Hashem.

The heart

Hashem wants the heart. The value of every act of serving Hashem depends entirely on how much one's heart went into it, as it says: "Give, my son, your heart to me" (Proverbs 23:26). Likewise, when it comes to mitzvot between man and his fellow man, the main thing is the heart. Rabbi Yochanan Ben Zakai said to his students: "Go out and discern a good way for a man to cleave to." Rabbi Eliezer said: 'A good eye.' Rabbi Yehoshua said: 'A good friend.' Rabbi Yossie said: 'A good neighbor.' Rabbi Shimon said: 'One who considers the outcome of a deed.' Lastly, Rabbi Elazar ben Arach said: 'A good heart.' Rabbi Yochanan said to them: "I prefer the words of Rabbi Elazar ben Arach to yours, because your words are included in his." Rashi explains: "Because everything depends on the heart" (Ethics of the Fathers, 2:9).

Acquiring a "good heart" takes work. Every message that a husband gives to his wife should be with his heart. He should strive towards feeling that his wife is part of himself.

Rabbi Aryeh Levin, of blessed memory, once accompanied his wife to the doctor. He said to him: "Our foot hurts." The doctor asked him: "Which foot?" He answered: "Our foot." The doctor asked him to point to which one, and Rabbi Aryeh pointed to his wife's foot. The doctor asked him: "Why didn't you just say that your wife's foot was hurting?" Rabbi Aryeh replied: "When my wife's foot hurts, my foot also hurts."

There are people who say nice things to their wives, but in a cold, heartless manner. You can fulfill all the tips for peace with your wife, but if you do so without feeling, she'll feel it deep in her own heart. She may not be able to pinpoint what's bothering her. Perfunctory "niceness" won't make a wife happy. She resents words and deeds that lack sincerity. If you really want to make her happy, you must give her your heart.

A wife needs her husband's constant attention. The Chazon Ish, of blessed memory, wrote: "Her nature is to delight in the favor she finds in his eyes, and to him, her eyes are lifted." Rabbi Wolbe, of blessed memory, wrote: "She puts on a dress and hopes for a compliment. She wraps herself in a scarf and hopes that he will like it." If the husband doesn't notice, or doesn't show any interest in whether the scarf is green or blue, she's very disappointed. The wife works hard to prepare a meal that her husband will like. If he wolfs it down and barely remembers what he put in his mouth - with no acknowledgement of her efforts - she's deflated.

Most of the things a wife does are with her husband in mind. She hangs a picture on the wall or puts a flowerpot on the table all for his pleasure. When he consistently ignores (or even fails to acknowledge) her efforts, she concludes that he isn't interested in the things that mean so much to her. In time, a schism develops between them and they begin to live separate lives.

When you take on the yoke of a wife, you are taking on the yoke of lavishing her with positive attention. Acknowledge all her efforts; don't take things for granted and don't be an ingrate. Show her that you're impressed by everything she manages to accomplish – including the cooking, cleaning, sewing, washing and management of the home. Show interest in her interests, even if they don't really interest you. Remember family dates like your anniversary and her birthday. When you buy her something, she doesn't measure its value by the price tag, but by how much thought you put into it. A thoughtful two-dollar trinket will make her happy, but a new car will upset her if she senses that it's insincere or that you bought the model that you wanted instead of what she wants. Just like Hashem, she wants your heart.

A listening ear

Our Sages said: "Ten units of speech came down to the world; of these, women took nine." Our Sages are not merely teaching us that women talk more than men. There must be something deeper.

In fact, our Sages are giving us an important key to understanding women's spiritual needs. Women need to express everything that's on their minds to others. "Worry in the heart of man, he should talk it out" (Proverbs 12:25), our Sages explain that both men and women should tell their worries to others, in order to feel better. But for women, this goes much further. A woman has a need to tell others not just her worries, but everything that's going on in her life - this is her nature. She looks forward to her husband coming home because she wants to share with him everything that happened to her that day, big and small. All he has to do is listen.

If a husband doesn't give his wife attention, he upsets her to no end and forces her to look for other people to talk to. She'll then spend long hours talking on the telephone, or going out to visit her friends or parents. Subsequently, on top of not giving her proper attention, her husband then also complains that his wife talks on the telephone and goes out too much. *He doesn't realize that he's responsible for all this.* Furthermore, her talking with others doesn't really satisfy her. What she really needs is patient listening and heartfelt attention from him; only this has the power to soothe her soul.

Jewish law states that a guest must not sleep in a room where a husband and wife sleep, even at times when they are forbidden to have relations. This seems surprising - if the couple can't be intimate anyway, how is the guest disturbing them? The answer is that he's disturbing them in a big way, because with a stranger in the room, the wife won't be able to tell her husband everything that's in her heart, and this upsets their relationship. The prophet Micha said: (2:9) "The women of my people you cast out from their pleasant houses", referring to a guest who sleeps in a couple's room and prevents the wife from speaking to her husband. This is equivalent to casting her out from her "pleasant home", because if she can't talk to her husband, her home isn't pleasant for her to be in.

A wife will talk about all the difficulties and burdens that she bears. She'll debate her problems with herself, and possibly even declare that she doesn't have the strength to carry on. A husband must know that even when she mentions problems connected to him – his character or behavior – her intention is not to blame or criticize; she's just letting off steam. She just needs to be heard and have her feelings acknowledged without her husband becoming defensive, judgmental, or snapping back at her. She doesn't need any solutions and doesn't want any advice. She just wants her husband to listen to her, lovingly, and to do his best to feel and understand what she's going through. She wants him to value her efforts and her achievements, and to let her know that he does. He must show her how pained he is that it's so hard for her; and he must give her the feeling that he's her best friend in the world, whom she can always lean on.

A husband should set aside at least half an hour every day to listen to and talk to his wife. This time should be entirely devoted to her – no eating or drinking, all phones switched off and no children present - just him and her, together. This is a daily opportunity for them to update one another about everything that happened to them during the day, in a relaxed and comfortable atmosphere.

A man reading this may think that to sit and listen to his wife for half an hour every day is a waste of time. This is definitely not the case. There is a mitzvah to perform acts of loving-kindness, and it's a great act of loving-kindness to listen to a person's pain. A husband would gladly listen to someone else's problems, and consider himself righteous for doing so, but here at home with his wife, where it's a daily occurrence, suddenly he feels that it's a waste of time. This is an example of where the evil inclination dresses up as an angel in order to trick us. A wife comes first: her feelings and happiness come before anyone else's. Listening to her alleviates her stress and worries and gives her the strength to carry on.

A wife's honor

There is a special mitzva at a wedding to tell the groom - within earshot of his bride - that his new wife is "beautiful and graceful". Even if she's neither, our Sages permitted bending the truth to increase the new couple's joy. It seems that if the bride knows that this is a mere custom, then such praises are meaningless to her. That's not the case, since our Sages understood how much women love to hear themselves praised in front of their husbands, no matter if the people giving the praise have been prompted to do so or not. Of course, the person a woman most wants to hear praises from is her husband. A husband must be very generous with his praises of his wife. The more he praises her, the more he is praiseworthy.

We express our honor for others with our words. If you want to honor your wife, compliment her and praise her and never say anything negative to her. Don't be lazy about this. Every word of encouragement, support, comfort, praise or honor is a gift of loving-kindness that you give to your wife. Each one plants in her the feeling that you value and cherish her, and this literally gives her new life. You build her self-confidence and fill her with vibrancy and joy, which make it easier for her to cope with the challenges of life. The words of praise that you tell her constantly echo in her heart. Every time she thinks about them, she's filled with joy. This strengthens the home spiritually, making it a joyous, happy and peaceful place. Words of praise give her the strength and will-power to manage her home and children in the best possible way. Tell her how happy you are with her and her deeds and that she is truly a 'woman of valor'. Tell her how impressed you are with her skills, alacrity and wit. Express all of this with emotionally-packed words – make her feel that she's your greatest treasure.

Be consistent with your compliments and never take them back. If she brushes them off, it's only because she wants to prove to herself that you really mean it. So as often as you can, at appropriate times, repeat your praises. The "Reishit Chochmah" writes that it is even permitted to falsely flatter for the sake of peace in the home.

But when, G-d forbid, a husband hurls insults at his wife, it's as if he plunged a knife into her heart. Insults reverberate in her heart louder than praises do, and every time she hears his words in her head, she relives the pain. It's therefore as if he kills her several times a day. She feels that her husband doesn't care about her, and perhaps even hates her, and her self-confidence disappears. There is no greater suffering for a wife.

A wife can't overlook an unpleasant comment from her husband. Rabbi Ben-Tzion Abba Shaul, of blessed memory, wrote: "It's an everyday occurrence that couples argue, fight, and get to the point of divorce, all because once, he said one cruel thing to her, and she can't forget it." Had the husband just thought for a moment, he wouldn't have said that thing, and he would've literally saved his marriage.

On the positive side, a husband can also win his wife's heart with one sincere compliment, to the point that she's willing to work all day long for the the praise that awaits her. Peace in the home depends on our choice of words.

The Zohar teaches us how Adam praised Eve: "How much love was there in what Adam said to Eve: 'You are the bones of my bones, and the flesh of my flesh' - so how could I despise or abandon you? Adam wanted to show her that they were one and that there was nothing that could separate them. When he said about her: 'To this shall be called woman', he meant: 'This is the woman whose equal cannot be found. She is the honor of my home and all other women are like monkeys compared to her. She is perfect in all her traits.' These are the words of love and affection that Adam said to his wife." The Zohar continues: "Every man should say even more words of love and affection [to his wife], for behold it is written: 'Many daughters did valiantly, but you exceeded them all (Proverbs 31:29).' By telling his wife that she is superior to all other women, he will increase the love and affection between them."

The self-righteous evil inclination may fly in at this point and object: "How can this be right, to tell lies and compliment a wife for characteristics and attributes that she doesn't have? Is this really what Hashem wants?!" To this the Talmud answers: "Whoever dwells without a wife dwells without joy, without blessing, without good, without Torah and without a protective wall." The Zohar adds that he also lives: "without peace, without help, without atonement, without wisdom, without life, without will, without wealth and without honor." If the Talmud and Zohar say all of this, then a husband can definitely say to his wife, in all sincerity: "You are my joy, my blessing, my good, my Torah, my boundaries, my help, my atonement, my life, my will, my wealth and my honor."

Love

The Torah instructs us to: "Love your fellow human as yourself" (Leviticus 19:18). Rabbi Chaim Vital writes that one's wife is also considered one's "fellow human". Our Rabbis interpret this commandment to mean: "That which is hateful to you, don't do to your friend. Rabbi Akiva said: 'This is a great rule of the Torah.'" Rabbi Akiva meant that this commandment contains all the other commandments concerning man and his fellow human. It means that we should treat others as we ourselves want to be treated. If you want others to love you and respect your wishes and property, then behave that way with them. If you don't want them to upset you, hurt you or cheat you, then be careful not to do these things to them. "Let your friend's honor be as beloved to you as your own" (Ethics of the Fathers, 2:10). The Torah's definition of loving others is to be good to them, to treat them well, and to avoid hurting them in any way.

There are those who say that they love their wives, yet if we would evaluate their 'love' against this definition, we would see that many times their behavior is far from loving.

The author of the 'Kehilat Yaakov', of blessed memory, writes: "A woman's greatest desire is that her husband should love her. If she sees that this is not the case, the pain and sorrow that she feels are so great that it's almost life-threatening. She feels so alone, like a widow while she's still married. A wife's world is her husband's love for her. If her husband doesn't give her confirmation of this love, her world grows dark." Our great Rabbis don't exaggerate. If they say that when a wife feels her husband doesn't love her it's "almost life-threatening", then that's how it really is. When couples come for marriage counseling it's not uncommon to find the wife spiritually broken and depressed, which makes her vulnerable to all sorts of illnesses.

King Solomon wrote: "As in water, a face reflects a face, so does the heart of man to man" (Proverbs 27:19). Rashi explains: "When a man looks into water and sees his reflection – it's smiling if he's smiling or sullen if he's sullen - so does the heart of one man reflect another man's heart. If he loves, he will be loved back; if he hates, he will be hated back." When a wife knows that her husband cherishes her, she loves him in return. This makes it easier for her to forgive him when he does make mistakes, because: "love covers all sins" (Proverbs 10:12).

For a wife to believe that her husband cherishes her, she must hear the words "I love you" from him every single day. At first, she may say that she doesn't believe him, but this is usually because she loves hearing the words so much that she wants him to say them again. Or it could be that he insulted her or hurt her feelings in some way, and the thought that he doesn't love her is embedded in her heart. In any event, he should repeat it to her every day, at every appropriate opportunity. He should also look for other words of affection, love and warmth to tell her too. [On days when she is ritually impure, it's forbidden to say things that may lead to intimacy, but he can still tell how much he values and appreciates her, and how grateful he is to her for everything she does.]

Shining faces

The Torah commands us to emulate Hashem's traits: "And you should walk in his ways" (Deuteronomy 28:9). The Chofetz Chaim explains: "We are commanded to emulate Hashem's traits, which are all good. Just like Hashem is merciful, so man must also be merciful. Just as He is patient, so man must also be patient. So too with all Hashem's traits, man must emulate Him." Hashem's Divine Countenance shines and illuminates; ours must also.

"Shammai says: 'One should receive everyone with a cheerful expression'" (Avot, 1:15). Rabeinu Yona explains: "Show them a joyous face. Everyone knows that if his friend would give him all the presents in the world, but with a sullen face, it would be as if he hadn't given him anything at all. But if his friend greets him with a cheerful face, even if he doesn't give him anything, he feels like he's received the greatest present in the world." A person's face shows what's in his heart. The word for "face" in Hebrew (*panim*) is related to the word for 'inside' (*pnim*) because a person's face reflects his inner state. It says in the book of Nehemiah: "And the King said to me, 'Why is your face bitter, seeing that you are not sick? This is nothing but bitterness of the heart' (2:2)."

A husband's face glowing with warmth and joy means more to his wife than all the material things that he provides. Therefore, a man must pause before he walks through his front door and prepare to greet his wife with joy, in a way that she'll feel that he's thrilled to see her. He must leave any anguish outside.

Rabbi Shlomo Zalman Auerbach, of blessed memory, eulogized his wife and declared that he didn't need to ask her for forgiveness, as is customary, because he never ever hurt or upset her in all their long years together. One great Sage said that he always wondered how it was possible to merit such a level – to never upset one's wife. Then one young man related to him how he once accompanied Rabbi Auerbach home on a very windy day. The wind had made him look slovenly. Before he entered his home, he smoothed and tidied his beard and clothes. The young man asked him if he was expecting guests at home, in whose honor he was tidying himself. Rabbi Auerbach replied that he wasn't expecting any guests, but that when he enters his home to meet his wife, he considers it equivalent to receiving the Divine Presence. He was therefore grooming himself in her honor. He added: "A wife doesn't need to see her husband untidy and unkempt. When a man enters his home, he should be neat and orderly with an affable expression on his face." After more than fifty years of marriage, he was still considerate to show a happy and illuminating smile to his wife. This was a great person.

A wife should also never see her husband with a frowning or angry face. Negative emotions change a person's appearance for the worse, as the Metsudat David (Nehemiah 2:2) writes: "Because of depression, the light of his face turned bitter." When a man enters his home with an angry or depressed face, he upsets his wife because her first thought is that he's upset with her. This alone can trigger a quarrel. When a friend looks at us with a miserable or angry face, our first reaction is that he or she is upset with us. A wife is especially sensitive about how her husband relates to her.

The trait of joy and a joyous countenance are not acquired overnight. A man has to work and pray to acquire them. The best way to acquire constant joy is to strengthen one's emuna in Hashem, and in His personal, tailor-made and loving providence.

Rebbe Nachman of Breslev, of blessed memory, writes: "Some people have tremendous and terrible tribulations, G-d forbid. It's impossible for them to relate what's in their hearts, or they have no one to talk to. They eaten up with afflictions and worries. But when a person approaches them with a joyous face, he can literally revitalize them." To revitalize someone is no small thing. If your wife's heart is full of pain and you come in and greet her with a warm and joyous face, you literally breathe new life into her and restore her soul.

A helping hand

Rabeinu Yona writes: "We are told to remove the trait of cruelty from our souls, and to implant in its place the trait of mercy."

The world generally defines cruelty in terms of overt acts of harm. But turning a blind eye to the suffering of others and failing to help them is also cruelty.

The Sefer Charedim writes: "When a person sees his friend's animal collapsed under its burden, he must help him. If he doesn't, he transgresses the negative commandment of: 'You shall not see your brother's donkey or his ox fallen down by the way, and hide yourself from them (Deuteronomy 22:4)'. When a fellow human's donkey has fallen under its burden, there is an obligation to help it. So too, when our fellow human himself has fallen under his burden, we must certainly do everything to help him." This means that if a husband sees that his wife is being bowed down by the weight of the household chores, he has a Torah obligation to help her. He has more of an obligation to help her than anyone else, because she is considered his own flesh, and the prophet Isaiah said: "Do not ignore your own flesh" (58:7).

The Torah says about Moses: "And it was in those days, Moses grew up and went out to his brothers and saw their suffering" (Exodus 2:11). Rashi explains that: "He set his eyes and heart to be troubled for them." This is the trait of bearing the burden together with one's fellow, to empathize with his situation and to feel his difficulties, fears and pain. In this manner, a husband must have compassion on his wife and must lend a hand to do the household chores and assist with tending to the children, when he sees that his wife needs help. A wife should have the confidence that her husband is always available and happy to assist her when she needs help. Knowing that her husband cares and is willing to help gives a wife extra strength to cope with her tasks.

A woman is in the early stages of pregnancy should be careful not to strain or overexert herself. If her husband doesn't give her sufficient support and assistance during this period, she may miscarry, G-d forbid. After the birth too, she needs a lot of help.

The Jewish code of law states that in the first month after giving birth, a woman has the status of an ill person. She needs to take it easy until her strength returns; and her husband is responsible for helping her to recuperate.

If, G-d forbid, the husband treats his wife like a slave and forces her to do hard work, he transgresses the Torah prohibition of forcing another person to do excruciating labor.

Rebbe Nachman of Breslev, of blessed memory, cautioned us to honor and value our wives. He said: "Women have great suffering and tribulations from their children. The pain of pregnancy and delivery followed by the strain of bringing them up - everyone knows the many pains, sorrows and afflictions that are involved, and how difficult they are to bear. Therefore it's only appropriate to have mercy on them, value them and honor them."

Everyone wants Heaven to have mercy on him. But Heaven only has mercy on people who have mercy on others. When a man has mercy on his wife, he opens the gates of Heavenly mercy for himself.

One who has compassion on his wife and who also helps her benefits even more, because he is granted wisdom that saves him from sin. Rebbe Nachman explains in Likutei Moharan (I:116): "When the Heavenly Court sees that a man is merciful, it decides to be merciful on him. But since the Talmud states that it's forbidden to have mercy on one who has no wisdom, they [the Heavenly Court] first give him wisdom, so that they can fulfill their decision to have mercy on him. Now that he has wisdom he will be saved from sin, since a man only sins because a spirit of foolishness enters him. This one who has merited wisdom will no longer tolerate foolishness and therefore won't sin." Happy is the one who has compassion on his wife.

The scale of merit

Hashem commands us: "With righteousness you should judge your fellow man" (Leviticus 19:15), which means that we our obligated to judge others favorably. When we see someone do or say something that could be interpreted positively or negatively, we are obligated to judge them favorably and assume that their intentions were earnest. After all, this is how we would want others to judge us.

This applies to everyone, but between husband and wife, this matter takes on another dimension. A husband who doesn't judge his wife favorably and give her the benefit of the doubt transgresses the commands of, "With righteousness judge your fellow man", and, "Love your neighbor as yourself." He also causes her indescribable anguish. Of all the people in the world, she looks to her husband to find the good in her and judge her actions favorably. These are signs of his love for her. When he doesn't do this, the message she receives is that he does not value, love or cherish her.

Husbands often fail to judge their wives favorably because they take their wives' mistakes and shortcomings personally. They think that their wives don't care about them or have done something intentionally to upset them, when this is seldom the case. For example, suppose a husband comes home to find the home in complete disarray; or no food prepared; or that his wife isn't home; or that she didn't send the children to school that day.

Rather than jump to the conclusion that she has been willfully negligent or spiteful, he should fulfill the commandment to judge her favorably and realize that there must be a good reason for what she did or did not do. He must be compassionate and remember that she's a human being with limitations to her strengths and resources. Something obviously happened. His wife will seek his compassion and reassurance that she's okay – that she did the best she could and he still cherishes her. The husband should focus on giving her this reassurance and see if there's any way that he can help her.

The *mashgiach* (spiritual guide) of the Kaminetz Yeshiva, of blessed memory, pointed out that we see this by Adam's treatment of Eve. Immediately after Eve brought about the decree of death on all of mankind and the decree of "By the sweat of your brow will you eat bread", Adam named her 'Chava' (life), which signified that she was the mother of all mankind. He didn't get angry with her, rebuke her or turn away from her. He was compassionate. He knew that she'd made a big mistake, and that she knew it too. He understood that after the fact, it was a time to build up her spirit, not break it down any further. So he gave her a name that proclaimed her as the giver of life to all humanity. Our Sages say that Adam was extremely pious. In this most difficult of situations, he managed to find the good in Eve and revive her spirit. That's greatness of soul and true piety.

Emuna

The Sefer HaChinuch writes: "A person should know and take to heart that everything that happens to him, good or bad, comes directly from Hashem and that there is a reason for it. No one can lay a hand on him, if it is not Hashem's will. When others harm him he should know that, due to his sins, Hashem decreed this suffering on him. He should not consider taking revenge on the one who hurts him, because he is not the true source of his suffering; his sins are the true source. King David, of blessed memory, when others wanted to stop Shimi ben Gera from cursing him said to them, 'Let him curse, because Hashem told him to'. He attributed his suffering to a Divine decree that was brought on by his own sins, and not to the agent of his suffering."

Peace in the home is a barometer of a husband's emuna. A man with emuna knows that Hashem's loving hand lies behind everything that happens to him, both within the home and outside the home. He knows that his wife is his mirror, and a vehicle through which Hashem communicates to him needed messages. Through the wife, Hashem shows the husband his weak spots that need reinforcing. Therefore, if his wife shouts at, curses or insults him, he should attribute these messages to Hashem. If she is careless with money, not as hygienic as he would like, disorganized or mean to him, he can accept the situation with love if he remembers that it's all from Hashem. With emuna, a person knows that his suffering is really a gift designed to cleanse his soul from the blemishes of transgressions, so he won't have to suffer in the world to come. A wife is merely a rod in Hashem's hands to arouse him to repent or atone for his sins. A husband with emuna therefore has no complaints about his wife, and treats her as a queen no matter what.

A man with emuna doesn't know the meaning of a 'bad wife'. He's grateful for everything she does even when she gives him grief. He doesn't lose his self composure since he knows that his tribulations from her are really from Hashem. Rather than retaliating against her, he works to correct himself, and treats her with love and respect. He says to Hashem, "You are just in all that is brought upon us; for you have done right, but we have done wickedly" (Nehemiah, 9:33). When our Sages said that "one who has a bad wife won't see the face of Purgatory" (Talmud Eruvin 41b), they stipulated that this applies only when a person accepts his situation with love and doesn't balk at his suffering. If he gets angry with his wife and retaliates, not only will the suffering not atone for his sins, but his debt of suffering will increase much more because of the pain he causes her.

Rabbi Shach, of blessed memory, writes, "Sometimes a man facing problems feels such sorrow that his world becomes dark and his spirit is broken inside him. When a person reaches such a state, it is due to a lack of emuna and trust in Hashem. One who fears Hashem and believes in His providence is never defeated by his problems and nothing oppresses or bothers him. As King David said, "Even when I walk in the valley overshadowed by death, I will fear no evil, because You are with me" (Psalms 23:4).

Rebbe Nachman, of blessed memory, writes, "All Torah and mitzvot depend on emuna." Emuna is the foundation and source of all Torah and Divine service.

Two Women in the Home

A man's role is to give and a woman's role is to receive - this is the way Hashem created the world. Attempts to reverse this order lead to disaster. A husband's role is to give to his wife and be a pillar of strength for her. A wife needs to feel secure both in her husband's love for her and in his ability to take care of her. When a husband displays weakness and needs *her* to boost *his* ego and give him honor, the foundations of his home crumble.

An honor-seeking husband loses his male status, since he wants to receive and is waiting for a handout. This creates a situation of two females in the home – an impossible state of affairs. His wife looks to *him* for honor, as she should, but because he's entangled in his own desire for honor, he is unwilling to give her any until she honors him, and a dead-lock ensues. Such a husband needs to understand two things: First, he has an obligation to honor his wife, not the other way around, and second, if he honors her properly, she'll honor him in return.

Rabbi Shlomo Wolbe, of blessed memory, writes, "There are husbands who claim, 'Surely our Rabbi's have taught, Who is a good wife? One who does her husband's bidding. If so, my wife should do what I ask her to, because only then is she called a good wife.' When such a husband sees that his wife doesn't do what he wants, he thinks that she is at fault and coerces her into doing his will. Such thinking flows from a distorted view of the world, and leads to the destruction of homes. This was certainly not our Rabbis' intention. If a man says to his wife, 'Don't observe the Sabbath,' she needn't listen to him. That which they said, 'Does the will of her husband' only refers to *when his will is in accordance with Hashem's will*, part of which requires him to treat his wife with honor and respect. Our Rabbis in the Talmud said that a man is obligated to honor and love his wife; their words are Hashem's will. Hashem also wants man to fulfill the oath that he swore on his wedding night to honor, respect and cherish his wife."

A husband has a Biblical obligation to honor his wife. On his wedding night he swears an oath, in the presence of two witnesses and the Rabbi conducting the service, that he will fulfill all that is written in the Ketubah – the Jewish marriage contract. One of the clauses of this contract states, "I will honor my wife in the manner of men who truly honor their wives." Rabbi Yeshayahu Pinto, of blessed memory, writes that the greatest honor for a wife is when her husband humbles himself before her and makes her his top priority. This is the greatest sign that he truly cherishes and values her.

When a husband fulfills his obligation to honor his wife, she then honors him in return. When she sees him treating her with love, honor and respect, she feels obligated and motivated to pay back his kindness.

The Vilna Gaon explains the difference between a king and a ruler as follows: a king is chosen by people who want him to rule over them; a 'ruler' is one who conquered a province and rules over it without consulting its populace. A groom is comparable to a king, since his wife accepted him to be her husband, but she expects him to 'rule' in the way of Jewish kings – with strength, compassion and sensitivity.

Laziness

Rebbe Nachman teaches that the bite of the primordial snake that represents the evil inclination is depression and laziness (Likutei Moharan I:189). The evil inclination overpowers man by trapping him in these two states. A husband's laziness can lead to the ruin of his home, because women find it very difficult to see their husbands wallowing in bed in the morning, even if they themselves get up later. Far worse is the situation where a wife gets up early to tend to the household and prepare the children for school, while her husband snores away in bed. She can't respect laziness. She will also sorely resent his doing nothing while she works so hard for the family. This resentment will strain their relationship, which will deteriorate until he alters his ways.

On the other hand, when a husband is diligent and an early-riser, his wife and children look up to and respect him. A Moroccan saying goes, "Be industrious and people will love you," and there is much truth in this. My teacher, Rabbi Levi Yitzchak Binder, of blessed memory, would say that one should go to bed early and set an alarm in order to wake up and start the day early. He said one should also pray to Hashem for help in rising early and with alacrity. Doing this has a positive effect on the whole rest of the day.

Wives can't stand when their husbands don't have an organized structure of work and/or study. They can't stand to see their husbands sitting idle. If a husband finds himself in such a state of limbo, he mustn't spend his days at home. He should rise early, pray and then stay out for the rest of the day, returning home only towards evening. During the day, he should make every effort to seek regular work and establish a fixed praying and learning schedule. Until he does, he can engage in short-term projects. Whatever happens, he must stay out of the house. In the evening too, a husband should occupy himself with constructive endeavors such as learning Torah, personal prayer, and devoting time to his wife.

A couch-potato husband can't possibly have a healthy relationship with his wife. Being around the house all the time, he gets in her way and frequently remarks about whatever she's doing. This upsets her - arguments and fights ensue, and the peace between them is lost. But when he's out all day, they have space from one another and look forward to seeing each other again in the evening.

We see that older couples sometimes get divorced. This seems very surprising because if they weren't getting along, why didn't they get divorced long ago and save themselves years of suffering? Why now? Once their children are grown, they usually have fewer expenses and no debt. They can sleep, rest, learn, go for leisurely walks and generally take it easy and enjoy the rest of their lives; they are free to serve Hashem without obstacles. What brings them to such a dire state that they want a divorce?

The answer is very simple: the very fact that they are spending so much time together is what pushes them apart. Our sages say, "A grandpa in the home is a stumbling block in the home," because an old grandfather in the home considers himself the tribal elder who sits all day giving instructions and advice. The tribal matron can't take this for very long, and if it doesn't stop, divorce may seem the only option to her. Despite many happy years together while marrying off children and grandchildren, she'll readily abandon him if he starts to constantly criticize and comment about everything she does.

The opposite of laziness is alacrity. The value of something done with alacrity is far greater than something done without it. Rabbi Moshe Chaim Luzzato, of blessed memory, said that when someone does something with alacrity it is a sign that he's enthusiastic. If a wife asks her husband to bring her something or do some chore in the home and he snaps to his feet, he shows her that he values her and is enthusiastic to do things for her. But, if he tarries and then sluggishly does whatever she wants, she'll be more aggravated than if he hadn't done it at all. "Run like a deer and be swift like an eagle, to do the will of your Father in Heaven." The will of your Father in Heaven is that you should "run like a deer and be swift as an eagle" to make your wife happy.

Wronging one's wife

The Torah Says, "You shall not wrong one another" (Leviticus 25:17). The Torah delineates two types of wronging: **monetary**, where one cheats someone else financially; and **verbal**, where one upsets and hurts someone else with one's words. Financial wrongs are relatively easy to rectify: apologize and return the money. Verbal wrongs are sometimes impossible to rectify. The words said can never be taken back or erased from the other person's memory. Even if they grant forgiveness, the pain in their heart and soul may never heal.

Women by nature are sensitive and emotional, and therefore readily vulnerable to verbal abuse. The Talmud says, "A man must be careful not to wrong his wife, for her tears readily flow." Her emotional sensitivity makes her feel the sting of any comments and criticisms. Jewish law specifically dictates that one must be extra careful with a wife's feelings.

The Talmud tells us of Rabbi Rachumi, who was extremely righteous. With his wife's agreement he would return home from the Talmudic academy only once a year, on the eve of Yom Kippur. Once, on this day, he became so absorbed in his studies that he failed to return home. His wife eagerly awaited his arrival, but when he failed to come, she shed a tear out of sadness and disappointment. At that very moment, the gallery on which Rabbi Rachumi was learning collapsed; he fell and died. In this extraordinary tale, the Talmud doesn't say that his wife suffered greatly or for an extended period. *She shed one tear.* This was enough to bring a decree of immediate death on her husband, although he had no evil intention of hurting her whatsoever.

Rabbi Chaim Shmuelevitz, of blessed memory, asks, "How did this punishment help his wife? Surely his death caused her only more pain and suffering, since she would now be a widow!" He explains that our Sages wanted to teach us the severity of upsetting others. Even in such circumstances, the punishment is severe and swift in coming. He would often say, "Upsetting a fellow human being is a burning fire!" The Talmud states that all punishments are delivered via a messenger, apart from the punishment for upsetting others, which Hashem delivers Himself.

The Sefer HaYeraiyim writes, "Just as one can upset people with words, one can upset people with a sour facial expression." Husbands often come home after a hard day with a bitter expression on their faces. This is problematic, for a wife sees this as a message that her husband is displeased with her. She doesn't think of attributing his frown to the ten people who aggravated him earlier in the day, or to the rush hour traffic jams. Even though it's sometimes difficult to avoid upsetting his wife, a husband must leave his aggravation outside the house and walk in smiling.

A breach of promise is another form of wronging. When a husband says that he'll come home at a certain time, he must keep his word. If he doesn't, his wife will be insulted because she takes it as a sign that she isn't important to him. Even for a mitzva, it's forbidden to be late. If he sees that he's going to be delayed, due to unforeseen circumstances, then he should phone her well ahead of the expected arrival time and tell her that - through no fault of his own - he won't be home on time. He should apologize in a pleasant tone, and make it clear that he's truly sorry that he won't be on time for her.

Entrenched in arguments

The road to peace in the home is paved with tests, obstacles and difficulties. A man shouldn't fool himself that he'll find a wife who matches him so perfectly that they'll always live together in harmony and bliss. All couples disagree with one another from time to time, and about a number of things. Disagreements are inevitable. To prevent disagreements from turning into arguments, a husband needs to familiarize himself with the areas where his wife feels differently than he does and with the situations and topics that are particularly sensitive for all women. He can then tread carefully whenever these cases surface.

The Satan dances wherever there is strife, so one must avoid arguments at all costs. If an argument has already been sparked, the husband should be quick to extinguish it, peacefully. If he doesn't, further arguments are likely to ensue. The nature of arguments is that one leads to another. The Sh'la writes, "At the beginning it says, 'And there was an argument between the shepherds of Abraham's flocks and the shepherds of the herds of Lot'. But when Abraham spoke to Lot he said, 'Let there not be strife between me and you'. He said 'strife' in the feminine tense, rather than 'argument' in the masculine. Why did he do this? Abraham was saying to Lot, 'The argument that began between the shepherds, let it stay as one argument, and not give birth to further ones, like a woman who gives birth.'" When a husband becomes entrenched in argument and refuses to concede his position, he transgresses what it says in the Torah, "Do not be like Korach and his congregation."

The Book of Proverbs says (16:2), "All the ways of man are pure in his own eyes". A person thinks that what he does and thinks is correct - this is natural. In every difference of opinion, if one side feels that he's right and the other side is wrong, he'll stubbornly argue his point. People have a very strong desire to defeat others. But, apart from where the topic is very serious, winning an argument is usually not worthwhile. Conceding a point preserves one's strength and the peace. Peace with others is true victory. Especially with one's wife, bowing to her wishes and placing her in first priority are the greatest show of strength and the greatest victory.

Rabbi Nathan of Breslev, of blessed memory, writes that argumentativeness is the worst of all bad traits. All other negative traits and desires can serve some positive purpose, if they are harnessed and used in accordance with Hashem's will. But, being argumentative serves no positive purpose and can uproot a man from this world and the next.

Rabbi Chaim Falagi, of blessed memory, testified that he had seen with his own eyes that every argumentative family never escaped without some serious damage to their health, wealth, or both. The vessel for blessings is peace. Where there are arguments, there are no blessings. In the story of Korach and his followers' argument with Moses, we see that the earth swallowed them alive with all their wealth. Arguments bring a person to anger, stress, depression, high blood pressure and heartache; nothing else does so much damage to a person's physical and emotional health.

Parents' quarrels sorely damages children's physical and spiritual wellbeing. Strife in the home destroys their capability to concentrate and learn, damages their souls, and can negatively affect them for the rest of their lives. A wife may make many mistakes in child-rearing, but her husband's quarreling with her about it will do more damage than any of her mistakes. If a wife is too stern with her children and her husband steps in to protect them, the damage to the child from the ensuing tension will be far greater than the damage from her stringency. In the case of strife between a mother and one or more of the children, a husband must first give her unconditional backing. The "Ben Ish Chai" writes that when one walks into a volatile situation, he should realize that the Satan is at work in attempting to stir up arguments and discord.

In many cases couples argue about matters of almost no consequence. The evil inclination incites the husband to be stubbornly insistent about something, and a fight follows. For example, the wife asks the husband to clean something or organize something for her that should take no more than half an hour, but he's resentful of her desire to take up his time so he doesn't do it. The resulting argument may then last into the wee hours of the night, when the whole episode could have been easily avoided. Had he granted her a mere half an hour of his time, he would have spared her untold anguish and spared himself of both migraines and wasted hours.

Often, a wife needs her husband for a short moment, to show or ask him something. The husband might be busy and fail to respond. Maybe he just calls out, "What?" and continues with what he's doing. When she vies again for his attention, he replies more impatiently with another "What?!" This lack of regard for his wife leads to strife. She may have only wanted his attention for half a minute; now he'll need hours on end to placate her.

The Talmud teaches that it's difficult to appease a woman. When husbands see this, but don't understand why, they feel that their wives are either spoiled or vindictive. They don't want to play this repeated game of humbling themselves before their wives while trying to appease them, so they decide to not try any more. They think that their wives are acting maliciously, so they apply a strong hand with no warmth or affection. In reality, their wives are longing for reconciliation and to be close with them again; they just don't know how to stop the vicious cycle of hostilities. With this in mind, a husband is careful to be loving and patient no matter what – his calm will neutralize any strife in the home.

A Tyrant in the House

Sefer HaBrit says, "There are people who are careful not to harm anyone, and love and honor others, yet hate their wives and insult them. They say that there is no sin in this. They don't understand that their sin is even greater than if they would do this to a stranger, for one's wife is the essence of one's own flesh. Furthermore, why should wives not be included in the commandments of 'Do not hate your brother in your heart', and 'Love your neighbor as yourself'?"

An ancient Jewish adage says, "Just as their faces are not alike, so too are their opinions different." Husbands and wives always have different preferences and goals to one another, but this needn't stop them from building a happy and successful life together. They know when they get married that there will be differences of opinion between them and their intention is that - when these arise - they will respect each other's wishes and arrive at a mutually-satisfying compromise. This works well.

A husband that feels that being man of the house grants him the last word and the power of veto over his wife's wishes is a tyrant. This was the attitude of the wicked Haman, "And all the wives will give honor to their husbands... so that each man will be the ruler in his home" (Esther 1:20-22). He wanted his wife and children to bow down to him, serve him like slaves, and accept whatever he said. Such a person feels that he has the right to insult his wife and children, and make them fear him.

The Talmud says that whoever places too much fear in his home will in the end come to transgress three major sins - forbidden sexual relations, bloodshed and breaking the Sabbath. Here's how:

Forbidden sexual relations - if the night of his wife's ritual immersion arrives but for some reason she does not manage to immerse herself, she'll be too afraid to tell him, so she'll have relations with him while she is still ritually unclean.

Bloodshed - she may run away out of fear of him and, due to her emotional duress, end up in a fatal situation.

Transgression of the Sabbath - if his wife forgets to kindle the Sabbath hotplate before nightfall, her fear of his reaction will lead her to turn it on after the Sabbath has commenced and he will eat food that has been cooked on the Sabbath.

Whenever one of the children has misbehaved, a terrorized wife will be afraid to tell her husband, for tyrannical husbands are usually tyrannical fathers that punish their children cruelly. The child in turn becomes progressively undisciplined and more difficult to handle. Were it not for the reign of terror at home, she could have kept her husband abreast and he could have helped his child before he or she slipped into a pattern of wrongdoing. In a household with fear, everyone will lie in order to escape the wrath of the despotic father and husband.

A man must never insult his wife or strike her, G-d forbid. The Jewish code of law states, "A man who hits his wife has committed a transgression and the power is given to the court to beat him and excommunicate him, because this is not the way."

Rabbi Chaim Vital explains that when our Sages said that anger is tantamount to idolatry, they were teaching us that a person with emuna shouldn't get angry. With emuna, he should know that everything that happens to him - even at the hand of others - is from Hashem. As such, there's nothing to be angry about. Anger shows a lack of emuna, and is therefore equated with idolatry.

King Solomon said, "Anger rests in the bosom of fools" (Ecclesiastes 7:9). A fool doesn't look beneath the surface of what he sees, so he never discerns Hashem's hand of providence underlying whatever happens to him. He therefore gets angry with whoever wrongs him and fumes whenever things don't go his way. A wise person, on the other hand, knows that when people wrong him, it is due to his sins. He knows that there is message for him in his suffering. He trusts his loving Father in Heaven who is guiding his life, so if something doesn't work out like he wants, he knows that it's all for the best.

Loads of time and effort go into preparing the meals for Sabbath and other festive occasions. Preparations frequently include some mishap - a child knocks over a bottle or breaks a glass, the wife burns something, or maybe the meat was gristly and tough. These incidents are tests of a person's emuna, to see if he'll be patient and understanding. Will he remember that everything is from Above or will he get angry and blame the people involved? If he passes the test, he and his family continue to enjoy a happy festive meal together. But if he fails the test, gets angry and shouts at his family, the meal is ruined. It's such a shame for so much to be lost for so little.

The Torah forbids us from taking revenge. The "Chinuch" writes about this commandment, "The custom of most of the world is that they do not rest from pursuing the one who wronged them, until they have retaliated to the degree that he hurt them. Hashem restrains us from this by commanding us, 'Do not take revenge'". Even if a husband feels that his wife purposefully upsets him, he must not react in kind. If he withholds good from her because of her behavior, he is taking revenge. Instead, he must strive to correct himself and treat his wife with love and respect. King Solomon wrote, "He that covers a transgression seeks love" (Proverbs 17:9). Rashi explains, "If one man sins to another and the latter covers it up by not mentioning it and by not showing him an angry face, this causes the one who sinned to him to come to love him." By not repaying his wife in kind, but on the contrary, by treating her with love and respect, she'll eventually reciprocate his love.

Quelling arguments

The book "Kochvei Ohr" tells about a man that came to Rebbe Nachman of Breslev, of blessed memory, and told him the sorrow he had from his daughter, who had been convinced by a non-Jew to give up Judaism, and had disappeared. The Rebbe told him that she was at the home of the local priest and that he should send two men in a wagon to the priest's house. They would find his daughter standing outside, and when she sees them, she'll want to come home with them. So it was. She returned to her family and to Judaism, and the Rebbe arranged for her to marry a certain young man. Before the wedding he told the groom, "If you ever get angry or argue with her, be very careful to not remind her of what she did. If you are careful about this, I promise you that you will have good children from her." The young man heeded the Rebbe's words and indeed had children who grew up to be outstanding Torah scholars.

Rebbe Nachman writes in Likutei Moharan that everyone has a lust of victory. This is what makes winning so sweet and losing so bitter. The evil inclination knows this and uses it to his advantage.

When people argue, the evil inclination encourages both sides to use every available means to win, no matter how hurtful or underhanded they may be. People know that cheap shots and bringing up dirt from the past are wrong, but in the heat of the argument when they're focused on winning, they can't resist the mudslinging. In an argument with one's wife, the damage might be irreparable, even leading to divorce.

To avoid trouble, one must establish clear boundaries and make a firm commitment never to overstep them, no matter how angry or hurt he is. For example, no matter what, he should never ever mention divorce. Some people spend years paying the price of a momentary slip of the tongue. If a husband conquers his evil inclination and doesn't overstep these lines, his reward will be very great, like the young man in the story above. Our sages say that the world is sustained in the merit of those who control themselves during an argument and refrain from saying what they could say.

A man whose wife returned to orthodoxy, or has been through some crisis or trauma, must be very careful to never remind her of her past mistakes and transgressions, or of the crisis that she went through. If he does, he transgresses the Torah prohibition of *onaat devorim*, of upsetting others. Even if he intends to help her, he shouldn't mention her embarrassing past unless she herself brings up the subject wants to talk about it. If he truly wants to help her, he should show her love and attention and do his best to make her happy, because joy is the best cure for the soul, as the prophet says, "They had happiness and joy, so sorrow and sighing fled" (Isaiah 35:10).

Rabbi Chaim Vital writes, "If one's wife rebukes him about matters of Heaven, he must accept her words, this is the way of humility." True humility is when one is humble with subordinates, like the members of his household and his servants. Listening to and accepting their words of rebuke and advice is a sign that one respects their opinion and is willing to learn from everyone. When one accepts chastisements and humiliations with love, his sins are atoned. The pain of the humiliations substitutes for the suffering that he was due. True repentance is to bear insult and remain silent (Likutei Moharan I:6).

Nobody likes a slap on the knuckles; in most instances, a person's pride prevents him from hearing a reprimand, no matter how justified. One tends to focus on finding fault in whoever is scolding or criticizing him, or he retaliates. A person's damaged pride stands in the way of teshuva and mending his ways. The Brisker Rov said, "When a person hears rebuke from another, sometimes his pride renders him incapable of saying, 'I sinned', even when he knows that he will suffer, and suffer he does. His pride doesn't permit him to admit his sin." When the people of Sodom attempted to capture and sodomize Lot's guests, they were smitten with blindness and other afflictions, yet they continued clamoring and trying to find the door to Lot's house and break it down.

The last person a man wants to hear a reprimand from is his wife. Sadly, most of her words of rebuke fall on deaf ears and have no effect. Too bad, for the husband is the loser on two counts:

First, his wife's rebuke is a growth opportunity for him. The old adage says that there's no smoke without fire. In that respect, even if he feels that her claims are exaggerated or unjustified, if he contemplates them earnestly, he's sure to find some substance in each one of them. A wife's feedback is invaluable, since it helps her husband grow and progress toward his soul correction, his life-long mission in this world.

Second, unloading whatever weighs heavy on her heart to an attentive husband has a magical effect on a woman. With each word she says, the pain and bitterness diminish and are replaced by a growing sense of calm and a warm glow. If she truly feels that her words are heard and accepted, then by the end of the conversation, or later in the day, she herself will approach her husband with renewed warmth and affection. The knowledge that he values her opinion and wants to improve gives her enormous satisfaction.

A husband whose pride rejects a wife's reprimand will eventually lose communication with her. She'll give up trying to tell him anything and his loss will be tremendous. He loses the opportunity to learn about himself and grow, and his wife will become more and more frustrated with him. They'll drift apart and their relationship will steadily deteriorate.

Dear husbands – our wives need to feel safe in telling us anything and everything that's on their hearts, and confident that we'll listen to them and heed their message without getting angry. Swallowing our pride is hard to do, but our rewards for doing so certainly merit the effort.

No Pressure

The "Chinuch" writes that it's impossible to list all the things that cause people pain, because each person is different. People have different degrees of sensitivity. What offends one person might not bother someone else. One must therefore be sensitive to the feelings of those around him and assure that his words and deeds don't hurt a soul, directly or indirectly, intentionally or unintentionally.

People nowadays suffer a great deal of stress. They worry about security, their income, their social standing and their future.

Some also worry about fulfilling their obligations to Hashem, and others are naturally stressed out. In any event, patience with others guarantees that we won't upset them, and also soothes their nerves.

Women are especially subject to stress. Housekeeping, child-rearing, shopping, banking, preparing meals, looking good for their husbands and, in many cases, holding down a job is a tough bill to fill. A caring husband does all he can to relieve the demands on his wife and make her life as stress-free and enjoyable as possible. By talking to her calmly and caring for her, he helps take the load off of her stress. By creating a happy and tranquil atmosphere in the home, he creates an environment that is, of itself, stress-reducing.

A sensitive husband acknowledges his wife's stress and does what he can to lighten her load. If he's smart enough to be patient and accepting whenever she doesn't get everything done, he's her best tranquilizer. By focusing on what she *does* succeed in accomplishing, praising her for it and expressing his gratitude, he recharges her batteries and gives her the strength to continue.

On the other hand, an insensitive husband adds to his wife's stress. If she's already struggling to deal with all her burdens and he asks her to do even more, or comments about what she hasn't done, he destroys her completely. Instead of caringly supporting her, he asks her curtly, "What are you so stressed about?" This makes her feel guilty for feeling stressed. If she feels pressured about things that wouldn't bother him, he makes her feel stupid about feeling pressure rather than acknowledging and appreciating her difficulties. Rather than offering his assistance, the insensitive and egocentric husband focuses on his own interests.

A tense husband must make every effort to appear calm and relaxed. He should learn from our patriarch Abraham. When

Abraham arrived in Egypt, he was worried that the Egyptians would kill him in order to take Sarah as a wife for their Pharaoh. The "Chizkuni" writes that despite this, he calmly requested of Sarah, "Please say that you're my sister, for my welfare and for your sake, and my soul will live in your virtue" (Genesis 12:13). Despite his fears, he spoke to Sarah calmly to prevent her from panicking or becoming distressed. Our sages say, "A pious person keeps his worries in his heart and joy on his face".

The man sets the tone of the house. If he's calm and easygoing, his wife and children will find their home a relaxing and happy place to be. If he's strict and ill-tempered, they won't want to be in his presence. Bad-tempered husbands wonder why their wives and children are never home…

To overcome stress and worry, one must trust in Hashem and not burden his family with his trepidations. They depend on him, and he has to depend on Hashem. If he is worried and insecure - as if he has no one to depend on - then they will lose their confidence in him. As a result, the wife and children will feel even greater stress.

Our sages teach us that late on Friday afternoon, a man should ascertain that his wife has made certain Sabbath preparations. One of these is the lighting of the Sabbath candles. Obviously, he can see if they've been lit or not. If they haven't yet been lit, he should instruct his wife to do so. Our Rabbis are careful to point out, though, that this instruction must be done in a calm and gentle manner. Lighting candles after sundown is a severe transgression of Torah, yet he is still not allowed to speak to her in a way that would upset her. If so, he certainly should be careful about maintaining a calm and pleasant tone of voice when talking to her about everyday matters.

At the end of a day's work, a husband must find time for his wife. By rushing in and rushing out again, he creates a tense atmosphere. His wife and children all want to see him and speak to him. They vie for his attention, knowing that he'll soon disappear again. This is stressful for everybody in the family. Ideally he should come home prepared to give them all some quality time and attention. If this isn't possible on a nightly basis, a father should set aside weekly one-on-one time with each of his children. A wife, though, needs quality time every day, preferably a half hour at least. Knowing that she'll have her own special time with him in the evening helps her to cope and to feel calmer all day long.

One of the sages of the Talmud would always begin his lectures with something humorous. He knew that his students were very much in awe of him, but also knew that they needed to feel at ease in order to fully absorb his teachings. The joke would relax them and open their minds for learning. The Talmud also tells a story of Elijah the prophet accompanying Rabbi Beroka in the marketplace. Elijah pointed out two men who had merited the world to come. Rabbi Beroka approached them and asked them what special mitzva they had performed. They answered that they were particularly jocular and that they would seek out the sad and downtrodden and cheer them up. The Maharsha explains, "They merited the world to come, for by cheering the downtrodden, they also brought joy to the Divine Presence, for Rabbi Meir teaches that when men are sad, the Divine Presence is sad with them."

A wife is comparable to the Divine Presence: by making her happy and relaxed, a husband also brings joy to Hashem's Divine Presence and will also merit the world to come. The Torah commands, "And he... shall cheer the wife that he has taken" (Deuteronomy 24:5) - a wife's happiness is a husband's responsibility. Her happiness is his most lucrative investment, both in this world and the next. When she's happy, he'll flourish and succeed in everything he does.

Lies

Rebbe Nachman writes in Sefer HaMiddot, "Where there is truth there is peace" (Truth I:22). Peace is only possible when a home is characterized by truth and honesty. Where there is falsehood and lies, the Divine Presence departs, for the Talmud says, "Liars will not receive the Divine Presence, as it says, 'One who speaks falsehood will not be stand before my eyes (Psalms 101:7)'." The Torah emphasizes that we must distance ourselves from dishonesty and says, "Keep *far* away from a false thing (Exodus 23:7)".

Sometimes a man is faced with the dilemma of wanting to do something that he knows his wife won't agree to. If he forgoes the idea in order to avoid arguments with her, he'll be frustrated and upset. If he goes ahead and does what he wants to, she'll be upset with him. He may then contemplate doing what he wants to secretly. He estimates that as long as she doesn't find out, they'll both be happy. In theory this works, but in practice, deceit is ultimately discovered. When his wife does find out what he did, her trust in him is shattered. Once she feels that she can't trust him, she won't be able to be close to him, and their relationship will be badly damaged. The more lies she discovers, the worse it will be.

He may have thought that he was justified in lying to her, relying on the rabbinical permit of deviating from the facts for the sake of peace, but this is mistaken. This permission was only granted for complex situations where selective truth adds to maintaining the peace. One is not permitted to tell an outright lie in order to avoid getting into trouble with others. Don't do anything wrong and you won't get into trouble.

The Vilna Gaon writes, "Lie and falsehood (two different words in Hebrew) have two different meanings. Falsehood is making a promise, intending to keep it, but ultimately reneging on it. A lie is uttering a promise that one never intended to fulfill, and words that from the start go against the truth." If you've already made a promise, then make every effort to fulfill it, otherwise you'll be guilty of falsehood. And in future before you promise, consider whether or not you'll be able to keep it. By doing this you fulfill the command to, "Guard what comes out from your mouth" (Deuteronomy 23:24).

Many men have told me that they entered into business ventures and had lied to their wives that they were only investing within their means, because they said to themselves that their wives didn't understand business matters. But in the course of time they got into huge debts and had to admit that had they listened to their wives' advice, not only would they have not got into such difficult predicaments, but they would have certainly been successful.

A very difficult challenge is a wife's telling her husband to not be in contact with his family. This puts him in a very awkward position. On the one hand, he wants to live in peace with his wife; on the other hand, he wants to honor his parents. Visiting his parents behind his wife's back will only deepen the problem. He must try to clarify the reason that she doesn't want him to visit or talk to them. It's quite possible that this is his fault, because he has been telling his about parents everything that happens in his home. This is not their business; what happens in his home is private between him and his wife. His exposing her privacy angers and insults her, especially when he tells his parents know what's going on behind her closed doors. No wonder that she wants him to stop talking to them.

A wife can't bear meddling in-laws, just as she can't bear comments and criticism from her husband. Nobody likes to feel like they're under a microscope. If a wife sees that when her husband returns from his parents his attitude towards her worsens, then she's positive that they've been badmouthing her. In that case, she'll demand that he no longer visit them.

A husband must never share his marital problems with his parents. Both he and they will definitely transgress the prohibition of slander and nothing positive will result from their discussions. His parents will no doubt take his side and deepen whatever rift has developed between them. Instead, he shouldn't tell his parents anything about it and should seek advice from a competent Rabbi. If a husband ever sees his parents trying to interfere in matters between his wife and himself, he must immediately put a stop to it and stand by his wife. His first allegiance is to her.

When it's forbidden to lie, the evil inclination encourages us to do so. When it's a mitzva to hide truth, he encourages us to be zealous with the truth. Whenever a husband returns from a visit with his family, he should say that they convey their warmest regards even though the reality may have been the exact opposite. A husband should praise his wife to his parents, even if he exaggerates. By doing so, he emulates Aaron the High Priest who would strive to bridge dissension and enhance people's love for one another. Peacemaking is a lofty mitzvah, for our sages tell us, "Be of the students of Aaron, loving peace and pursuing peace" (Avot 1:12).

Truth is the cornerstone of a home. Maharam Shik in his commentary on tractate Avot writes, "'Love truth and peace' – why is truth placed before peace? Because peace is impossible if there is no truth; when there is truth, then there is peace." Rebbe Nachman writes in Sefer HaMiddot that truth redeems one from all sorrows.

Self Correction

Self correction is our greatest and most challenging obligation in life. By improving our character, we merit a good life both in this world and the next, marital peace and success in raising our children.

Throughout the Talmud and the Zohar, our Sages that emphasize the importance of character improvement. Our sages say, "When the spirit of men is pleased with a person, the spirit of Hashem is pleased with him" (Ethics of the Fathers 3:10). Our Sages equate anger with idolatry, and arrogance with denial of Hashem's existence. They teach that the traits of humility and modesty invoke the Divine Spirit to rest on a person. Elijah the Prophet, of blessed memory, said, "The Torah can only be expounded by someone who isn't stern, and I too will not reveal myself except to someone who isn't stern. 'Who is one who merits the world to come - he who is humble'."

In the book "Tanna D'bei Eliyahu," Elijah the Prophet teaches a golden rule for how a man should conduct himself with his family. Coming from the mouth of Elijah, this rule is tantamount to a Divine directive. He says, "Be lowly and humble to all men, and to the members of your family more than to any man." We are told be "lowly and humble to all men", which means to bear insults without retaliation, and listen when others rebuke us, and we are to do this to an even greater extent with our wives.

Rabbi Chaim Vital, whose teachings come from the holy Ariza'l Rabbi Yitzchak Luria, of blessed memory, writes in his "Gates of Holiness" that, "Bad character traits are worse than actual transgressions." Hashem wants us to be more exacting about our character traits than with adhering to all the positive and negative commandments, for with good character traits, keeping the commandments is easy.

A few steps are involved in acquiring a good trait. First, one must learn about the nature of the desired trait, the paths that lead to acquiring it and the factors that detract from it. He should also weigh the benefits of acquiring the trait against the losses incurred by not doing so. Then, he should evaluate himself daily in regard to that particular trait. He should thank Hashem for whatever progress he makes and pray to Him to help him truly change and acquire the desired trait.

The journey to correct just one character flaw is long and arduous, filled with successes and failures, traps and tests. One must be incredibly tenacious to complete the journey. But when we work, we see results. As our sages say, "If you labored and achieved, you can believe it!"

The Premarital Guide

The final two chapters are a premarital guide devoted to those readers who are not yet married, and are either searching for their soul-mate or are engaged to be married. Chapter Thirteen deals with finding a mate and Chapter Fourteen provides premarital instruction for those who are engaged.

Chapter Thirteen
Finding a Mate

A person who goes on *shidduchim* (arranged dates,) and relies on the fact that he knows how to find his proper mate, is making a big mistake. Even if he makes every effort in the world, and carefully screens the prospective match – he cannot see into the depths of other souls. Since he doesn't know his previous incarnation, and the previous incarnations of others, he will never be able to know for sure which soul is his true soul mate.

This knowledge is known only by a very few great Tzadikim (righteous people) such as the Arizal (Rabbi Yitzchak Luria, the famous 16th century father of Kabbalah), who with one glance, could see the soul of the person standing before him, the correction that particular soul needed, and her previous incarnations, etc. Since this type of knowledge is concealed from simple people like us, and we lack the ability to know these things, it is therefore understood that the results of any number of screenings or investigations where a person is relying on his own limited perceptions and judgment will be no more than illusions.

Good advice

From the Torah's account of finding a soul mate for our forefather Isaac (see Genesis 24:3-27), we can learn several good pieces of advice on how to find our soul mate.

Success

When our forefather Abraham sent his servant Eliezer to find a wife for his son Yitzchak, Abraham said to Eliezer (see Genesis 24:7): "Hashem, the G-d of Heaven, will send His Angel before you." That is to say, he promised Eliezer that he would receive help from Heaven in finding a good and worthy match for Yitzchak. From here we learn that success in finding one's soul mate comes from Heaven. Since only the Creator truly knows who is a good and true match for each individual, the essence of finding one's soul mate is therefore to ask the Creator to help him in his search.

Preparation with prayer

When Eliezer set out on the mission for his master Abraham, he first prayed, and only then, took action. Our ancestral mother Leah prayed such a great deal and shed so many tears in order to merit a worthy soul mate, that her eyes were weak from so much crying (see Genesis 29:17). From here, we learn that we need to pray before taking any action. Before we turn to *shadchanim* (matchmakers) or friends or acquaintances to help us find our soul mate, we must begin by praying and asking assistance from Hashem. Hashem determines all matches! So, the way to find a good match is to pray that Hashem give us our genuine soul mate.

Hashem sees the heart

Because, in the matter of matches, we have nobody to depend upon other than Hashem, the one who is seeking his soul mate must turn to Hashem with complete trust, and not depend upon his own perceptions or intellectual assessments. Because: "A person sees the eyes, but Hashem sees the heart (Samuel I 16:7)."

A person should just increase his prayers and ask for his soul mate from Hashem. He should depend upon Hashem to lead and guide him in the right way throughout the process, until the wedding, and afterwards as well.

Therefore a person must rely on the Creator and say to Him: "Creator of the world! Only You know who my soul mate is, and I rely only on You. Please! Help me meet up with my soul mate with no confusing thoughts or obstacles!" Hashem will certainly not disappoint a person that seeks His help and guidance, and He will swiftly send him his true soul mate. Regarding this, King David said in the Psalms: "Happy is the man who trusts in You," and also: "Happy is the man who trusts in Hashem." And there are many more such examples of verses that speak of trust in Hashem.

Before every *shidduch* (prearranged date with marital intentions), a person should ask Hashem - who is the Number One Matchmaker - to help him and enlighten him in making the right decision, free from doubts and fears, etc. And he should say: "Creator of the World! Please have mercy on me, and help me to make the right decision on this date, because You know that I completely lack the ability to know anything in the matter of soul mates."

Paving the way

Prayer paves the way to a successful match. First, one should pray to find his soul mate. Then, he should pray for the success of the meetings with his prospective soul mate, which hopefully should accomplish their purpose easily and quickly and without a need for excessive meetings, which often lead to suffering and confusion. That's not all; he should pray for every imaginable detail, such as the success of the wedding. Nothing should be taken for granted. Both bride and groom should pray that their families should get along, that they find a suitable and affordable place to live, and that they have an adequate income. Both should pray for marital bliss, peace, harmony, mutual respect, and a communicative, loving, and healthy relationship. They should ask for Hashem's blessing that they'll always help one another, that neither he nor she will be sterile or infertile, and that they merit having righteous children. A man should pray that his wife have a good and charitable character, and so forth.

Up until now, we have learned the first and most important lesson from the story of our Forefather Isaac's search for his soul mate: Prayer.

Good character traits

The second thing we learn from the story of our Forefather Isaac's search for a soul mate is the importance of good character traits. Like the great sage Rabbi Shach, of blessed and saintly memory, said: "The main thing you should look for, is that she possess good character traits, for this quality encompasses all others." We see that even Eliezer, Abraham's servant, checked only to see that Rebecca possessed a good character, and that she performed acts of loving-kindness and generosity.

Even when the well-waters rose up toward her, (see Genesis 24:16), it wasn't this miracle that proved to Eliezer that Rebecca was suited and destined for his master's son Isaac, but rather, when she acted towards him and his helpers in an extremely charitable manner. Rebecca's kindness proved to him that she was the woman worthy of Isaac.

The great Rabbi Yechezkel Levenstein explains this in a similar fashion: "Although it was necessary that the wife of Isaac would continue in the path of our Foremother Sarah, peace be upon her, in converting the women, and helping to spread emuna in the world, nevertheless, Eliezer didn't look for a woman with sophisticated religious philosophies, but rather, a generous, kind, and loving woman, who was not selfish or self-centered. A woman like this has the ability to receive truth, and give it over to others.

The task begins

Beyond checking the obvious and basic criteria, one should not try to be too clever by probing, testing, and analyzing too much. Why? Before the wedding, it is impossible for the couple to really know each other in depth, for that's the work that only begins when the couple begins to live together. Only then do they truly get to know one another. And then they begin to build and establish a true bond - a marriage built upon much compromise, patience, concerted effort, and a true desire to build together.

It is very important that a person does not fool himself into thinking that he is marrying a perfect person, because there is no such thing. One must know from the start that every person has shortcomings and failings. Just as each individual knows that he himself is not perfect, so too his wife is not perfect. The whole purpose of the wedding is to learn to live together with love, and to help each other perfect themselves.

Character improvement doesn't happen overnight. Even when a person puts forth much effort, prayer, and study, character improvement is a slow and painstaking process. Like the great Gaon of Vilna said: "It is easier to know the entire Talmud, than to fix even one character trait."

Therefore, the first thing the husband needs to learn is to live with his wife's shortcomings. His focus should always be on her positive traits and on the fact that her shortcomings are nothing compared to the wonderful qualities she possesses. The bottom line is that he should deeply love his wife just the way she is.

A prospective husband must remember – getting married means hard work. Until now, you lived in your parents' home and they didn't ask much of you. On the contrary, they pampered you and understood you. Or, maybe you lived in a different framework such as a dormitory, that didn't involve much emotional attachment or mutual responsibility. In such a non-committal framework, any person with even minimal social skills can get by. Now that you are married, life's real work begins. Know and remember this well: The whole purpose of your getting married is to enable you to truly get to work on improving your character. Realizing that the entire purpose of the wedding is to prepare a person for the true service of Hashem is the best possible preparation for married life. When a person knows this - and prepares himself for this - he will gain the strength and the patience to withstand anything, and he will certainly succeed in building an everlasting edifice in Israel. A home of beauty and harmony, from which beautiful and good fruit will be brought forth into the world.

Every good home that produced upright generations, righteous people and our nation's spiritual leaders did so through much toil, effort, and serious work. There isn't a couple in the world, even amongst the very righteous, that had it easy right from the start of their marriage with instant *shalom bayit* (marital peace). Rather, it is certain that they had a big task to complete. The strength they had to work so hard for peace in the home stemmed from the fact that they knew what to expect. They knew that a marriage is hard work, and they prepared themselves for this. Therefore, they were able to withstand all the difficulties and challenges. Happy are they, and happy is their lot.

The arrogant lose

It's vital a man not be arrogant and picky, because ultimately, they are liable to miss out on meeting their soul mate. The Steipler Rav, of blessed and saintly memory, commented on the phenomena of the many older and unmarried Yeshiva students: "This is a sickness, when those because of their excessive arrogance, lose their true intended matches with their own two hands."

He with the inflated ego imagines himself to be something really special, and in need of a woman like him, who possesses every conceivable attribute. Subsequently, every girl he meets is not good enough for him. Time goes on and he wastes some of the best years of his life, searching for the *shidduch* worthy of him - a woman who's a mere product of his imagination. Ultimately, he drops out of Torah learning, becomes a ball of nerves, and the years march on. In the end, with no other choice, he just marries anybody.

The Steipler Rav added with great emotion and heartache: "Behold! Many older men come to me, with tears on their cheeks. 'Where is my *bat ploni*?' (Forty days before a baby is conceived, a Heavenly voice decrees: '*bat ploni*, The daughter of such and such, for *ben ploni*, the son of such and such'). I reply, 'you already met her, many years ago, when people first began recommending *shidduchim* to you, and you rejected her. She didn't find favor in your eyes because of some foolish reason. She got married long ago to somebody else.'" This is the fate of an arrogant heart walking a twisted path.

Young men forfeit their intended when they reject a marital proposition without consulting a reliable spiritual guide. *Da'at Torah* (a Torah-based opinion from a rabbinical scholar,) would have advised them not to turn down a certain proposal, namely, the *shidduch* most likely destined from Heaven.

The choice is up to you

The Steipler Rav also said: "When our Sages say that forty days before a child's conception, a Heavenly voice issues forth and proclaims, 'the daughter of so-and-so for the son of such-and-such' - this is not a decree which must happen, and it is not certain that they will marry. Rather, the Heavenly voice proclaims that this is the right way, and she is suitable for him, and he can find her with ease, and the Heavenly assistance will be in this direction. But even so, there remains free choice. A person, through his actions, can cause it to come about, that he will not merit her, and she will not be his."

The current circumstance is what counts

In light of the above, a person might be mistaken and think that he lost his soul mate, especially if he knows that he committed many transgressions. Not So! *Teshuva* is always effective, and Hashem can do anything. He has plenty of matches, and can find one for anyone. Therefore, pray to Hashem, and ask Him for forgiveness in acting with arrogance up until today and rejecting the proposals that Hashem sent, since one of them could have been the true soul mate. Ask Hashem for a new beginning, and to mercifully send your true intended. Hashem will have mercy and will send a good match, as we have witnessed with our own eyes. Many young men who came to the Yeshiva and did *teshuva* merited good wives and righteous children. Happy are they.

And it is said in the name of the great Saint, Rabbi Eliyahu Lopian, of blessed and saintly memory: "A person's match is made according to the deeds he performs now - in the present - at the time of his *shidduchim*, and not according to his deeds of the past, and not according to his future deeds. Rather, he is matched according to his deeds now, as he is today."

Chapter Fourteen
Premarital instruction

The most beautiful life

Mazal Tov! You are about to begin a new life of partnership, love, peace, and joy. The step you are about to take and the bond you're about to make are the loveliest things there are in this world. Nothing is comparable to the beauty of love between a man and a woman.

Read the vital advice in these pages to prepare yourself for receiving the happiness that awaits you. This premarital instruction manual will help you attain long-lasting success in your married life.

Prepare yourself for life

Proper preparation is the key to marital success. Like anything else in life, the better the preparation, the higher the chances of success, especially in the case of marital bliss.

It's no problem to get up in the morning and get married. You don't have to be a genius to rent a hall, hire a band and a photographer, or to choose the menu. The important part is what happens *after* the wedding ceremony and reception, being able to live in peace and harmony. This is no small problem, since modern reality shows that few couples succeed in attaining true marital harmony. On the contrary, disagreement, faulty communication, and misunderstanding characterize most marital relationships. Unfortunately, that's why divorce rates are so high.

Marriage isn't a summer vacation or a walk in the park; it's much more complex. A husband and a wife must learn to live together for years. With Hashem's blessing, they'll have children and will need to educate them. These are not simple endeavors. Not only do they require serious instruction, but a large measure of help from Above.

It's amazing that in any serious field where one person affects another person – such as driving a car, practicing law or medicine, or even cutting hair – one is required to learn theory, acquire practical skills, and gain experience as an intern or understudy. Then, the person must prove his knowledge by passing a series of exams, frequently both in theory and in practice. Only then does he receive a license for driving a car, practicing law or medicine, or giving another person a haircut.

Getting married without premarital instruction is tantamount to getting behind the wheel of a car without ever having learned to drive. We all understand how an untrained and unlicensed driver could wreck other people's lives. Marriage is much more complex than driving a car; untrained people often lack understanding about the true meaning of marriage and its responsibilities. Therefore, they're prone to head-on collisions with their spouses.

Although the law doesn't require premarital instruction, any person with common sense would obligate himself to prepare adequately for marriage. One eats the fruit of his own proper preparation, as do all those that are and will be dependent on him. Indirectly, the whole world will benefit as well.

The wedding day

A well-known rule says that everything goes according to the beginning. If the beginning is good, the continuation will be good as well. The beginning of married life is the wedding day.

The Kotzker Rebbe said: "The wedding day is the biggest day in a person's life... too bad it's wasted on children!" His connotation is that young couples have no idea about the unfathomable value of the wedding day, a day when it's possible to move mountains and to set the tone for their entire lives together.

Therefore, before you stand under the *chuppa*, the wedding canopy, you should know what's about to take place and how you should act. The customs of the Jewish matrimonial ceremony are not only rooted in ancient tradition, but they have deep inner meaning. As such, this section of the book will help familiarize you with the order of the day.

Stage One – The Ketuba

When the *chattan*, the bridegroom, arrives at the wedding hall, the officiating rabbi sits with him and fills out the details for the *ketuba*, the Jewish marriage contract.

The *chattan* must know that the *ketuba* is no joke – it's a binding and obligating agreement. As soon as he signs the agreement, he is duty-bound to fulfill its conditions.

Usually, before a person signs a contract, he reads the fine print, consults experts and especially a legal advisor, and clarifies all the ramifications of each clause. Then, he deliberates on each clause, its pros and cons, and so forth. Frequently, a single word in the contract can become the subject of hours of negotiations.

In short, a prudent person doesn't sign an agreement without knowing what he's signing.

By signing the *ketuba*, one assumes a life-long obligation not only to his wife, but to Hashem as well. He does this in the presence of parents, family, rabbis, and the whole congregation. This behooves him to know what he's signing.

By knowing his obligations, a *chattan* spares himself untold grief in the future. Much of the agony that men suffer in marriage stems from their failure to fulfill the conditions of the *ketuba* and therefore invoke upon themselves severe judgments from Above. This is because they signed an agreement and accepted a solemn obligation which they fail to fulfill. Ignorance about the terms of the agreement is no excuse for breaching the terms of the agreement. Therefore, learning the terms and nature of the agreement is extremely important. Hidden within the *ketuba* are intrinsic instructions as to how a husband should act, as well as hints for marital success.

The text of the *ketuba* is written in Aramaic. Here, we present an approximate but comprehensible translation in English, to make it easier on the English-speaking bridegroom to familiarize himself with the *ketuba*.

The monetary denomination that appears in the ketuba is the *zuz*. The ketuba deals with three different sums: **the basic ketuba, the dowry, and the supplement**. The basic ketuba is a fixed sum of 200 zuz (the currency in Talmudic times) for a first marriage and 100 zuz for a second marriage. The woman's dowry consists of the possessions she brought to the marriage, which the husband's estate must return to her upon death or divorce. Originally, the dowry was itemized but in order to avoid public humiliation, the sum is fixed at 100 pieces of pure silver (about $14,000) for a first marriage and half of that for a second marriage. The third sum in the ketuba is the supplement that the groom adds to enhance his obligation. The accepted supplement is designed to equal the dowry. In some communities and in rich families, an additional supplement is added.

Text of the Ketuba

With Divine assistance

On the _____ day of the week, the _____ day of the month of _____, in the year five thousand seven hundred _____, as we reckon time here in the city of _____, the groom _____ son of _____ said to the bride _____ daughter of _____: "Be my wife according to the statutes of Moses and Israel. And I will work for, cherish, feed and support you as is the custom of Jewish men who work for, cherish, feed and support their wives faithfully. And I will give you _____ and I will provide you food and clothing and necessities and your conjugal rights according to accepted custom." And the bride _____ agreed to become his wife. And this dowry that she brought from her _____ house, whether in silver, gold, jewelry, clothing, furnishings or bedding, the groom _____ accepted responsibility for all in the sum of _____ zuzim, and agreed to add to this amount from his own assets the sum of _____ zuzim, for a total of _____ zuzim. The groom _____ said: "The obligation of this ketuba, this dowry and this additional sum, I accept upon myself and my heirs after me, to be paid from all the best part of all my property that I now possess or may hereafter acquire, real and personal. From this day forward, all my property, even the shirt on my back, shall be mortgaged and collateral for the payment of this ketuba, dowry and additional sum, whether during my lifetime or thereafter." The obligation of this ketuba, this dowry and this additional sum, was accepted by _____ the groom with the strictness established for ketubot and additional sums customary for the daughters of Israel, in accordance with the decrees by our sages, of blessed memory. This ketuba is not to be regarded as a mere formality or as a perfunctory legal form. We have established the acceptance on the part of _____ son of _____ the groom to _____ daughter of _____ the bride, of this contract, all of which is stated and specified above, with an article fit for that purpose.

And all shall be valid and clear and binding.

Signed_____ Witness

Signed_____ Witness

Although there are many different texts, the above is the text most widely used in Orthodox communities of the USA, Canada, and the UK.

The power of giving

The first characteristic of the ketuba that grabs our attention is that it's one-sided. The groom gets nothing but gives everything – ring, food, clothing, necessities, livelihood and obligations, both emotional and material. He promises to cherish her and obligates himself to sell the shirt off his back to meet his responsibilities, yet she doesn't commit to anything other than agreeing to marry him. What's going on here?

We see that the ketuba is a list of the husband's commitments to his wife, both on a spiritual and on a material level, signed in his own free will with a smile and an open hand.

According to Kabbalah, the male is the giver and the female is the recipient. The principle is expressed in the ketuba, and it teaches us a prerequisite to happy and healthy married life: Just like the sun shines its light on the moon, the husband should be the giver while the wife should be the recipient.

For example, a husband must respect his wife, compliment her, give her gifts, and fulfill her needs. The wife isn't required to do likewise.

If a husband never forgets the rule that the male is the giver, then he'll always enjoy marital peace. The notion of the male as the donor and the female as the recipient is intrinsic in creation. The reproduction process operates in this manner. So, as soon as a man wants to be on the receiving end, he's going against the grain of creation. If he demands respect, attention, and other amenities, then he takes on the role of a female, since he now wants to be a recipient. When that happens, the whole household turns upside down. Two females cannot possibly connect like a male and a female can.

She looks to you

The ketuba is the husband's public declaration that: "With Hashem's help, I'll work for, cherish, feed and support you as is the custom of Jewish men who work for, cherish, feed and support their wives *faithfully*." Faithfully means straightforward, in truth, without shirking responsibility or acting contemptibly, Heaven forbid.

Later in the ketuba, the husband accepts and assumes complete responsibility to fulfill all the obligations of the ketuba, even if he must sell *all* his worldly assets, including the shirt off his back. He signs his name in public to these commitments, thus giving his word of honor.

Get a job!

The very first words at the top of the ketuba are: "With Divine assistance." By invoking Hashem's help in all his obligations, the bridegroom binds himself to emuna, the pure and complete faith in Hashem. Emuna is the only way he'll be able to fulfill his obligations. Yet, right after invoking Divine assistance, the husband commits to work. In this manner, our sages are teaching us by way of the ketuba text that a husband is obligated to supply all his wife's needs honorably, even if he's required to do hard labor. Our sages thereby silence the lazy, the irresponsible, and the "holy believers" that send their penniless wives to Hashem, saying: "The Almighty provides! Go ask Him for what you need."

The assorted "deadbeats" not only fail to fulfill their solemn obligations, but they complain about the lack of faith of their wives. A typical "holy deadbeat" preaches to his unfortunate wife: "Don't you have any emuna? Our lack of money comes from Hashem – that's the way Hashem wants us to live! Accept poverty with love! Don't you believe that everything is for the best…" The deadbeat husband doesn't provide his wife with money to pay the bills; instead, he gives hours of his warped sermons. Even worse, he's angry at her "lack of trust" in Hashem.

Our wise sages knew all about the proverbial deadbeat; they therefore incorporated the clause within the ketuba that obligates the husband to work. They virtually tell him: "If you lack the wherewithal to provide for your wife in an honorable manner, then get a job! The ketuba doesn't require you to teach your wife emuna, and certainly not on her expense. Your ketuba says that you'll 'work for, cherish, feed and support' your wife, and not lecture her about emuna and trust. Nothing in religious law requires a wife to sign an obligation to attend her husband's lectures."

Cherish

The husband's commitment to cherish the wife is so important that it precedes his obligation to support her, since the ketuba requires him to "work for, **cherish**, feed and support." "Cherish" includes both love and respect. Our sages in their wisdom understood that a woman needs love and respect even before she needs bread and water. Even if a husband gives his wife an unlimited budget and an open checkbook, if he fails to give her love and respect, he starves her soul. Suffering emotional malnutrition, she loses all joy and her life isn't worth living with such a man.

Cherishing a wife means no comments or criticism, and certainly not exposing her to anger and verbal abuse. You don't argue with a person you cherish. When a husband cherishes his wife, he compliments her incessantly; he ignores her faults and focuses on her virtues, and gives her the feeling that she's the best woman on earth.

Another reason that "cherish" comes before "support" is that Jewish law requires a husband not only to provide for his wife, but to do so in a respectful and loving manner. If he gives her a cashier's check for a million dollars while snarling and hissing through his teeth, then it's worthless to her.

Faithfully

After the husband commits to cherish his wife, he obligates himself to provide all her necessities, "faithfully." Faithfully means that it's not just word of mouth, but a solemn commitment. It also means that he doesn't have the attitude that he's doing her a favor, for on this condition, she agreed to marry him.

"Faithfully" also reminds the husband of the very first words that are written at the top of the ketuba: "With Divine assistance."

Faith, or emuna, is the best way to invoke Divine assistance. Therefore, the primary requirement of a husband is that he be a man of emuna. All his commitments – his wife's food, clothing, necessities, and conjugal rights – should all be fulfilled in a faithful manner.

A good husband must constantly reinforce his emuna. Emuna enables him to weather life's difficult tests, to strengthen and encourage his wife, to promise her whatever she wants even if he temporarily lacks the wherewithal to fulfill her request, and to avoid showing her a worried or troubled countenance. She should never feel that he's shirking his responsibility.

A husband should never say no to a wife's request with an answer like: "I can't afford it" or, "I don't have any money." He certainly shouldn't throw the responsibility on her shoulders, either. Even if he doesn't have a dime to his name, he should comfort her, encourage her, and promise that he'll fulfill her wishes as soon as he possibly can. And, when the wife sees her husband making every effort to provide all her needs, then her soul shines with joy. The illumination of a wife's soul is a wonderful vessel for the blessings of livelihood and abundance.

The same goes for the blessing of children. Our ancestral great grandmother Rachel complained to her husband our ancestral great grandfather Jacob that she wanted children. He replied impatiently: "Do you think that I'm Hashem, that I can make such a promise?" Hashem was upset with Jacob for his curt and inconsiderate response to his wife. It seems that Jacob was right; how can he promise his wife children? Our sages answer that he should have soothed and comforted her, promising to do everything in his power – both physically and spiritually – to obtain for her the blessing of children. He shouldn't have forsaken his share of responsibility.

When a husband shines the light of emuna and trust on his wife, she becomes a vessel for whatever blessing of abundance she needs. Even if her wishes fail to materialize for the time being, his encouragement and empathy comfort her so much that she doesn't feel the sting of want.

Conjugal rights

Conjugal rights are an important mitzvah that the husband commits to. He must be available to her on her immersion night and at least once a week during the days when she's ritually pure. A husband that slights his wife in this area causes her untold anguish, not because her sexual appetite is so great, but because her soul needs to feel that her husband loves her. This is one of the best times to strengthen and cement a relationship.

Jewish law states that conjugal relations are only permissible with the wife's consent. If she's angry or upset, he should first placate her.

Truly beautiful conjugal relations require modesty and complete privacy. Children shouldn't be in the same bedroom with parents, or in a situation where they might see or hear what's going on. *Halacha* (Jewish religious law) does allow a baby that can't yet speak to be in his or her own crib in the same room.

Kosher witnesses

The two witnesses should be chosen according to halachic requirements, and not according to considerations of prestige and the like. A witness should be an upright Sabbath-observant individual that is not related to either the bride or the groom. Many people make the mistake of bestowing family members or people that don't observe the Sabbath with the honor of being a witness. Not only is this erroneous, but it invalidates the entire marital ceremony.

Kosher ketuba

A couple must have a kosher ketuba to marry. Once, a couple failed to have children for many years. It turned out that their ketuba was invalid; shortly after a rabbinical judge wrote a corrected ketuba for them, they were blessed with a child.

On an esoteric level, the soul signs a solemn commitment to observe all the Torah's mitzvas when it's still in the upper world. As far as the mitvas listed in the ketuba go, the husband signs a commitment in this world as well.

Married already?

Even if you're already married or if you've been married for years now, if you've never learned about your ketuba and what it obligates you to do, do so now without further delay.

Stage Two – Veiling the bride

Before the chuppa ceremony, the groom covers the bride's face with a veil. According to esoteric tradition, this custom is propitious for being blessed with children. As such, this is a wonderful time for the husband to pray in his heart for children. Tradition states that a transparent veil does not have this propitious quality, so one should use a veil that's not transparent.

Remember, the chuppa is not just a ceremony of perfunctory rituals. Everything done under the chuppa is deeply rooted in ancient tradition. The fact that our forefather Jacob didn't know that Rachel was switched with Leah under the chuppa testifies that Leah wasn't wearing a see-through veil.

The groom sanctifies his bride when he says: "You are hereby sanctified in matrimony to me according to **the laws of Moses and Israel**, and not according to the laws of the photographer or the program director. A couple with emuna shouldn't let anyone else sway them into forfeiting the blessings that a traditional chuppa ceremony invokes. This is a once-in-a-lifetime affair, so they should ignore extraneous considerations like social pressure and do things right.

Every custom under the chuppa is important. Therefore, one shouldn't allow those who are not faithful to Jewish tradition to "run the show." Jewish tradition shouldn't be bent or warped by the considerations or the convenience of the waiters, the photographers, the band, the wedding hall manager or anyone else.

Dear bridegroom, maybe you and your kalla don't adhere to the Jewish laws of modesty. Yet, since the evening of your chuppa is holy of holies that will influence the rest of your lives together, try to avoid foreign customs such as kissing under the chuppa or wearing provocative dress, Heaven forbid! This is the most important day of your life, and it's therefore critical to begin on the right foot, without sin and transgressions.

Jewish customs exemplify the holiness of the Jewish people. This separates them from the nations of the earth that do all sorts of lewd things during the wedding ceremony and end up divorcing shortly thereafter.

The custom of completely covering the bride's face under the wedding canopy symbolizes the fact that from this moment on – for the rest of her life – looking at her face is the privilege of her husband only. For that reason, the groom walks over to the woman's side of the partition to cover the bride's face, rather than having the bride come to the men's side, where other men would see her.

The moment the bride's face is covered, she is no longer considered single. No one has the right to look at her – neither the officiating rabbi nor the witnesses, and certainly not the guests. The bride's beauty now becomes the special treasure of her husband. She should no longer desire to make herself attractive for anyone else in the world. She is his and he is hers.

The two fathers and the two witnesses accompany the groom when he goes to cover the bride's face. The two witnesses must see with their own eyes that the groom covers the bride's face. The groom alone must cover her face with no outside assistance.

Afterwards, the men escort the groom to the *chuppa*, while the bride, escorted by both mothers, follows. The groom should always take the first step up to the *chuppa* with his right foot, for the right side in Jewish esoteric thought symbolizes *chessed*, or loving-kindness.

Stage Three – Under the Chuppa

Actually, the groom should recite the nuptial blessings. But, our sages prescribed that someone else should recite the blessings, to avoid embarrassing a groom that doesn't know how to recite them properly.

The nuptial blessings are very important, for they invoke blessings for the newly married couple that will accompany them all the days of their life together. Therefore, only those people who know how to pronounce the blessings properly and to say them with the proper intent should recite them during the ceremony. He who recites the blessings must also have the intent to say them in behalf of the *chattan* and *kalla*.

Preferably, the officiating rabbi should say all the blessings, unless there are upright and learned guests who are capable of doing so with proper intent. At any rate, the *chattan* and *kalla* should listen carefully to the blessings with the intent of fulfilling their obligation as if they themselves recited them. If not, then the blessings are in vain.

Blessing of the wine

This is the first blessing under the chuppa:

Blessed are You, Hashem, our God, King of the universe, Who creates the fruit of the vine.

Our Talmudic sages said (tractate Berachot, 35): "One should recite songs of praise with wine." Therefore, Jewish ceremonial occasions begin with a blessing over wine. Wine has a special importance. We begin our Sabbath meals with Kiddush, the blessing over the wine, for the Torah commands us to "remember and observe" the Sabbath. Our sages teach that the "remembrance" should be with something of importance, namely, a cup of wine, since wine is considered the most prestigious of drinks in the Jewish tradition.

Betrothal

Immediately after the blessing of the wine comes the blessing of betrothal:

Blessed are You, Hashem, our God, King of the universe, Who has sanctified us with His commandments, and has commanded us regarding forbidden unions; Who forbade

betrothed women to us, and permitted women who are married to us through canopy and consecration. Blessed are You, Hashem, Who sanctifies His people Israel through canopy and consecration.

This is a blessing over the mitzvah that prohibits forbidden unions. The husband hereby accepts the solemn commitment that his wife is now the only woman in the world that's permitted to him, and even this is conditional on proper ritual consecration. As long as she is not consecrated properly, she too is forbidden to him.

At this point, a husband accepts the commitment to refrain from forbidden unions, to guard his holy covenant by refraining from any illicit sexual activity, and to look at no other women other than his wife. Adultery begins with the eyes; therefore, our sages warned that looking at other women is tantamount to adultery.

When the bride's face was covered with the veil, she committed to reveal her beauty to her husband only and to refrain from any personal relationship with any other man. Now, the husband accepts his reciprocal commitment with a solemn blessing that's said with Hashem's Holy Name. He pledges thereby not to look at any other woman other than his wife, and certainly to avoid any personal connection with any other woman.

Consecration and ring

Now, the groom places the ring on the kalla's index finger and says: **Behold, you are consecrated to me by means of this ring, according to the ritual of Moses and Israel.**

The term "consecrated to me" means especially and exclusively mine. This behooves the woman to distance and separate herself from any other man in the world. Even though the woman is commanded to maintain her modesty, her power to do so depends on her husband. In other words, if her husband fulfills his obligations to meet her emotional needs – particularly love, respect, and attention – then she won't have any problem remaining faithful to him always, since she lacks nothing. But, if her husband fails to meet her emotional needs, she'll develop a thirst for love, attention, and respect. At first, she'll complain bitterly and become belligerent. Ultimately, her faithfulness might be ruined.

The Shehechiyanu Blessing

At this point, Sefardim make the Shehechiyanu blessing over a new tallit (prayer shawl). In addition, they keep in mind all the wonderful new blessings in their life – the occasion of the wedding ceremony, the new bride, the new clothes, apartment, furniture, and so forth. The groom says the blessing for himself and for his bride; her intent is to thank Hashem for all the new blessings in her life.

Reading of the Ketuba

The officiating rabbi or a guest scholar reads the ketuba, followed by the groom and the witnesses signing of the ketuba.

Acquisition, oath, and signature

The groom commits to ten basic things in the ketuba: food: clothing: conjugal relations: a sum of money assigned to the ketuba: medical care when the need arises: redemption from captivity: burial if she dies within his lifetime: to allow her to remain in his house if he dies before her: food for her daughters: and rights of inheritance of the ketuba to her sons.

The principle obligations include other side obligations such as a place to live, a promise not to take another wife, a commitment not to sell or mortgage her property without her express consent, and many other fine points that we won't elaborate on now. For the ketuba to assume full legal validity, the groom must do an act of acquisition, by raising an object such as a clean handkerchief or a fountain pen.

The Seven Marriage Blessings

The seven marriage blessings under the chuppa and afterwards during each of the seven festive days are obligatory blessings for the chattan, but as mentioned above, our sages prescribed that someone else should recite the blessings, to avoid embarrassing a groom that doesn't know how to recite them properly. One who can understand and pronounce the blessings properly should recite them. It's very important that the chattan and kalla listen to the blessings with the intent of fulfilling their obligation through the person that is making the blessing.

The first blessing: **Blessed are You, Hashem, our God, King of the universe, Who creates the fruit of the vine.**

As we explained previously, Jewish ceremonial occasions begin with a blessing over wine.

The second blessing: **Blessed are You, Hashem, our God, King of the universe, Who has created everything for His glory.**

This is a message to the chattan: you should be taking a wife in order to enhance Hashem's glory, and not for your own glory and enjoyment.

The third blessing: **Blessed are You, Hashem, our God, King of the universe, Who fashioned the Man.**

The chattan now blesses Hashem in becoming a complete person, for up until now - before he found his soul mate - he was incomplete.

The fourth blessing: **Blessed are You, Hashem, our God, King of the universe, Who fashioned the Man in His image, in the image of his likeness and prepared for him - from himself - a building for eternity. Blessed are You, Hashem, Who fashioned the Man.**

Here, the chattan expresses his gratitude to Hashem for creating mankind in the Divine image. From this human created in the Divine image, Hashem took a rib and built from it a "building for eternity." The wife, created from that rib as in the story of Adam and Eve, is therefore the husband's "building for eternity." Without her, he has no house and no home. Our sages therefore would refer to their wives as their "home."

Don't think that only Eve was created from a part of Adam. An intrinsic part of creation is that each man feels (when he's doing his job as a husband) that his wife is a part of him like his own limbs. Therefore, our sages said: "One's wife is tantamount to one's own body."

A husband should therefore avoid anger at all costs, for being angry at her is like being angry at his own body. He should always empathize with her, rejoicing in her happiness and cringing at her pain. Rabbi Aryeh Levin of blessed memory once escorted his wife to the doctor when she experienced severe leg pains. When the doctor asked what the problem was, Rabbi Aryeh spoke up and said: "Our leg hurts us!" He felt her pain as if it were his own.

The fifth blessing: **Bring intense joy and exultation to the barren one through the ingathering of her children amidst**

her in joy. Blessed are You, Hashem, Who gladdens Zion through her children.

This blessing is a prayer for the rebuilding of Jerusalem and the ingathering of the exiles. The text compares Jerusalem to a barren woman, and we pray to see the rejoicing of Jerusalem, the full redemption of our people, and the ingathering of the exiles. With her children (the Jewish people) in her midst, Zion (holy Jerusalem) is no longer childless.

Any home built on the foundations of peace and love hastens the *Geula*, the full redemption of our people. Therefore, when a husband and wife build such a home, it's as if they rebuilt one of the ruins of Jerusalem.

Since a proper matrimonial ceremony hastens the full redemption of our people, this is the proper time to pray for the rebuilding of Jerusalem.

The sixth blessing: **Gladden the beloved friends as You gladdened Your creation in the Garden of Eden from of old. Blessed are You, Hashem, Who gladdens groom and bride.**

This blessing is very deep. First, the groom and bride are called "beloved friends." This teaches us that friendship should be the basis of a relationship. First of all, a husband and wife should be best friends that enjoy each other's company, cooperate and help each other, communicate freely and openly, and are loyal to one another.

The main part of the blessing is asking Hashem to bless the young couple as he blessed Adam and Eve in the Garden of Eden. In effect, this is a blessing that they be satisfied with their lot in life – the husband should be satisfied with his wife and the wife should be satisfied with her husband. Adam and Eve had each other and no one else to compare to; as such, they had no jealousy or competition. A relationship devoid of jealousy and competition is truly a blessing.

The young couple is blessed with joy because a person's main joy is happiness with his lot in life, when he never looks at other people of compares himself with them. He's happy with whatever Hashem gives him. The husband and wife should feel just like Adam and Eve: just as they were created especially for each other, so should a husband and wife feel like they, too, were created especially for each other.

The seventh blessing: **Blessed are You, Hashem, our God, King of the universe, Who created joy and gladness, groom and bride, mirth, joyous song, pleasure, delight, love, brotherhood, peace, and friendship. Hashem, our God, let there soon be heard in the cities of Judah and the streets of Jerusalem the sound of joy and the sound of gladness, the voice of the groom and the voice of the bride, the sound of the grooms' jubilance from their canopies and of youths from their song-filled feasts. Blessed are You, Hashem, Who gladdens the groom with the bride.**

This is a very special blessing. Hashem created a spiritual couple – joy and gladness – to accompany the physical couple, the groom and the bride, along with all the other spiritual guests of honor, mirth, joyous song, pleasure, delight, love, brotherhood, peace, and friendship.

The more the groom and the bride cling together in a true spiritual union, the more the spiritual "guests" of the wedding ceremony and the week of *sheva berachot* (seven days of feasting) will become permanent residents in their home.

With love, brotherhood, peace, and friendship in the home, one can expect to hear the joy and gladness of the full redemption of our people. A home of peace and love in the material world creates unity between The Holy One (Hashem) and the Divine Presence (the Shechina) in the spiritual world. Unity between the material world and the spiritual world invokes the Divine Presence to dwell in the material world as well. Therefore, when couples live in peace, they literally build the Holy Temple in Jerusalem, since they make this world a suitable dwelling place for holiness.

The opposite also holds true. Strife in a household and divorce are tantamount to the destruction of the Holy Temple. They perpetuate exile and Diaspora, since the Divine Presence can't stand a world of turmoil. Peace is the best vessel for holiness. As such, the chuppa is a unique opportunity to invoke the Divine Presence and to expedite the *Geula*, the full redemption of our people, especially when the young couple is committed to building a home of love and peace.

Remembrance of the destruction

After the blessings, the groom stamps on a glass and shatters it in remembrance of the destruction of the Holy Temple in Jerusalem. He recites a passage from Psalm 137, and says: "If I forget you, O Jerusalem, may my right hand wither! May my tongue stick to my palate if I don't remember you, if I won't ascend to Jerusalem ahead of my greatest joy!" Our sages require us to remember the destruction of Jerusalem at every joyous occasion, to remind us that no joy is complete without the Divine Presence within our midst. Until Hashem rebuilds his Holy Temple in the material world, we can't fully rejoice.

Summary

The objective of the Jewish wedding ceremony, the rituals, and the blessings are all designed to teach us the proper way of married life. The foundation principle is that the male is the giver and the female is the receiver. The groom takes on a long list of obligations and responsibilities, while the female obligates to nothing other than being a wife.

Our sages thereby teach us the respective roles of the husband and the wife. The husband gives and plays the role of the "influencer", in Hebrew *mashpia*, he who gives abundance. The wife receives and plays the role of the "influenced", in Hebrew *mushpa*, he who receives abundance. When this is the case, the marriage is healthy and there is a climate conducive to peace and harmony. In an opposite situation, when a husband expects to receive, he takes on the spiritual role of a female. With two competing females, the home becomes a battleground since it goes against the grain of nature and creates friction rather than harmony. Therefore, a husband must give freely with no expectations of anything in return.

Enjoy the sweetness

In effect, there's no reward and punishment in the world. Hashem says: (Devorim, ch. 30) "I have given you today life and the good, and also death and the bad." With no surprises, the Torah describes two different path – that of the blessings and that of the curses. Each person has the free choice to choose whichever path he or she wants.

If we choose the path of Torah, and we listen to the teachings and advice of our sages, we enjoy the sweetness of this world. Torah, mitzvoth, and emuna are all like honey on our tongues. On the other hand, the path of agnosticism, transgressions, arrogance, and stress give life a bitter aftertaste. We alone decide what we want – the choice is ours.

If a person decides to drink poison, contaminate his brain with lewd images and thoughts, and to gaze at women, he shouldn't be surprised if he feels bad...

Hashem pleads with us: "For your own welfare – choose life!"

In Psalm 34, King David says: "Evil topples the wicked," in other words, the transgressor suffers from tribulations that he brought on himself with his unfortunate choices. The suffering of the evil is not a punishment, but merely the outcome of making choices that go against the Torah.

If a person chooses life, in other words, a life according to the advice of Torah, he can expect to enjoy the sweetness of a good and satisfying tour of duty on this earth. Even if up until now he has consumed spiritual poison, there's still hope. Hashem, in His magnificent compassion, has given us a spiritual antidote that completely reverses the negative effects of bad choices and spiritual poison. The name of this antidote if *teshuva*, returning to Hashem in penitence, with a strong resolution that from this moment on, he'll begin to walk the path of Torah and mitzvoth.

The chattan and kalla should decide to make their new home a worthy dwelling for the Divine Presence. That means a home of decency, with as little contaminating influences from the unholy outside world as possible. Holiness and peace go together with blessings, while lewdness and immodesty in any shape or form (pictures on the wall, DVDs, mode of dress, improper speech, and so forth) are closely related to curses, since they and the Divine Presence are mutually exclusive.

Jewish tradition, Shabbat candles, Kiddush, the Shabbat table, celebration of holidays and the like all impart an aura of tranquility and holiness on the home. When a husband and wife discuss emuna and trust in Hashem, love and joy, or Torah and mitzvoth, the Divine Presence illuminates their home.

Family purity enables a couple to enjoy the real sweetness of marriage. Here are some of the dividends of family purity:

* **Rejuvenation** – the monthly days of conjugal abstention that result from a woman's unclean days create a beautiful climate of monthly rejuvenation. The days of physical separation create a longing for one another; the immersion night therefore becomes like a wedding night revisited every single month.

* **Children** – children born within the context of family purity are sweet and well-adjusted; those born from a mother that didn't immerse in a proper mikva are rebellious and insolent.

* **Livelihood** – Observing the laws of family purity is conducive to a good income. Those couple that fail to observe the laws of family purity frequently suffer debt and financial difficulty.

The main preparation

The main and most important preparation for marriage is prayer. A person who is contemplating marriage should have an entire savings plan of prayers, not taking a single detail for granted. He should pray to find the right match, for all the preparations before the wedding and for everything he'll need after the wedding. One should pray for peace in the home, understanding, communication, fulfillment, peace of mind, emotional and physical health, successful children, adequate income, upright neighbors...leave no prayer stone unturned! The more prayers accumulated, the better the chances of success in marriage.

A single person would do himself an enormous favor by setting aside an hour a day for personal prayer, especially in asking Hashem to send him his true soul mate. Each prayer creates a mighty angel that assists a person at some point in their life. When a groom has prayed extensively before the wedding, all these angels stand with him under the chuppa. Also, nothing invokes Divine assistance like prayer.

A basic principle of emuna is that a person's life is determined by the Heavenly Court. When a person's prayers prior to marriage precede severe judgments, then those prayers will be the blueprint for the young couple's future, rather than the severe judgments dictating their future. As such, with prayer, a person can literally design his own future.

On the other hand, when a person begins to pray *after* the need arises, he must contend with a complicated set of severe judgments. It's much more difficult to rescind a severe judgment that has already manifest itself in this world, than it is to cancel a severe judgment that has not yet manifest itself. That's why preemptive prayer and daily personal prayer are so important.

Mutual prayers have special power. The bride and groom should not only pray for their mutual success and for their lives together, they should pray for each other. They should pray for mutual aspirations, for love, friendship, communication, and understanding. Such prayers are the foundation of unity in the home.

They shouldn't forget to pray for fertility and for successful children.

The main responsibility of prayer falls on the husband's shoulders, because *shalom bayit* depends on him. He therefore must pray that he'll succeed in respecting his wife, that he'll refrain from comments and criticism, and that he'll love her unconditionally.

A person can't know what to pray for unless he learns. Therefore, he should study this book seriously and listen to our CDs as well. "Respecting Your Wife," "Peace in the Home," and "First Place" all have valuable information that's critical to success in marriage. Learning is not enough; after learning, one must pray that Hashem help him internalize and apply everything that he has learned.

Prayer and learning are critical before the wedding - before a person can err, and G-d forbid, destroy, or ruin a marriage that's just beginning. Repairing a badly damaged building is much more difficult that building a sturdy building from scratch. The same holds true in marriage. Therefore, the combination of prayer and premarital instruction (such as this book and the aforementioned CDs) are a wonderful preparation for marriage.

Prayers on the wedding day

The wedding day is a special time to devote to prayer and teshuva. The chattan and kalla should not have any last-minute errands to do. This holy day should be free for the spiritual preparation for the rest of their lives together.

If one lives in Israel, then a visit to the Kotel in Jerusalem or to the gravesites of our great tzaddikim is most propitious. If one is outside of Israel, he should try to find a room or a secluded place where he can pray and commune with Hashem without being disturbed.

First, one should thank Hashem for all the blessings in life up until now, especially for the awesome imminent occasion of his wedding. Then, he should do serious soul searching and ask Hashem's forgiveness for all his wrongdoings from the day he was born to this very day. Confession, sincere remorse, and firm resolution to do better comprise the type of teshuva that completely cleanses a person's soul. Once the soul has been purified with teshuva, one should ask for true and unswerving emuna in Hashem and His Torah.

On this wonderful day, the chattan and kalla should pray for the rest of their lives together. The most important things to pray for are emuna and *shalom bayit*. They should ask Hashem for love, friendship, understanding, mutual respect, and holiness so that their home will be a worthy place for the Divine Presence. The chattan and kalla should also pray for their material needs, especially good health, adequate livelihood, and success. This is also *the* day to pray for fertility and for upright and successful childen, sound in body and in spirit. They should pray for peace and good relations between their families. Nothing should be taken for granted. With so many things that can go wrong, they should pray that the wedding ceremony and celebration should be a success, with much rejoicing and dancing. With so much to pray for, one would be best advised to make a prayer list on a notebook or pad. One can also take advantage of prescribed prayers, such as those of Rebbe Natan of Breslev that appear in *Likutei Tefillot*.

We learn the power of prayer on the wedding day from a Breslever anecdote: Rebbe Nachman heard his married daughter yelling at her cleaning woman. He asked her: "Why didn't you ask for dependable domestic help on the day of your wedding, so you wouldn't have to be yelling and losing your temper today?"

Arriving at the chuppa from a day of prayer makes a chattan and kalla shine like the rarest of gems. Nothing could be loftier.

May Hashem help you succeed!

Glossary

A
Amalek (Biblical) – evil grandson of Esau; nickname for the Yetzer Hara, the evil inclination

B
Baal Tshuva (pl. Baalei Teshuva) (Hebrew) – spiritually awakened Jew

Brit mila (Hebrew) – ritual circumcision

C
Chassid (pl. Chassidim) (Hebrew) – literally "pious person", but alludes to the disciples of the Chassidic movement, founded by Rabbi Yisroel Baal Shem Tov in the early 18th Century CE

Chattan (Hebrew) – bridegroom

Chuppa, or chupah (Hebrew) – marital canopy

D
Dinim (Hebrew) – the spiritual forces of severe judgments that are created by a person's misdeeds.

E
Emuna (Hebrew) - the firm belief in a single, supreme, omniscient, benevolent, spiritual, supernatural, and all-powerful Creator of the universe, who we refer to as God

Emunat Chachamim (Hebrew) - the belief in our sages

Epikoris (Greek) – skeptic, heretic

Epikorsis (Greek) – heresy, skepticism

G

Gemara (Aramaic) – The 2nd-5th Century CE elaborations on the Mishna, which serve as the foundation of Jewish law

Gett (Aramaic) – Jewish writ of divorce

Geula (Hebrew) – the redemption process of the Jewish people

H

Halacha (Hebrew) – Jewish religious law

Hashem (Hebrew) - literally means "the name," a substitute term for The Almighty so that we don't risk using God's name in vain.

Hitbodedut (Hebrew) – personal prayer

K

Kabbala (Hebrew) - Jewish esoteric thought

Kedusha (Hebrew) – holiness

Ketuba(h) (Hebrew) – Jewish marital contract

M

Malchut (Hebrew) – monarchy; in Kabbalah, the seventh sphere

Midrash (Hebrew) – collection of Jewish homiletic literature, mostly from Talmudic sources

Mikva(h) (Hebrew) – Jewish ritual bath

Mincha (Hebrew) – daily afternoon prayers

Minyan (Hebrew) – a quorum of ten men for prayer or ceremonial occasion

Mishna (Hebrew) – The oral elaboration of the Torah as given from Hashem to Moses, finally codified by Rabbi Akiva, his pupil Rabbi Meir, and his pupil Rabbi Yehuda HaNassi, 1st-2nd Century, CE

Mitzva(h) (Hebrew) – a commandment of the Torah; good deed.

Mitzvot(h) (Hebrew, pl.) – literally, the commandments of the Torah; good deeds

Moshiach (Hebrew) – Messiah

N
Neshama (Hebrew) - soul

O
Onaat Devorim (Hebrew) – a transgression of Torah where one person insults, saddens, humiliates, or misleads another person

P
Pgam Habrit (Hebrew) – literally "a blemish of the holy covenant", connotes a breach in personal holiness

R
Ruach Hakodesh (Hebrew) – holy spirit

S
Sandek (Hebrew) - godfather
Shabbat (Hebrew) – Sabbath, day of rest
Shadchan (pl. shadchanim) (Hebrew) - matchmaker
Shalom Bayit (Hebrew) – literally "peace in the home", marital bliss
Shechina (Hebrew) – The Divine Presence
Shidduch (pl. shidduchim) (Hebrew) – a match between a man and a woman for the sake of marriage
Shlemazel (Yiddish) – literally, a person with no luck. Refers to someone clumsy and inept
Shlit'a (Hebrew) – suffix used after a contemporary rabbi's name, acronym for "may he merit long and good days"
Shmirat Habrit (Hebrew) – literally "guarding the covenant"; male holiness in thought, speech, and deed, particularly the use of one's reproductive organs only in the performance of a mitzvah
Shmirat Eynayim (Hebrew) – "guarding the eyes," or refraining from looking at forbidden objects, particularly at a woman other than one's wife
Shulchan Oruch (Hebrew) – Code of Jewish Law, compiled by Rabbi Joseph Caro of Tzfat, late 16th Century CE
Siyata D'shmaya – Divine assistance

T

Tallit (Hebrew) – prayer shawl

Talmud (Hebrew) – Jewish oral tradition, comprised of the Mishna and the Gemorra

Tanna (Aramaic) – Mishnaic sage, $1^{st} - 2^{nd}$ Century CE

Tefillin (Aramaic) - phylacteries

Tfilla (Hebrew) - prayer

Tikkun (Hebrew) – correction of the soul

Tikkun Habrit (Hebrew) – literally "correction of the holy covenant", connotes a state of personal holiness

Tikkun Klali (Hebrew) – A compendium of ten Psalms (16, 32, 41, 42, 59, 77, 90, 105, 137, 150) revealed by Rebbe Nachman of Breslev which are conducive to purification of the soul and personal holiness

Tikkunim (Hebrew) – plural for tikkun

Tshuva (or Teshuva) (Hebrew) – literally "returning," the term that refers to the process of atoning for one's misdeeds

Tzaddik (Hebrew) – extremely pious and upright person

Tzaddikim (Hebrew) – plural for tzaddik

Tzedakka (Hebrew) – charity

Y

Yesod (Hebrew) – literally "foundation"; in Kabbalah, the sixth sphere that represents personal holiness

Yetzer Hara (Hebrew) – evil inclination

Yetzer Tov (Hebrew) – inclination to do good

Yir'at Shamayim (Hebrew) – literally "the fear of Hashem," a term for sincere piety

Z

Zohar (Hebrew) - the 2nd-Century C.E. esoteric interpretation of the Torah by Rebbe Shimon Bar Yochai and his disciples

Did you enjoy this book?

If so, please help us spread the message of emuna around the world. Send your contributions to:

Chut Shel Chesed
POB 50226
Jerusalem, Israel

Or call:

Brooklyn: 718-577-2975

Los Angeles: 323-271-0581

Israel: 972-2-532-3339

Dear reader!

The book You have just finished reading has changed the lives of many. Please note that this book is the outcome of a wonderful enterprise that is dedicated to the goal of spreading Jewish wisdom and emuna to hundreds of thousands of people around the globe.

We turn to you, dear reader with a request to become a partner in this enterprise by contributing to our efforts in spreading emuna around the world.

For your convenience please fill in the form on the back and send it to us.

With blessings always
"Chut Shell Chessed" institutions

"Chut Shell Chessed"
p.o. **50226**
Bucharim mail box office
Jerusalem zip code: **91050**
Israel

Attach here

Support The Important Work of "Chut Shel Chessed"
Thank you for supporting "Chut Shel Chessed".

Recommended Operation Support Levels:

$ 15.60 (30¢/week) ☐
$ 26.00 (50¢/week) ☐
$ 39.00 (75¢/week) ☐
$ 52.00 (1.00$/week) ☐
Other Amount: $ _____

Recommended Support Levels:

$ 100
$ 250
$ 500
$ 1000

Please include your email address, We will keep you informed about

E-mail address: _____

Name: _____

Street address: _____

City, State, Zip: _____

Phone: (_____) _____

Contribute by Credit Card:

Credit Card Type:

☐ Visa ☐ MasterCard ☐ Discover ☐ American Express

Credit Card #: _____

Expiration: _____ (Month / Year)

Cardholder Signature: _____

Contribute by check :
send a check to the address listed on the back of this card

Attach here